Defiant Dads

Defiant Dads

Fathers' Rights Activists in America

Jocelyn Elise Crowley

Cornell University Press
Ithaca and London

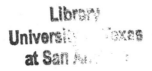
First published 2008 by Cornell University Press

Printed in the United States of America

Library of Congress Cataloging-in-Publication Data

Crowley, Jocelyn Elise, 1970–
    Defiant dads : fathers' rights activists in America / Jocelyn Elise Crowley.
        p. cm.
    Includes bibliographical references and index.
    ISBN 978-0-8014-4690-0 (cloth : alk. paper)
    1. Fathers—Legal status, laws, etc.—United States.
2. Divorced fathers—Legal status, laws, etc.—United States.
3. Custody of children—United States.   4. Child support—
Law and legislation—United States.   5. Self-help groups—
United States.   I. Title.

    KF547.C76 2008
    346.7301'7—dc22   2008020312

Cornell University Press strives to use environmentally responsible suppliers and materials to the fullest extent possible in the publishing of its books. Such materials include vegetable-based, low-VOC inks and acid-free papers that are recycled, totally chlorine-free, or partly composed of nonwood fibers. For further information, visit our website at www.cornellpress.cornell.edu.

Cloth printing   10 9 8 7 6 5 4 3 2 1

For my mother, Patricia Ann Sheffield, with love

Contents

Acknowledgments

This project would not have been possible without the assistance of many different people. For all of their time and insights, I first must thank my interview respondents and those whom I observed while conducting this research. Family dissolution is a difficult process, and all of the people who participated in this project generously provided me with a valuable view into their lives. I hope that my respect for them—even when we do not agree—is evident throughout this book.

Second, I would like to thank the many individuals at the Edward J. Blousstein School of Planning and Public Policy at Rutgers, The State University of New Jersey, who encouraged me at different stages of my research. Dean James Hughes, Associate Dean Michael Greenberg, Professor Carl Van Horn, Professor David Listokin, and Professor Cliff Zukin provided enormous encouragement and advice regarding the financial support of my work. Professor Nancy Wolff, chair of the Public Policy Program, was also extremely supportive throughout the writing process. The Rutgers University Research Council offered direct funding as well, for which I am very grateful. I also was fortunate to work with excellent research assistants, including Nicole Dempsey, Margaret Watson, Kimberly Kierstead, and Mary Kate Feeney. Ellen Oates kept me organized with her excellent secretarial support, and Raymonde Pozzolano did a wonderful job transcribing all of my interviews.

Third, the Russell Sage Foundation was indispensable in helping me complete this book by providing me with a Visiting Scholar Fellowship during the academic year 2005–2006. Special thanks go to Eric Wanner, Suzanne Nichols, Catherine Winegard, Nicole Radmore, and Lauren Porzelt, all of whom made the foundation a rewarding place to be for a year. I must also thank the wonderful people responsible for moving the book through the editing, marketing, and publicity phases: Peter Wissoker, Susan Specter, Jonathan Hall, Mahinder Kingra, Susan Schwartzman, David Prout, Bruce Acker, and Tamara Swedberg.

Fourth, I am lucky to have the best friends a person could hope for! Theresa Luhm, Esquire, and Amy Schapiro read through the manuscript at different stages and provided excellent feedback. In addition, Sandhya Verma Higgins made me laugh when I most needed it! I thank them from the bottom of my heart.

Fifth, I would like to thank my family—including the late Florence and Stanley Baron, and M. B. Crowley—and especially my husband, Alan Colmes, who brings light into every single one of my days. Dr. Monica Elizabeth Crowley deserves a special thank you for reading the book in its entirety and offering insightful comments. As this list of acknowledgments suggests, I am very fortunate that God has blessed me with such a wonderful support system, and I honor Him every day. Finally, this book is dedicated with love to my mother, Patricia Ann Sheffield, who, while I was growing up, was both mother and father to me. I love you, Mom.

Defiant Dads

1

A Coming Revolution in Fathers' Rights?

A local fathers' rights group, Superdads, is meeting in a business office in a relatively highly populated city in the West.[1] It is around 8:00 p.m., and the office's employees have long since left. Juan, a middle-aged man with a broad smile and intense eyes, is the charismatic leader of this group. A total of eight racially diverse people, including Juan, are gathered around a small conference table. One of the eight is a woman. It is a hot summer day, and group members have been describing their problems with the family court system for more than an hour.[2] Finally a man who has been quiet up until this point breaks his silence.

1. All group names in the vignettes that introduce each chapter as well as the individual respondent names that appear in this book are pseudonyms, as explained in appendix A.
2. Throughout this book, I will frequently use the words "group members" and "fathers" interchangeably. Indeed, the majority of individuals participating in these groups are men. However, readers should also keep in mind that many women are actively involved in these groups as well (as in the meeting described here), and these women also have much to critique about contemporary family policy in the United States. My generic use of the term "fathers" should not be understood as a way to marginalize women's voices or patterns of participation.

SUPERDADS MEMBER 1: What are fathers' rights groups doing to change the fucked up rules that favor women?

JUAN: The Violence Against Women Act clearly protects women. State by state, however, things are improving. There is one Internet support group that is very helpful. But in our state, it is primarily a select group of assemblymen and state senators that continually block legislation and hold up fathers' rights in the Unites States. (Our organization's) problem is that we have no money.

SUPERDADS MEMBER 1: I know what we should do. We should get the unions involved.

JUAN: The problem is, we don't have the money to influence voting.

SUPERDADS MEMBER 1: We should be able to change this.

JUAN: The National Organization for Women is highly funded. Women have their shit together.

SUPERDADS MEMBER 1: We don't have equal rights.

JUAN: If you accept your life as a noncustodial parent, then you are in 2nd place. Face it, most men give up custody.

SUPERDADS MEMBER 2: We go through this entire process in ignorance. . . . But the system isn't fair. How is it that we are taking this? I am ready for action.

JUAN: We need to take action. Our state laws have not kept up with this trend of divorce. Petitions might help, but you have to make sure that people are registered voters.

SUPERDADS MEMBER 2: This system stinks. Sometimes I want to drop out of my children's lives.

In scenes like this all across America, angry, dispossessed fathers are demanding rights. They argue that since the breakdown of their own families, they have been deprived of their most basic parental joys: the freedom to love and experience their children in the fullest ways possible. They call themselves fathers' rights or children's rights groups, and some of the most prominent ones in the United States include the Children's Rights Council, Dads Against Discrimination, the National Congress for Fathers and Children, and the Center for Children's Justice.[3]

3. In contrast to the group names that are all pseudonyms in the introductory vignettes of each chapter, the names of the groups listed here, in a footnote in chapter 4,

These groups bring together mostly men in small venues to speak their minds about the state of the American family and, more specifically, to articulate their objections to current child support and child custody policies. Indeed, their grievances are manifold. But they all start from the same place of frustration: the stories of what happened to them and their families.

On the individual level, their personal histories are compelling. A father reports that he has not seen his two sons in ten years as his ex-wife continually moves the children from school district to school district in order to avoid detection. Another describes the boarding house room that he can barely afford to maintain for himself once he has paid his child support in full each month. One haggard father shares how he tried to explain to his seven-year-old daughter that the reason he missed her first Holy Communion service was not because he does not love her, but rather because he was never informed of the date by her mother. A diligent older man discusses his numerous attempts to visit his daughter in a distant southern state, only to be prevented from actually spending time with her because of his ex-wife's overriding mission to keep them apart. He carries memories documenting these failed efforts close to his heart every day of his life. He also has kept detailed computer spreadsheets recording his fruitless trips, saved under the file name "Sabrina: Visitation Attempts."[4] The file name is perfectly fitting; they were all attempts, never successes.

At fathers' rights group meetings everywhere, these sad details are reported member by member, month after month, year after year. And the number of such groups is likely to grow, since the percentage of children living with a sole parent—typically the mother—more than doubled (to 28 percent) between 1970 and 2006, and it now includes

---

and in the middle of chapter 9 are real. However, they are specified for illustrative purposes only. Their inclusion does not imply that these particular organizations or their members/leaders were studied in this project.

4. Some fathers' rights activists object to the term "visitation" when describing the time that they spend with their children. They argue that the term visitation denigrates their level of parental authority, and they prefer the term "parenting time." However, since other activists do not oppose the term visitation, and since it is still commonly used in the courts as well as in the media, it will be incorporated into this book and used interchangeably with the term "parenting time."

about 20 million out of 73 million children living in America.[5] What are these fathers looking for when they attend these groups? Is it a chance to share their pain? Is it a political organization that will help remove government-imposed impediments to them showing their love for their children?

This book is grounded in the assumption that in most family policy debates, there are rarely pure angels and pure villains whose positions provide clear signals regarding what steps should be taken in pursuit of the public good. Instead, the needs of mothers, fathers, and children must all be considered in any proposal for reform. More to the point, this book takes a hard look at fathers' rights organizations in order to understand their concerns and how these concerns affect the entire family unit. It pools the knowledge gained from 158 in-depth interviews with leaders and members of fathers' rights groups, observational analysis of eight groups in action throughout the country, and a thorough reading of these organizations' published material, all of which let fathers speak for themselves about the current trajectory of their lives.[6] Readers will find answers to the following questions: What reforms do fathers' rights groups want in terms of child support and child custody? Are their claims truly worthy of consideration or, if enacted, would they damage other members of the family? What kinds of help do fathers' rights groups offer their members, and how well can they deal with fathers' interpersonal issues with their ex-partners and children? In the end, whom do these organizations help, and do all members of a family benefit in equal ways from the services that they provide? And finally, given their array of activities, what are the prospects that fathers' rights groups can achieve their goals?

The answers to these questions are complex, with activists reporting a wide range of beliefs, attitudes, and behaviors regarding their relationships to their children, a diversity of thought that reflects earlier periods of identity struggles regarding the definition of fatherhood in American history (La Rossa 1997).[7] Because of their diversity, fathers' rights groups

5. U.S. Census Bureau. 2006.
6. Details describing the methodology used in this book can be found in appendix A. The interview protocol is contained in appendix B.
7. An important point to note is that fathers' rights activists are mostly heterosexual in orientation and thus concerned with the children whom they have

provoke a range of reactions among the public at large, from fear and anger to sympathy and encouragement. Indeed, throughout the following chapters, the reasons for this strong public response to their activities will become apparent. But this complexity in public response does not mean that important, substantive conclusions cannot be drawn about the nature of these organizations and the worldview that they aim to impress upon others. With this in mind, three central themes about their mobilization efforts are interwoven throughout this book, the first of which is most important. Unlike most other historical attempts at male organizing,[8] fathers' rights groups have *two* faces: a political side—focusing on transforming the society in which they inhabit—and a much lesser-known personal side—focusing on their intra-family relationships. Although individual groups might emphasize one over the other, understanding these two faces is key to understanding the nature of these groups and their collective identity.

Consider first their political "face." If Americans have any image in their minds about fathers' rights groups, the political identity of these organizations is this image. Indeed, their political personality is emotionally charged, with these groups comparing their fight for family law reform to the gay, women's, and black civil rights movements that have come before them (Crowley 2006a). Their political character is also international in scope, with their grievances and message of family "crisis" similar to those expressed by parallel groups in Canada (Bertoia and Drakich 1993; Boyd 2003, 2006; Kenedy 2004), the United Kingdom (Collier 1995, 2006; Collier and Sheldon 2006), Sweden (Eriksson and Pringle 2006), Australia (Flood 1998, 2004, 2006; Rhoades 2006), and other nations. The shape of the fathers' rights movements in these countries, of course, is informed by their own national culture and values. However, all of these groups, including those in the United States, have incorporated notions of what constitutes a "good father" into

---

biologically fathered or adopted with a female partner. The discussion of issues throughout this book, thus, follows from this common premise of heterosexual parenthood.

8. Note that men have organized in the past, but usually with an emphasis on the political *or* the personal. For discussions of men organizing around political themes, see Messner 1997; Connell 2005b; Gavanas 2004. For discussions of men organizing around personal themes, see Bly 1990; Kimmel and Kaufman 1993; Moore and Gillette 1991; Schwalbe 1996; Coltrane 1989; Quicke and Robinson 2000.

their mission and stress that the current legal infrastructure prevents them from becoming the best fathers that they can be. In other words, these groups have rejected the idea that their own members are to blame for their current predicaments; instead, the legal system is the culprit, and it must be contained and reformed. How then do they advocate for reform and on what issues do they focus their attention?

With their nonprofit status, most of the groups in the United States cannot directly lobby state or federal legislators, but they can engage in various forms of publicity-seeking behavior, personal persuasion, and political education to further their view of equality (Coltrane and Hickman 1992; Williams and Williams 1995). In many ways, they hope to reform family law, which can play a key role in determining the relationships between two parents and between parents and children at the time of a family's dissolution (Dewar 1998). Indeed, the main focus of fathers' rights groups rests on two public policy areas: child support and child custody reform.

Child support payments are simply financial transfers that take place between two parents in the event of a family breakdown. In the majority of cases, money is transferred from the father to the mother due to the relative disadvantage she faces economically when a family dissolves. Fathers' rights activists, as we will see, have many problems with the current child support system, including the amounts that they are required to pay, how these monies are spent, and, in their view, the excessive intrusiveness of the state in pursuing enforcement. However, most activists also complain about the child support system because of its direct link with a second area of policy concern: custody laws that necessitate the transfer of this income. Mothers in American society today retain primary physical custody of their children in the overwhelming percentage of family dissolution cases, either by mutual parental consent or, to the consternation of fathers' rights activists, by judicial decree. Why, these activists ask, should mothers automatically receive custody and fathers have to succumb to a "visitor" status in their own children's lives? Why, they wonder, should they always have to accept this second-rate status? From their perspective, each state should maintain a presumption of joint legal and physical custody—or true "shared parenting" laws, as they put it—with only circumstances of abuse, violence, or neglect sufficient to void this presumption.

It is also important to note that although the issues of child support and child custody dominate the agenda of fathers' rights groups, they are also concerned—to a lesser extent—with other policies related to family law. Most organizations, for example, maintain that domestic violence laws need to be reformed, especially in the area of what they call "false allegations." In the heat of a custody dispute or simply out of a desire for vengeance against their former partners, mothers, according to these activists, will frequently accuse fathers of domestic violence—even sexual violence—against themselves or their children. The proliferation of false allegations of abuse, in their view, has led judges to flagrantly and unlawfully strip men of their rights to see their children, a practice that fathers' rights groups want to permanently stop. Fathers' rights groups also work toward ending the injustice of "paternity fraud," which they argue is fundamentally unfair to men (Sheldon 2003). State laws expressly dictate that any child born into a marriage is a child of that marriage—that is, the parents are assumed to be the married couple in question. The problem of paternity fraud most often occurs when a family breaks down, divorce proceedings begin, and the father, through whatever means possible, obtains biological proof that a particular child born into the marriage is not really his. This can also occur in a nonmarital case when a man assumes he is in a monogamous relationship, only to be proven subsequently by genetic evidence taken from the child born to his partner that he is wrong. In the past, states have pressed these men into continuing to pay child support in order to promote the continuity of parenthood that is presumed to be in the best interest of the child. In recent years, however, fathers have argued that such practices amount to nothing more than robbery. Currently, states are reconsidering these laws with heightened scrutiny.

Note, then, that fathers' rights groups are very different in their goals than other organizations that also have fatherhood at the core of their agenda, two of which include promarriage and economic empowerment groups (Crowley 2006c; Gavanas 2004). Promarriage groups argue that misguided progressives have advocated new family forms that wrongly assert a moral equivalence between two-parent and female-headed households (Blankenhorn 1995; Popenoe 1996). This moral equivalence has led to the proliferation of single parent families, either by choice, separation, or divorce. In contrast to this liberal belief system, promarriage adherents argue that men and women perform unique tasks within the American family that should not be undertaken by the opposite sex (Coltrane 2001). For societies to function fully and effectively, mothers and fathers must again cherish monogamy within a lifelong commitment to their partners. Examples of organizations that promote this agenda include the National Fatherhood Initiative, the Institute for American Values, the Institute for Responsible Fatherhood and Family Revitalization, and the National Center for Fathering.

Economic empowerment organizations are also sometimes confused with fathers' rights groups. However, these groups distinguish themselves from their fathers' rights counterparts by focusing on the significance of economic opportunity for low-income and especially African-American men (Doolittle et al. 1998; Doolittle and Lynn 1998; Gavanas 2004; Mincy and Pouncy 1997, 1999). In their view, men face extremely difficult circumstances in their family lives when they do not have access to jobs (Wilson 1996). If they are living in cities where there is little work, or if they themselves have not been exposed to a quality education, they may father children but then be unable to support their offspring (Sorenson and Zibman 2001). These organizations thus attempt to provide men with labor skills so that they can parent their children with the assistance of as many financial resources as possible. Examples of these organizations, also known as fragile-family organizations, include the National Partnership for Community Leadership, the National Practitioners Network for Fathers and Families, and the Center for Family Policy and Practice.

In sum, both promarriage and economic empowerment groups have political agendas, but these agendas are very different from that of fathers' rights organizations. Moreover, the promarriage and economic empowerment groups described here are mostly populated by grassroots service providers and other professionals working in the field, although members of the public may "join" by making a financial contribution. These "members" never physically come together, however, to discuss the current state of public policy. Thus fathers' rights groups are also different in that they are populated by ordinary citizens who meet on a regular basis to act on issues of importance to them.

Beyond fathers' rights groups' "political face," much less known among the general public is that fathers' rights groups also have a strong "personal face" as well. In fact, for some organizations, meeting these "personal" goals is much more important than pursuing their political goals. What, exactly, do we mean by "personal" goals? Much of the time and attention of these groups goes toward addressing the individual problems of their members. These groups are often the first stop for men who are seeking basic information about the court system, both because they have never encountered the legal system on issues related to family breakdown before and because some cannot afford to hire a lawyer on their own.

Although these groups cannot, by law, provide legal *advice* because they are not accredited, they can provide legal *information* to their members. It is chiefly the responsibility of group leaders, who have acquired information about judicial processes simply through time and experience, to dispense this knowledge at each meeting. However, more often than not, attorneys also attend these meetings and offer free legal guidance as well. These attorneys may be interested in fathers' rights issues or they may be looking to solicit new clients. Standard newcomer and member inquiries at these meetings involve finding the location of the local family court and child support customer service offices, understanding how to go about enforcing a visitation order, determining whether or not to undertake a paternity test, and establishing which legal forms to fill out under which conditions in pursuing a custody case.

Beyond information about the legal system, fathers' rights groups also engage in the "personal" by helping members with their relationship concerns. Broadly speaking, fathers' rights organizations provide two central categories of guidance: support in relationships with their ex-partners and support for relationships with their children. In the event of a family breakdown, many fathers clearly struggle with both types of interactions. For example, fathers' groups offer men the opportunity to voice concerns about how to speak constructively with their former partners, especially over issues that affect their children. Veteran members may instruct newcomers to use specific, concrete communication techniques in order to protect their youngsters from witnessing their parents argue in a heated fashion. In addition, fathers may worry about reconnecting with their children after a painful separation. With the aid of mental health experts, members sometimes use the time allotted at monthly meetings to discuss the problems of parenting that arise when they have not been fully present in their children's lives for a significant period of time.

The second theme of the book is that in addition to fathers' rights groups being relatively unique in their concern over both political and personal goals, the strategic focus of these groups is also remarkable in its antistate orientation. Unlike many other modern rights-based movements, fathers' rights activists are not asking for more state intervention to fix their particular familial situations; *they are asking for less.* More specifically, in the political realm, they view the state as hyper-involved in family life. They see the current system of regulating families after a dissolution as an interlinked maze of legal professionals, bureaucrats, and other self-proclaimed experts all seeking to profit from their personal pain. They therefore aim for a world where family dissolution practices involve as little government interference as possible. Pursuant to this goal, the concrete policy recommendation of fathers' rights advocates would be for both parents to automatically receive joint physical custody of their children, a standard that would also, in the view of these advocates, obviate the need for any child support to exchange hands.[9] Any future disputes that might arise over child-oriented issues would be resolved by a trained mediation expert, not the already out-of-control court system.

Interestingly, their personal goals share this same antistate theme. For instance, the work of these organizations in the area of legal assistance centers on providing alternatives to hiring high-cost attorneys to represent members' interests, including encouraging their members to represent themselves *pro se* in judicial proceedings whenever possible. In addition, these groups offer members guidance in conducting their own legal research, instruction regarding how to navigate the maze of the local court system, and other informal advice in order to help them circumvent the standard "government-imposed" method of protecting their rights. In the area of improving relationships with ex-partners and children, these groups also set out to provide a viable alternative to the court-affiliated divorce education programs that are currently (and

9. Interestingly, and somewhat paradoxically, fathers' rights activists need more state intervention in the form of new family policy laws in order to ultimately "push the state out" of their lives.

sparingly) in place to help with these same issues. Court-based programs are mixed by gender and cover legal and relationship issues that are of interest to *both* mothers and fathers. In contrast, fathers' rights activists repeatedly proclaim their desire to offer similar information specifically to *men* in need, thereby creating programs that are not bound to any other competing constituencies (i.e., women). Overall, then, this omnipresent distrust of the state permeates these groups' meetings, discussions, day-to-day activities, and long-term vision for the type of society that they want to achieve. This book thus seeks to map out these antistate dynamics and to understand their origins and implications.

Finally, the third theme of the book is that although the combination of political and personal goals may distinguish fathers' rights groups from other types of men's organizations, the uniqueness of this mission does not automatically mean that their objectives have merit. One of the key arguments presented in this book is the double-edged nature of their efforts to secure reform in the area of family policy. More specifically, there is an extreme tension between their political goals and their personal goals: the political goals of fathers' rights groups are highly problematic in terms of their capacity to strengthen American families, while their personal goals can be extremely beneficial to most parents and children facing the dissolution of the core family unit.

In terms of their political goals, the push by fathers' rights groups for equality with women completely discounts the disadvantages women must confront in contemporary American society. As a result, their arguments for public policy reform are overly simplistic, not based in the strong social science research that documents the negative effects of these inequities, and at times demonstrate an alarming level of antifeminism and overt negativity toward women as a group. More specifically, fathers' rights groups hope for a world where mothers and fathers share equally in the financial provision for their children, yet in doing so, they neglect the variety of ways in which women are disadvantaged relative to men in today's economy. Simply put, women work for less pay than men in occupations that remain segregated by sex, and suffer enormous financial instability when their adult relationships fall apart. Without substantial and effective child support, women and children would face enormous economic hardship. Fathers' rights groups also long for equal caretaking responsibilities for their children after their families break down. Yet, in doing so, they ignore the fact that in the majority of intact families, mothers do the most significant share of child-rearing—work that is underrewarded and undervalued in modern society, but ironically becomes the focus of deep contestation by fathers when their families dissolve. Unfortunately, breaking mothers' primary caregiver ties after the family separates, which fathers' rights groups advocate, may result in more harm than good to all involved parties, children and parents alike. The lack of attention by fathers' rights advocates to all of these grave matters understandably creates opposition among women's groups that have been fighting on behalf of formal recognition of women's economic and caregiving contributions for decades. The political goals of fathers' rights groups, therefore, are fundamentally flawed in content.

Although the political goals of fathers' rights groups have few, if any, links to research that points to the ways in which women and children can emerge from their systematically disadvantaged position in American society, their personal goals are much more laudable and consistent with the compelling academic literature that suggests their efforts are beneficial for families in flux. As will be demonstrated throughout this book, modern fathers' rights groups play a critical informational role in providing men with the knowledge that they need to guide themselves through the court system. Fathers learn what they must do to protect their interests in the family, and they acquire valuable insight into the role of lawyers, judges, and other professionals who operate within the court system. More important, these groups also engage in a variety of activities that show fathers how to effectively bridge their relationships with both their ex-partners and their children. By attending regular meetings, fathers learn practical communication strategies for relating to their former partners, strategies that ultimately can help them avoid further disruptive interactions that might, under different circumstances, bring them back to court for resolution. In addition, members who buy into the group "identity" also come to preach a new philosophy that places their children's well-being at the core of their day-to-day activities, with stronger bonds with their offspring the best potential outcome.

Problematic, then, for fathers' rights groups today is the tension that exists between these political and personal goals. One set of goals has no merit, while the other has significant value. This particular combination of strategic activity results in a quagmire of missed opportunities for fathers' rights groups to help strengthen American families on the political level. At the same time, it creates positive changes in their members' lives at the individual, relationship level. Their struggle to pursue this complex, dual agenda is the focus of this book.

2

The Origins of Fathers' Rights Groups in the United States

The eight people belonging to the local fathers' rights group Dads Forever are sitting in a small, windowless office in a southern city. The racially diverse group is cramped around a tiny table when they hear a voice from the adjoining hallway yelling out, "Make way for the television and the VCR." At this request, everyone shuffles his chair slightly to the right. One member appears at the door, pushes the television into the tiny room, and then scrambles to find an electrical outlet within reach. Luckily, he finds one nestled between two large books on a nearby table. Without further delay, he presses "play," dims the office lights, and begins the video.

The topic is establishing paternity for unwed parents, and the video is full of scenes of happy couples with their children. The video's narrator informs the audience that there are currently two ways to establish paternity: by acknowledging it voluntarily through the signing of a standardized form or via the court system through a DNA test. Remarking that financial and medical benefits can accrue to a child who knows the identity of his or her father, the narrator also warns that signing a voluntary acknowledgment form waives a father's right to ask for a court trial to contest the paternity, once established. Even with this risk in mind, however, the narrator declares that fathers should seriously consider stepping up to the plate in order to be truly "full parents" to their children.

What, exactly, do fathers *do* within modern families? The answer, of course, varies across racial, ethnic, and class lines. But even *within* these broad socioeconomic categories, a high degree of diversity exists in the attitudes, aptitudes, and behavioral styles of individual fathers. Some fathers are emotionally very close to their children, listening to their school-day struggles on a regular basis; others are not. Some fathers spend significant amounts of time playing with their children outdoors; others do not. Some fathers place primacy on the financial benefits that they can bestow upon their children; others do not. Some fathers regularly undertake household chores with their children; others do not.

The important point is that whatever goes on within a family unit is usually a matter of private determination. At times choices regarding the allocation of parental responsibilities are made consciously. A husband and wife or unmarried couple may come together and verbally negotiate how child-oriented activities will be divided between them, and then commit themselves to executing that plan. More often, however, these decisions are made without a comprehensive discussion. Personal preference in terms of childraising activities, gender norms of acceptable behavior, and external, contextual pressures—job obligations, extended family responsibilities, travel commitments, and so forth—all intersect to influence fathers in their daily approach to parenting. And barring accusations of abuse or neglect, fathers are generally free to exercise their own personally designed paternal practices without state interference.

All of this "freedom" changes when traditional families break down, as the paternity establishment video shown at the Dads Forever meeting at the beginning of this chapter indicates. In these cases, the government takes an active stance in deciding the roles fathers must assume in their children's lives. Two areas of activity are of primary concern: financial support and custody, both legal (which pertains to decision-making authority) and physical (which refers to where the children live). The ways in which the state has determined a father's responsibilities across these two domains, however, have varied over time. Most recently, major sociodemographic changes—the rising divorce rate and the rising nonmarital birthrate in the post-World War II era—have fundamentally altered the state's approach to the care of children when families dissolve. Both child support and child custody laws have evolved to meet the demands of these transformative socio-demographic trends, but these legal changes have met with resistance in the form of the emergence of fathers' rights groups across the United States.

Children in Limbo: Trends in Divorce and Nonmarital Childbearing in Post-World War II America

In the traditional two-parent, white, middle-class family of the mid-twentieth century, American children could rely on both a mother and a father for stability within the home. The standard division of labor in the family unit produced a father who typically worked outside the home and a mother who stayed at home caring for the children. Although black mothers were more likely to work outside the home than their white counterparts, their labor force participation rates were under 50 percent during this period (England, Garcia-Beaulieu, and Ross 2004). These dynamics changed as the result of multiple cultural shifts in American society that ultimately produced both a rising divorce rate and a rising nonmarital birthrate. Consequently, beginning in the 1960s, children no longer had the financial and emotional security that they were virtually guaranteed in previous years. In fact, increasing numbers of children assumed a precarious state in American family life.

Recent Divorce Trends

Broadly speaking, since the Second World War two primary factors have contributed to the rising divorce rate: women's increasing economic independence and women's growing interest in individual fulfillment as shaped by the women's movement. First, World War II brought many women into the paid labor market for the first time in American history. As their husbands and brothers went off to war, women had to assume positions in the work force that men had traditionally held in order to keep the economy afloat. Although the returning soldiers forced these women out of their jobs and back into the home, this temporary

TABLE 2.1.
Female Civilian Labor Force
Participation Rates, Ages 16 Years
and Older, 1950–2000

Year	Female Labor Force Participation
1950	33.9
1960	37.7
1970	43.3
1980	51.5
1990	57.5
2000	59.0

Sources: Fullerton, Howard N. 1999.
"Labor Force Participation: 75 Years of Change,
1950–98 and 1998–2025." *Monthly Labor Review*
(December); U.S Census Bureau. 2002. "Profile
of Selected Economic Characteristics." *Census
2000 Supplementary Survey Profile.* Table 3.

economic independence provided them with a taste of what life could be like without dependence on a male breadwinner. Financially speaking, women quickly recognized that they had new opportunities to live their lives on their own, if they so chose. Indeed, as table 2.1 demonstrates, women increased their labor force participation rates from 33.9 percent to 59 percent from 1950 to 2000.

The women's movement also played a role in prompting women to reconceptualize their lives outside the boundaries of the traditional family, especially when it came to matters of individual happiness. Along with the other types of civil unrest that dominated the 1960s, the women's movement stressed the importance of personal fulfillment as a noble and worthy goal for all human beings, regardless of gender. Indeed, during the 1950s most citizens viewed marriage as the only acceptable status for female adults, but by the 1970s this conception had changed considerably. Personal fulfillment could mean a life with marriage as one option, but no longer was marriage a necessity in constituting an acceptable family form (Furstenberg and Cherlin 1991). As a result of all of these developments, the divorce rate climbed upward throughout the second half of the twentieth century. As table 2.2 demonstrates, in 1950 the divorce rate was only 2.6 divorces per 1,000 individuals in the population. By 1980 the rate had jumped to 5.2 before falling to 4.1 in 2000.

TABLE 2.2.
Divorces in the United States,
1950–1997

Year	Rate per 1,000 Population
1950	2.6
1955	2.3
1960	2.2
1965	2.5
1970	3.5
1975	4.8
1980	5.2
1985	5.0
1990	4.7
1995	4.4
2000	4.1

Source: U.S. Census Bureau. *The 2007 Statistical Abstract.*

Economic independence and personal fulfillment goals driven by the women's movement also provided the foundation for the reform of divorce law in the United States—a complex web of state statutes that gradually moved from a fault-based system to a no-fault system during this volatile period in family jurisprudence. For a significant part of the twentieth century, an individual seeking a divorce had to show just cause for exiting the marriage, such as his or her partner's abandonment, abusive behavior, addiction, adultery, or alcoholism. In other words, for the union to be terminated, an individual had to demonstrate that the other spouse had engaged in some type of serious misconduct while married (Buehler 1995). In the courtroom, one party was usually found to be "guilty" and the other party "innocent" (Weitzman 1985). Once blame for the breakdown of the marriage was properly attributed, then the divorce action could proceed to completion.

With the introduction of the no-fault standard, however, an individual could seek a divorce by convincing the court that the marriage had simply irretrievably broken down (Jacob 1988). Unhappiness, in other words, became justification enough for those seeking to end their unions. Throughout the 1970s, the no-fault revolution spread throughout the states. By 1991, the revolution was complete, as Arkansas became the last state to add some type of no-fault provision to its books.

Appendix C provides a summary of the introduction of no-fault laws in the states.[1]

What were the motivating factors behind this no-fault revolution? The reasons were manifold. First, reformers hoped to reduce the bitterness and hostility of those involved in the divorce process. Former partners had enough problems to confront without having to engage in the adversarial process of fault-finding, which was then common in the divorce courtroom. Second, advocates of the no-fault system hoped to restore integrity to the judicial system. In the fault-based system, lawyers were known to encourage their clients to distort the truth in order to receive favorable treatment from the presiding judges. This practice resulted in decreased confidence in the judicial system overall, as perjury became commonplace. Third, prior to the no-fault revolution, a distinction existed between the law-as-philosophy and the law-as-actually-applied. On the books, partners seeking divorce had to experience the strict adversarial system. Off the books, there was already a movement toward a de facto standard of no-fault divorce; for example, most states had enacted laws based on a loose definition of the cruelty provision or some other type of incompatibility standard by the 1980s. The passage of no-fault laws, then, was simply a way to standardize and publicize those guidelines that were already in use. Finally, straightforward pragmatic reasons led to the adoption of no-fault rules. To reformers at the time, relationships were complex, and determining who actually "caused" a marriage to break down was next to impossible. In this view, courts should remain as evenhanded and neutral as possible in granting divorces (Wardle 1991).

Several decades later, people still debate whether or not no-fault laws have had their desired effect in changing the fault-based divorce culture described above, and in some states opponents of these reforms have actually mobilized to roll back these statutes (Ellis 2000). However, one fact is certain: No-fault laws did provide adults with another

---

1. It is important to note that these dates are not without controversy. Researchers have reported different dates for the same state, with some using the date when a law was passed and others using the date a law became effective. Complicating matters are different definitions of what constitutes a "no-fault" law and the fact that many states have amended or repealed such laws over the past three decades. For a further discussion, see Vlosky and Monroe 2002.

mechanism for legally ending their marriages, and many couples took up this option. Children from these families thus had to face the same types of emotional stressors when their families broke down as they did before under the fault-based regime. Where would they live? Who would take care of them? When would they achieve stability in their lives once again? These were questions that not even the most liberal no-fault law could easily answer. Children of divorce were joined in their uncertainty by the rising number of children born into nonmarital circumstances whose biological parents either never lived together or had subsequently broken up after their birth.

Recent Nonmarital Birth Trends

In the post-World War II period, the United States witnessed a massive increase in the number of unmarried couples having children. In 1950, only 4.0 percent of all births were to unmarried women. By 2004, this number reached 35.8 percent. During this period, the absolute number of births to unmarried women increased from 141,600 to over 1.47 million. In addition, the birth rate per 1,000 unmarried women aged 15–44 climbed from 14.1 in 1950 to 46.1 in 2004. Appendix D summarizes these trends in greater detail.

A variety of factors contributed to these changing dynamics. In absolute numbers, as described above, more unmarried women chose to have babies during this time period. Cohabitation and unmarried women keeping their children rather than placing them up for adoption became more acceptable as well, which also produced an increase in the number of children born under nonmarital circumstances. However, when focusing on births to unmarried women as a percentage of all births, the story becomes much more complex. First, there was simply an increase in the number of unmarried women in the population at large as the baby boom generation aged and delayed or even completely put off marriage as a lifestyle choice. A second significant factor behind these birth-related statistics, surprisingly, was the number and behavior of married women. During this same time period, they were declining in population (especially in the 18–29 age group), and they were having fewer children overall. In sum, the percentage of births to unmarried women was rising because of the demographics and behavior of *both* unmarried and married women (Burnes and Scott 1994; Ventura and Bachrach 2000).

The increase in children born to unmarried mothers produced many of the same problems as the rising divorce rate. In numbers never seen before, children were spending either all or part of their lives with a single parent, creating a situation of potential confusion and turmoil. Two parents had created the child, but now the two parents were living apart. American family policy had to catch up to these new realities, and the first area ripe for reform was child support law.

Transformation in the Policy Environment

Changing Child Support Laws

Congress first became involved with the issue of child support for welfare families, or those receiving Aid to Families with Dependent Children (AFDC) benefits, as a way to save taxpayer dollars (Crowley 2003). Over time, the AFDC caseload was transitioning from one composed primarily of widows and their children to one made up of unmarried women and their children. With this change, fathers could actually be found and held responsible for their children's well-being. Toward this end, in 1950 Congress passed Section 402 (a) (II), an addition to the Social Security Act, which mandated that state child welfare agencies notify local authorities if a child had been abandoned by his or her father. The Social Security Amendments of 1965 (Public Law 89-97) permitted state welfare agencies to access absent parents' addresses through the U.S. Department of Health, Education, and Welfare. By 1967, states were required to organize separate administrative units to establish paternity and collect support for AFDC children (Social Security Amendments of 1967, Public Law 90-248). States could also turn to the Internal Revenue Service to secure delinquent parents' addresses.

The most significant change for welfare families came with the passage of the Social Security Amendments of 1975 (Public Law 93-647), which created the Federal Child Support Enforcement Program. In addition to structuring the main federal office, this legislation enabled the Department of Health, Education, and Welfare to supervise the opening of independent child support agencies in the states (Crowley 2000). The law also imposed new financial penalties on mothers who were unwilling to identify the fathers of their children. All monies collected from fathers would pass to the states as reimbursement for welfare expenditures already laid out on behalf of these families, with the exception of a $50 pass-through provision in force during the years 1984–1996; in 2006, this pass-through was reactivated at the states' discretion up to $200 per family. Congress initiated an additional enforcement mechanism with the Omnibus Reconciliation Act of 1981, which required states to withhold a percentage of a father's unemployment benefits for child support purposes (Public Law 97-35).

Although Congress was extremely active in devising ways to locate and secure support from fathers of families on welfare, it was much less active in the area of securing support for nonwelfare families, composed predominantly of divorcing rather than nonmarital couples. In fact, Congress left it to the state court systems to assign and enforce support in these cases. Typically, a mother would seek support relief from the judge granting her a divorce. However, the system was extremely arbitrary across the fifty states. Some judges would order support; others would not. There were also no uniform rules determining the size of the awards. Some were large; most were very small. Most egregious, however, was the complete lack of enforcement. Contempt of court citations were possible but did little to change fathers' behavior. Most fathers who refused to pay simply did so with impunity.

The 1984 Child Support Enforcement Amendments (Public Law 98-378) changed all of this. As a result of pressure from women's groups and women legislators, nonwelfare families were incorporated into the child support enforcement program that had been established for welfare families nine years earlier. After this point, any family, regardless of income, could request the government's assistance in securing support. Moreover, instead of the money being intercepted by the state for welfare reimbursement purposes, all monies collected would go to the families in need. This expansion of the child support caseload is critical in the program's development, because fathers of nonwelfare children form the core foundation of fathers' rights groups. After the 1984 legislation brought more economically advantaged men under the auspices of this administrative system, laws regulating the child support program quickly became tougher and more far-reaching in their powers. In fiscal year 2005, for example, the program collected $23 billion in support for its caseload of 15.9 million families, of which only 2.5 million families were receiving benefits from the Temporary Assistance for

Needy Families (TANF) program, which replaced the AFDC program in 1996 (Office of Child Support Enforcement 2006). In serving all of these families, the current program engages in four central tasks: (1) locates missing parents, (2) establishes paternity, (3) issues order awards, and (4) enforces awards.

State intake workers attempt to gather as much data as possible on the whereabouts of missing parents. States can also turn for assistance to the Federal Parent Locator Service, which collects individual identification information from a variety of different state and federal databases such as the Selective Service System and the Department of Defense. Child support orders are then matched against the information contained within these databases on a regular basis to locate parents. Further enhancing this process, since 1996 the Personal Responsibility and Work Opportunity Reconciliation Act (PRWORA) (Public Law 104-193) has required employers to report all new hires to their state employment agencies based on employers' W-4 forms. These new hire reports are then matched against outstanding child support orders, providing another potential opportunity for parental location. In making these matches, states can also access the National Directory of New Hires, which pools employment and unemployment records from state directories of new hires, state employment security agencies, and other federal agencies.

Paternity establishment is the second task required of the state child support agencies, and since 1984 it has increasingly become a critical component of support policy. Under President Reagan, the Family Support Act of 1988 (Public Law 100-485) created new paternity establishment standards and provided financial incentives to the states to pursue DNA testing. In addition to the use of genetic science, another key innovation in this area was the development of processes for fathers to simply acknowledge paternity on their own (Crowley 2001, 2002). More specifically, the Omnibus Reconciliation Act of 1993 (Public Law 103-66) required that each state move in the direction of instituting a voluntary civil process for establishing paternity. In response, states created opportunities for parents to file standardized paperwork that automatically generates a rebuttable or conclusive presumption of paternity. In 1996, to further expedite these processes, PRWORA instructed the states to begin to establish and publicize voluntary paternity acknowledgement programs in hospitals at the time babies are born.

In terms of issuing orders, the Child Support Enforcement Amendments of 1984 required the states to establish award guidelines or formulas in determining support payments, and the Family Support Act of 1988 required that all judges actually use the 1984 order guidelines when determining support. In general, states have converged on a core set of four formulas under which they award support: the percentage-of-income standard, the income shares model, the Melson formula, and a hybrid formula. Under the percentage-of-income standard, fathers must pay a specified proportion of their income as child support based on the number of children that they have; the custodial parent's income is not considered. The income shares model—by far the most common model currently in use—adds both parents' incomes together, calculates an appropriate child-rearing sum, and then prorates each parent's responsibility to pay into this fund based on his or her income. The Melson formula begins by setting aside a self-support income level for each parent and then calculates a child's support allowance based on his or her needs and a standard of living adjustment. The hybrid formula employs the percentage-of-income standard when a father's income falls below a specified level, and the income shares method when his income is above this level. Under PRWORA, states must review and modify awards every three years based on changes in parental circumstances.

Finally, the child support program engages in aggressive enforcement. The 1984 Child Support Enforcement Amendments began significant movement in this direction by focusing on developing punitive policies toward parents who had not lived up to their obligations in the past. More specifically, the law made wage-withholding mandatory if support payments were delinquent by one month; mandated liens against real property and instituted the withholding of tax refunds to secure overdue support; reported delinquencies to credit agencies; and ordered that all individuals who had been delinquent in the past post bond or some other type of security to guarantee future payments. The Family Support Act of 1988 went even further by requiring wage withholding for all new cases, with the aim of preventing delinquencies before they begin. Within four years, the Child Support Recovery Act of 1992 (Public Law 102-521) imposed a federal criminal penalty for the nonpayment of interstate support, and the Ted Weiss Child Support Enforcement Act of 1992 (Public Law 102-537) required consumer credit agencies to include child support delinquencies in their reports. Two years later, the Full Faith and Credit for Child Support Orders Act (Public Law 103-383) required states to enforce child support orders from other states by clarifying issues of enforcement jurisdiction, and the Bankruptcy Reform Act of 1994 (Public Law 103-394) prevented child support obligations from being discharged in bankruptcy proceedings. Legislation passed in 1998 imposed a prison term on parents who deliberately and proactively seek to avoid paying interstate support (Public Law 105-187). From all of this législation, Congress made its message clear: lack of compliance with child support obligations would be taken extremely seriously, with incarceration as the ultimate punishment looming for those parents who flouted the law. Table 2.3 tracks the growth of the child support program across a variety of measures from 1978 to 2002.

Although policymakers have stressed the importance of effective child support policy over the years, it has become increasingly expensive to run these programs. Currently the states fund their programs through three sources. First, the federal government reimburses the states for 66 percent of their administrative expenditures for locating parents, establishing support orders, and collecting payments; the federal government also pays 66 percent of the laboratory costs associated with determining paternity. Second, the states receive a share of all collections made on behalf of families receiving welfare with the federal government and can spend this money in any way they see fit. Third, the federal government provides the states with incentive payments based on their performance in establishing paternities and support orders and collecting current and past-due support and on their overall level of cost-effectiveness. The money that the states receive from these incentive payments must be reinvested back into the child support program.

Given these financing mechanisms, does the child support program "make money" for either the federal government or the states? The answer to this question, simply put, is no. Like most other social programs, the child support system provides to families a service that upholds a strong value-system of parents providing for their children, but does so at a direct high cost.[2] Table 2.4 demonstrates that the program has never earned more than it has expended at the federal level. How-

---

2. Of course, these costs might be mitigated in the long run if the program prevents families from experiencing the devastating and multifaceted effects of economic hardship.

TABLE 2.3.
Summary of National Child Support Program Statistics, Selected Fiscal Years, 1978–2002 (Numbers in Thousands, Dollars in Millions)

Measure	1978	1982	1986	1990	1994	1996	1998	1999	2000	2001	2002
Total child support collections	1,047	1,770	3,246	6,010	9,850	12,019	14,347	15,901	17,854	18,958	20,137
In 2002 dollars	2,629	3,158	5,081	8,018	11,823	13,716	15,808	17,159	18,644	19,260	20,137
Total TANF collections	472	786	1,225	1,750	2,550	2,855	2,649	2,482	2,593	5,592	2,893
Federal	311	311	369	533	762	888	960	922	968	895	950
State	148	354	424	620	891	1,013	1,089	1,048	1,080	1,004	1,180
Total non-TANF collections	575	984	2,019	4,260	7,300	9,164	11,698	13,419	15,261	16,366	17,244
Total administrative expenditures	312	612	941	1,606	2,556	3,049	3,584	4,039	4,526	4,835	5,183
Federal	236	459	633	1,061	1,741	2,040	2,385	2,680	3,006	3,222	3,432
State	76	153	308	545	816	1,015	1,199	1,359	1,519	1,613	1,752
Federal incentive payments to states and localities	54	107	173	258	374	410	385	361	391	413	450
Average number of TANF cases in which a collection was made	458	597	582	701	926	940	790	912	822	774	806
Average number of non-TANF cases in which a collection was made	249	448	786	1,363	3,169	2,618	3,071	5,688	6,409	6,687	7,013
Number of parents located	454	779	1,046	2,062	4,204	5,808	6,585	NA	NA	NA	NA
Number of paternities established	111	173	245	393	592	733	848	845	867	777	697
Number of support obligations established	315	462	731	1,022	1,025	1,093	1,148	1,220	1,175	1,181	1,220
Percent of TANF assistance payments recovered through child support collections	NA	6.8	8.6	10.3	12.5	15.5	20.0	NA	NA	NA	NA
Total child support per dollar of total administrative expenses	3.4	2.9	3.5	3.7	3.9	3.9	4.0	3.9	3.9	3.9	3.9

Source: U.S. House of Representatives. House Committee on Ways and Means. The 2004 Green Book. Washington, DC: U.S. Government Printing Office.

TABLE 2.4.
Federal and State Share of Child Support "Savings," Selected Fiscal Years
1980–2002 (in Millions of Dollars)

Fiscal Year	Federal Share of Child Support Savings	State Share of Child Support Savings	Net Public Savings
1980	–103	230	127
1985	–231	317	86
1990	–528	338	–190
1991	–586	385	–201
1992	–605	434	–170
1993	–740	462	–278
1994	–978	482	–496
1995	–1,273	421	–852
1996	–1,147	409	–738
1997	–1,282	469	–813
1998	–1,424	286	–1,139
1999	–1,758	66	–1,692
2000	–2,038	–87	–2,125
2001	–2,327	–272	–2,599
2002	–2,252	–463	–2,715

Source: U.S. House of Representatives. House Committee on Ways and Means. *The 2004 Green Book.* Washington, DC: U.S. Government Printing Office.

ever, in the aggregate, the states earned more than they expended through 1999. After this point, the states started losing money, with an aggregate loss of $87 million in 2000. By 2002, the federal government was losing approximately $2.3 billion and the states were losing a total of $463 million. This change in fortunes primarily has to do with the major transition in the composition of the caseload over the past several decades. States were able to retain most of what they collected when the program was dominated by welfare cases. However, as nonwelfare applicants increased, the states were legally bound to collect support on their behalf but could not keep these payments for cost reimbursement purposes.[3] Monies had to go directly to the families on behalf of whom they were collected.[4]

3. States do, however, routinely charge families small fees for processing their child support cases.
4. Recent research, however, has indicated that the poorest fathers, specifically those attached to mothers resistant to exiting welfare, have difficulty paying their current obligations. This reality has always limited the state from maximizing its collection capacity among this population. This research is discussed further in chapter 5.

Changing Custody Laws

Policymakers not only have to determine who will provide financially for children after a divorce or a breakup among nonmarital partners, they also have to ascertain who will take care of these dependents. American law, as broadly defined by policymakers, has always contained provisions designed to protect children. Part of this concern, undoubtedly, is the result of altruistic motivations. Most citizens, even those with the most libertarian leanings, would agree that those who cannot protect or provide for themselves—children—should be protected by those who have the capacity to do so. Another component of this concern, of course, involves self-interest. Healthy families provide one of the cornerstones of modern societies and act as strong institutions of social control. To the extent that mutually supportive and functional families break down, so does social control. Governments, therefore, have a stake in preventing families from dissolving, and to the extent that families do break down, preserving the well-being of all involved parties becomes a significant priority (Friedman 1995).

In its role as protector, American family law gradually evolved to address the rising numbers of children in legal limbo as a result of the increasing divorce rate and the surge in nonmarital births. Broadly speaking, from the 1950s through the 1970s, mothers were the typical recipients of sole physical custody, mostly as a result of negotiated settlements rather than court-ordered directives. In contested cases during this period, and as early as the late nineteenth century, judges advanced the "tender years" doctrine, which specified that children were especially vulnerable from birth to ages seven or eight (Luepnitz 1982).[5] Society viewed the mother as holding a special place in the family, and in particular as the parent who "specialized in addressing the needs of children of tender years" (Ellis 2000). Of course, mothers had to be of righteous character in order for this standard to prevail; adulteresses, for example, could not rely on the tender years doctrine to work on their behalf in custody disputes (Barnes 1999).

---

5. Interestingly, prior to the advancement of the tender years doctrine, the presumption was in favor of sole father custody.

In following this placement rule of thumb, not only were judges attempting to respect the tender years doctrine, they also were aiming to replicate the living arrangements of most children at that time. With fathers working outside the home, mothers tended to be the primary caretakers. Judges granted fathers visitation, which usually translated into weekend time that they could spend with their children in any way that they saw fit. In this model, therefore, there were clear winners and losers in the custody system. Not unexpectedly, many fathers viewed this system as unconscionably biased against their gender.

The tender years doctrine did not, however, go unchallenged for long. As a result of the women's movement's emphasis on equality and individual rights, women's increasing participation in the labor market, and a renewed interest in the psychological well-being of children that valued the emotional contributions of both parents, the "best interest of the child" became the new standard for evaluating custody cases during the 1970s. In this new world, state legislators stripped all gender-related assumptions from custody law (Mason 1999). No longer would women automatically be given preference in custody battles. Instead the child's needs would be considered paramount, and fathers hoped to earn an equal right to parent with their female counterparts (Brown 1984).

What factors did judges begin to take into account when determining what the best interest of the child actually meant in practice? Although each case commanded individual attention and review, courts normally started to weigh the following issues when considering with whom a child should reside: (1) the child's physical, emotional, mental, religious, and social needs; (2) each parent's capacity to meet these needs; (3) the child's preference; (4) the parents' preferences; (5) the child's relationships with his or her parents and siblings; (6) the identity of the primary caretaker; (7) the ties between the child and each parent; (8) the current living arrangement of the child; (9) each parent's desire to encourage the child's relationship with the other parent; (10) any record of domestic violence, child abuse, or child neglect; (11) the mental and physical health of all parties; (12) each parent's degree of cooperation in the custody process; (13) the child's age and gender; (14) each parent's moral standing; and (15) the child's cultural needs (May 2001).

As this list suggests, the process of deciding custody is far from a precise science. One way judges have attempted to produce order across this ambiguous terrain is through the promotion of joint custody arrangements. This standard assumes that parenting roles are interchangeable and that children are most well-protected against negative behavioral or psychological outcomes when they maintain contact with both parents (Mason 1994). Joint legal custody laws give both parents the right to make decisions about their children's well-being; joint physical custody laws permit children to alternate between their parents' houses on a fixed schedule. When parents live near one another, children may switch households at the end of every week or month. When parents live geographically far apart, children may spend the school year with one parent and all vacations with the other. Of course, a multitude of other options are also available depending on the needs of the family under consideration. About half of the states also require separating parents to create parenting plans, which can be especially useful in families where physical custody is shared (Schepard 2004). These plans detail the rights and responsibilities of each parent in the day-to-day care of their children and contain provisions for the resolution of disputes that may arise.

The best-interest standard, when combined with the newfound predilection of the courts to consider joint custody solutions, was promising to many families who opposed the old, winner-take-all system of determining a child's living arrangements. Whereas the introduction of no-fault laws in the case of divorce removed the judicial system from the private, interpersonal conflicts between adults involved in a familial dissolution, joint custody, many reformers hoped, would do the same for decisions regarding the proper placement of children. The new system would provide discretion to the involved parents to determine their own best plan for sharing access to their children. Joint custody would also promote the then-emerging idea among mental health professionals—an idea that had only started to be investigated as to its merits in the academic research—that children need both parents in order to become emotionally and developmentally successful citizens. Finally, the new system would remove the stigma of gender discrimination against fathers and recognize that both parents, regardless of gender, have the power to contribute to their children's well-being in positive ways (Brown 1984).

Despite the promising potential of this new custodial philosophy, the real life results in courtrooms across the country have proven far less revolutionary. Although joint legal custody is a common outcome in contemporary family dissolution cases—42 states had made some provision for joint legal custody under certain circumstances as of 2002 (Elrod and Spector 2002)—the majority of children living under these joint legal rules continue to live with their mothers (Williams 2000). In addition, sole maternal physical custody, rather than joint arrangements, remains the dominant form of physical custody. In fact, in 2002 approximately 84 percent of all custodial parents were mothers (Grall 2003).

Why has maternal custody continued to predominate? One explanation is simply that the mechanics of joint physical custody are difficult to manage. Only when cooperative parents are dedicated to the idea of true, shared parenting can such a plan be successful. Because many family breakups end acrimoniously, such civility is often lacking (Mason 1999). A second explanation is simply that old habits die hard. Judges have traditionally awarded custody to mothers, and that mindset is difficult to break. Third, judges' consideration of the identity of the primary caretaker while the family was intact increases the likelihood that children will go to the mother in cases of family dissolution. A fourth, extremely controversial explanation is that most fathers do not want custody, leading to negotiated settlements designating the mother as the primary custodian that are never presented to a judge for adjudication.

Finally, three other developments related to custody disputes deserve mention here because, as we will see, fathers' rights activists have a lot to say about them as well (Schepard 2004). The first of these trends relates to the use of alternative dispute resolution (ADR) procedures to resolve outstanding custody issues. All ADR methods attempt to address custody disputes without a judge's intervention or an adversarial court proceeding; however, they differ in terms of their formality and level of third-party decision-making power. At one end of the spectrum is negotiation. Parents using negotiation methods often do so through their lawyers, who simply seek to settle outstanding disputes prior to standing before a judge. No standardized rules govern negotiation proceedings, and participants are not bound by these agreements. Next along the spectrum is mediation, which is the most common form of ADR and which a handful of states have required parents to pursue once they separate. Parents who engage in mediation hire a neutral third-party to help them work out their differences over custody matters (Beck and Sales 2000). Through numerous meetings and hearings, mediators attempt to facilitate problem-solving between parents and promote positive communication. However, parents are not bound to the recommendations of the mediator and may ask a judge to intervene with a trial if they cannot resolve their conflicts. A final ADR procedure involves arbitration, which is similar to mediation in that a neutral third-party is called on to devise a workable custody arrangement. However, unlike mediation, arbitration is adversarial in nature in that each parent attempts to persuade the arbitrator with concrete evidence that he or she is better-suited to make decisions on matters related to the children. In addition, all arbitration decisions are final and the courts will normally enforce them.

The second trend in custody disputes involves methods that have been developed to deal with high-conflict families. In these cases, the court may appoint a special master—also known as a parenting coordinator—to help troubled families resolve their disputes and to reduce the burden on the court system (Coates et al. 2004; Guyot 2005). Parenting coordinators typically are lawyers, mediators, or mental health officials who manage the day-to-day conflicts of couples as they attempt to parent their children in two separate households. They may meet with the parents and children regularly and document progress in relationships in regular reports for the court. The courts may also order "supervised visitation" if there is a suspicion of domestic violence or other type of high-risk circumstance facing a family. Supervised visitation may be appropriate when the court has a strong interest in promoting parent-child contact but, at the same time, wishes to protect the involved children from potential harm. To facilitate such meetings, the courts may order an individual of the couple's choosing to monitor all visits or may require that the visitation take place at a qualified center monitored by trained supervisors who document and report to the court the nature of all scheduled parent-child interactions.

The third trend in custody matters relates to the court's use of outside experts to help judges make the best possible decision when it comes to child placement. More specifically, courts can use mental health evaluators, guardians ad litem, or attorneys for the child in evaluating the merits of a custody case. Mental health evaluators, also known as forensic evaluators, conduct neutral investigations into a particular family's life and generate a report to the court on their findings regarding the health, safety, and well-being of the children under consideration (Gould 1998; Stahl 1994). These evaluators have the power to interview parents, children, and other adults such as teachers and doctors in order to ascertain which living arrangements might be in the children's best interest. The courts then consider these evaluations when making their custody determinations. In contrast, guardians ad litem or attorneys for the child may be used when the courts believe that the dependents in question need representation in the custody dispute at hand (Mason 1994). Guardians ad litem need not be attorneys; their role is to protect the children, and their primary allegiance is to the court. Guardians ad litem weigh the preferences of the child in a custody matter as only one of many factors that they may consider when presenting their views to the judge. By contrast, attorneys for the child act as lawyers and serve as advocates for their child clients in custody disputes. Their role is to directly represent the children's preferences regarding residential arrangements to the court.

Mental health evaluators, guardians ad litem, or attorneys for the child may play a particularly important role in documenting the ways in which children may be alienated from one parent as a direct result of the actions of the other parent. Some children's advocates argue that judges should consider the impact of what they call Parental Alienation Syndrome (PAS) when making custody and visitation determinations (Schepard 2004). According to these advocates, PAS exists when one parent systematically denigrates the other parent in the presence of the children. It can involve negative actions, words, or accusations of abuse, any or all of which result in the children expressing a strong desire not to be in the presence of the alienated parent (Carbone 2000). Those who believe that PAS is a rampant problem that needs to be corrected argue that if this syndrome is "discovered" by child advocates investigating a dissolving family, the court should order the children to live with the targeted parent as a form of immersion therapy to undo the damage that has been inflicted by the alienating parent. PAS is extremely controversial: currently no large-scale academic studies document its existence, nor does it appear in the *Diagnostic and Statistical Manual of Mental Disorders,* the manual that is used by mental health professionals to diagnose and treat psychological disorders.

The Response: The Emergence of Fathers' Rights Groups

In the post World War II era, then, American families underwent a dramatic transformation. A rapidly increasing divorce rate, as well as a rise in the number of nonmarital children, produced a strong demand for laws that would regulate the ways in which these new family forms would operate on a daily basis. Policymakers ultimately responded by producing a range of initiatives in the areas of child support and child custody. Of course, any new regulatory scheme has its political supporters and opponents. These new family-oriented measures were no different. Across child support and custody issues, women were likely to gain, and men perceived themselves as much more likely to lose.[6] Growing male political mobilization first emerged in the form of divorce reform activists and men's rights activists during the 1960s and 1970s (Crowley 2003). These two sets of groups served as the forerunners of contemporary fathers' rights organizations in operation today.

Organizations dedicated to the reform of divorce law from the male perspective constituted the first set of precursors to modern fathers' rights groups in the United States. Ruben Kidd and George Partis were two of the earliest leaders in this area when they formed "Divorce Racket Busters"—later renamed United States Divorce Reform—in 1960. Located in Sacramento, California, the group attempted to bring men together to protest what they viewed as unfair treatment by the courts in terms of divorce settlements. They primarily focused on economic judgments, which in their view overwhelmingly favored women, and they drew support for their position from the work of Charles Metz, who published his critique of family law in *Divorce and Custody for Men* (1968). In his treatise, Metz argued that in modern society, men engage in submissive behavior in order to be chivalrous or to curry favor with women. Because of this male subservience and the fact that women are so well-organized politically, lawmakers and judges have become fearful of rejecting a woman's demands during a divorce. As a

---

6. Of course, many feminists would argue that women were definitely not gaining in the area of child custody with the rise of joint legal custody laws. According to this view, when men acquire joint legal custody with their ex-partners, they obtain decision-making power over their children's lives but not day-to-day responsibility, see Williams 2000.

result, women can get anything they want financially in a divorce settlement. To remedy this situation, men need to come together in groups to fight off any further infringements on their rights. While Kidd's and Partis's early efforts to reform the system by creating family arbitration centers throughout the state of California were not successful, they did raise dissolution issues from a male perspective that had been unaddressed by policymakers.

Other significant divorce reform groups began at the urging of author and activist Richard Doyle. Doyle's scope of complaints in terms of the societal treatment of men was much broader than those of Kidd and Partis. He argued that men face multiple disadvantages in society in comparison with women and submitted a broad critique of male "second rate status" in the following areas of public policy: criminal justice, child abuse, affirmative action, paternity actions, and welfare for unwed mothers. However, he ultimately chose to focus in particular on men's experiences in the courtroom when their relationships with their partners broke down. In 1971, he started the Coalition of American Divorce Reform Elements (CADRE) as a way to bring divorce reform activists from all over the country together to exchange policy ideas. The organization held three incorporation efforts in Elgin, Illinois, but ultimately failed to sustain itself due to internal infighting over competing operational strategies and goals. Notably, after CADRE folded, Doyle joined forces with Kidd in 1973 to create the Men's Rights Association, which began providing attorney referrals for divorcing men across the United States. Doyle later published *The Rape of the Male* (1976), which systematically catalogued his emerging ideas on what he viewed as the problem of rampant discrimination against men, and formed MEN (Men for Equality NOW) International, or MI, in 1977. This organization ultimately narrowed Doyle's broad, pro-male agenda to issues of false allegations of abuse and molestation between feuding couples. Sensing his contribution to the male cause was still incomplete, Doyle later turned his attention to editing and publishing a father-friendly newsletter entitled "The Liberator," which is still in print today.

The second set of precursors to the modern fathers' rights movement involved men's rights groups that pursued reform on a wide range of male-oriented issues during approximately the same period. As an early voice in this movement, Herb Goldberg attracted widespread attention when he wrote *The Hazards of Being Male: Surviving the Myth of Masculine Privilege* (1976). The argument Goldberg laid out started from the basis that modern society places men in a truly difficult bind; men, in Goldberg's view, suffer from a dual set of onerous, gender-specific pressures. On one level, they must be solid, unfailing economic providers for their families. They cannot select potentially more fulfilling but much less lucrative types of work because of the financial expectations that are placed on them. At the same time, society convinces men that they cannot show their emotions, as this display would constitute utter humiliation in the face of the masculine ideal. In Columbia, Maryland, in 1977, Richard Haddad, Dennis Gilbert, Allan Scheib, and Allen Foremen used Goldberg's thesis as the foundation behind the formation of a group that they called Free Men. They later renamed themselves the Coalition of Free Men and have largely served as an educational body on men's rights over the past several decades.

Another significant men's rights group that emerged in 1980 was the National Congress of Men (NCM), which began in Utica, New York. After several meetings, NCM, which aimed to bring together several sets of groups that desired to fight on behalf of men's rights in multiple arenas, selected James Cook as its first president. Cook, who was then leading the Joint Custody Association in Los Angeles, California, attempted to pool and then pare down the broad policy agendas of each individual member organization that advocated on behalf of diverse issues such as equality in the draft, increased aid for disabled veterans, and enhanced funding for male health needs.

Modern fathers' rights groups, then, or those that grew in strength during the late 1980s and early 1990s, emerged with similar sets of claims honed from both streams of activism that had come before them. However, although they share a common heritage, they learned from their predecessors which types of political rhetoric were likely to be most palatable to the public at large. In practice, this meant that the demonization of women in its most venomous forms had to be set aside in favor of political campaigns that would stress their relationships with their children (Crowley 2003). Toward this end, sometimes men's rights groups changed their names to promote a more child-oriented focus. The National Congress of Men, for instance, changed its name twice in the years between 1986 and 1995, initially becoming the National Congress for Men and Children and then transitioning to the National

Congress for Fathers and Children. Second, fathers' rights groups started to de-emphasize child support as their sole area of concern—with its concomitant strategy of calling all women gold-diggers and financially irresponsible—and began channeling their energy toward equal physical custody goals as well. In this way they hoped to soften their image by de-emphasizing their financial disagreements with their former partners and instead placing the father-child bond at the center of their efforts.

In addition to these image transformations, fathers' rights groups began adopting more far-reaching and responsive organizational structures to best do battle in the contemporary political environment. Some started to maintain strictly a national office, usually located in Washington, D.C., and focused on pressing their cause on federal policymakers. Others set up national-level organizations with state-level chapters. Currently, the most common type of structure is a state-level organization with or without regional chapters. Alliances also form among these organizations, and these networks provide members with the opportunity to receive the benefits of many groups specializing in different father-oriented issues. Individuals may also join multiple, nonallied groups, as indicated in chapter 1, in order to take advantage of as many available activities as possible.

A critical question, however, still remains when we consider the relative power of fathers' rights groups today: How many people, exactly, are involved in these groups? This question is not easy to answer. Groups are quite reticent about releasing membership numbers, as these counts undeniably affect their prospects for political success. Moreover, it is difficult for the groups themselves to "count" their own members. Some organizations maintain a tight hold on their members' participation based on whether or not these individuals are current with their dues. Most groups, however, do not restrict access to their organizational activities based on this principle. Making matters even more challenging, some members pay dues and are supportive, but do not regularly attend meetings. Based on my observations and conversations with group leaders about the relationship between membership and attendance patterns at regularly scheduled meetings, I estimate that approximately 100 members are currently active in one or two viable groups per state. This leads to a total upper-level estimate of approximately 10,000 members nationwide, a figure that has been reported elsewhere (Goldberg 1997).

Fathers' Rights Groups Grow Up

Fathers' rights groups currently operating in the United States, then, did not appear from "out of the blue" to contest policy in the areas of child support and child custody reform. Instead, these groups emerged out of the convergence of two important sociodemographic trends and the political response that these trends triggered. More specifically, the rising divorce rate and the skyrocketing nonmarital birthrate in the post-World War II era prompted policymakers to think about caring for the children involved in these new family forms in both innovative and aggressive ways. Enhanced child support enforcement became the panacea for these children's financial needs in the post-breakup context, whereas the "best interest of the child" custody standard evolved as the primary tool in decisions regarding children's physical and emotional requirements. These policies produced fairly predictable results for both mothers and fathers. Child support payments most frequently flowed from fathers to mothers, and mothers most often became the primary physical caretakers of the children in the post-family dissolution period.

In response, fathers' rights groups, drawing on the experience that many of their forerunners had gained in the divorce reform and men's rights organizations of the 1960s and 1970s, sprung into full action during the late 1980s through the present day. In groups diverse both in organizational and numerical strength, these organizations methodically began staking out claims in opposition to the mounting tide of legislation and judicial rulings that were increasingly, in their minds, designed to hurt them. But who exactly are the individuals who continue to join these groups across the country? What specifically do they hope to gain from participation in these groups, and do they feel a responsibility to recruit others? These are the questions to which the next chapter turns.

3

Membership Dynamics in Fathers' Rights Groups

It's 7:00 p.m. and Bruce, the leader of Dads Unite for Kids, has been at the meeting location for more than thirty minutes. In the corner of the room, a small group of people who are already members are gathered around an attorney, who is doling out advice about their upcoming custody and child support cases.

It has been a hot day, and Bruce looks tired. Dads Unite for Kids has its own headquarters in a high-rise located in a midwestern city that has seen better economic days. Walking to the building at night, prospective members have to make their way through the loud pleadings of panhandlers who line the mostly desolate urban streets.

Bruce checks his watch one more time. It is 7:10, and he decides to begin his pitch, all the while complaining to anyone who will listen that he has no tolerance for lateness. The potential draw tonight of newcomers who are not yet members, when it is still over ninety degrees outside, is small. Only one white woman and three black men have shown up. Nonetheless, Bruce pushes forward. Never hinting that he has given this speech countless times before, he launches into the hard sell.

BRUCE: Thanks for coming tonight. I would like to begin this evening with a simple question: What can this group offer you? There are a couple of points I want to make.

1. This group is like having "legal insurance." The attorneys here can help you. They are hoping to have you hire them, but you don't need one usually. Most cases can be resolved by default or agreement, not trial. But you will be prepared if you need to go to trial.
2. We sell and have onsite our state's family law code book. You might need to consult this book in your case.
3. We try to reform family law in our state.
4. We sell and have onsite our state's rules of the court, which you will need to know.
5. We have onsite Black's Law Dictionary so that you can understand the terminology involved in your case.
6. I have been at this job for years. I can help you with my experience.
7. We also have advanced family law manuals onsite.

I want you to know that I have gone through what you are going through. My teenage daughter decided to go and live with her mother even though I had custody. I did not think that she was mature enough to make this decision. My strategy, and what I can teach you, was to bury my ex in legal fees. It worked and I won! I can also "coach" you with respect to what to do with your case, and to be as organized as possible. The average custody battle costs $27,000 per side (for those who need a lawyer), but this organization can help minimize these costs.

(Bruce then proceeds to give all of the attendees the opportunity to present their issues before the group as a whole.)

DADS UNITE FOR KIDS ATTENDEE 1: I am a Christian man, and my ex committed adultery. I have been married for eight years, and this is a very difficult situation. I want joint custody of my kids.
BRUCE: Well, you have to have a positive attitude and sell the joint plan to her. Understand something right away. All women are born

control freaks. You have to pretend that they have a choice, but really you must guide her and control her options. You first must file for divorce.

DADS UNITE FOR KIDS ATTENDEE 2: In 2002 my son came to live with me, but I was still paying child support. Eventually my ex gained custody, and my son went to live with her in 2004. Now my son wants to move back with me. I am officially "behind" in my child support payments, but I think I should have a child support credit for the years when my son lived with me. I know my ex used my child support to buy crack cocaine.

BRUCE: My advice is to offer her a fraction of what you owe as a lump sum and see if she goes for it. She might, given that she needs the money to buy crack cocaine.

DADS UNITE FOR KIDS ATTENDEE 3: I have a simple problem. How do I file paperwork to punish my ex for all of her violations of my visitation rights?

BRUCE: First, call the police if she violates the order. You can also send her a letter saying that you will execute all visitation rights. This is key. Judges are recognizing relationships with both parents. Kids need both parents.

DADS UNITE FOR KIDS ATTENDEE 4: My husband is in jail right now [because] he owes $9,500 in child support arrearages. He has a work release so he can work during the day, but he must go to jail at night.

BRUCE: Try to get an early release for him. He will have to only serve less than six months, but the judge can keep him in jail [if he wants].

DADS UNITE FOR KIDS ATTENDEE 4: My husband's ex kept saying she is going to drop the case, but she didn't.

BRUCE: Be humble!

(Bruce then checks his watch and notes that about forty-five minutes have passed. He looks around the room and makes his final pitch.)

BRUCE: There is a $160 membership fee to join. I can help you through every case, and the attorneys are here for you to use. If you decide to hire an attorney, you can negotiate fees with him or her and save money. Does anyone want to join?

(Two out of the four people raise their hands, and a third asks for a reduced fee. Bruce collects the money from the "joiners" and directs them to the attorneys who are waiting for them in another room. He then quickly ushers the non-joiner toward the door.)

One of the most difficult challenges facing groups seeking to transform social life in America is attracting committed members. Interestingly, this is only a fairly recent problem. As Theda Skocpol (2003) has described in *Diminished Democracy*, throughout the nineteenth and early twentieth centuries, Americans easily formed large, cross-class organizations that afforded their members a strong sense of purpose. Examples included the Independent Order of Odd Fellows, the Knights of Pythias, the Knights of Columbus, and the Benevolent and Protective Order of Elks. More often than not, these groups had a brotherly, patriotic dimension, serving to support their fellow countrymen in times of both war and peace. In addition to instilling nationalistic sentiment, these organizations also played a fundamental role in providing individuals from vastly different backgrounds with opportunities to socialize in their broader pursuit of a greater, public good. In these forums, members—rich and poor alike—educated each other on the importance of participation in group decision-making, which ultimately had positive spillover effects for all different types of democratic institutions. Group members remained connected to state and national politics through their own local organizations, which maintained offices at these higher levels of government for exactly these purposes. During this period, then, group membership was a natural part of the American social fabric.

With the rise of the rights-based movements of the 1960s, however, the trajectory of organization-building was fundamentally altered. First, with the rapid spread of television and alternative sources of diversion, group involvement in general became less attractive to Americans as a way to spend their time (Putnam 2000). Second, narrowly defined issue-oriented groups and business associations replaced the large-scale, cross-class organizations of the past. Examples include the Concord Coalition, the Children's Defense Fund, and Common Cause. Dues became a less important revenue stream, as groups looked to foundations and donors with deep-pockets to fund recurring organizational operating expenses. Most important, little by little, these new, professionally run organizations engaged in what they viewed as more effective types of political mobilization strategies, such as creating mailing lists and requesting action from their members "from a distance"—for example, by encouraging them to make calls to their legislators on specific issues (Verba, Schlozman, and Brady 1995). These types of tactics gradually obviated the need for regularly scheduled meetings; in this new world, all business transactions could happen remotely. Across the majority of emerging organizations, therefore—and quite remarkably, in fact—one member of a specific group need not know the identity of a single other member.

Interestingly, fathers' rights groups operating in America have flouted these trends by building "brick and mortar" groups that continue to meet in-person all across the United States. They are, in other words, doing the unthinkable in many ways by engaging in a type of group activity that has fallen out of favor with most Americans. This strategy of developing a unique identity, as one might imagine, has not been without sizeable difficulties. Against a backdrop of competing opportunities for people's time, fathers' rights groups must publicize their presence within the community at large and effectively communicate their mission. Most important, they have to convince people to actually show up and stay dedicated to the cause. Given these challenges, this chapter seeks to answer the following questions: Who are the people who join fathers' rights groups today? How did they become involved, and what types of issues are they hoping to address by their activities? Finally, what responsibility do members sense that they have in attracting other, like-minded individuals to participate in their groups?

Membership Characteristics

Contemporary media portrayals of fathers' rights groups paint them in a variety of different ways, but most commonly as organizations composed of conservative, white males. In order to verify that this perception is correct, we would need to collect information from the entire universe of fathers' rights groups, or at least from a random sample, in order to make inferences about the population. Unfortunately, as described in appendix A, no formal, comprehensive directory exists of groups or members involved in fathers' rights groups. This study therefore used a snowball sampling method to attract participants. As a result, the characteristics of study participants described below may not accurately represent the characteristics associated with the actual membership of fathers' rights groups across the United States. However, they can help in understanding the types of people who are likely to be involved and are essential in contextualizing the multitude of family-oriented experiences and attitudes that are presented throughout this book.

Table 3.1 presents numerous sociodemographic characteristics of this study's sample. The majority of members in these groups were in their thirties and forties. Although the mean age of the sample was forty-six, the range of ages represented was from twenty-three to seventy-six.[1] Surprisingly, wide variation in the number of children was reported by these respondents. Although the average number of biological children of members in this study was close to two, one respondent had twelve children. Also notably, some members of fathers' rights groups are simply activists; they do not have any biological children of their own. In addition, 15 percent of the sample were actually women, an interesting finding that will be discussed in more detail below.

What about their relationship situations at the time of the interview? About 41 percent of the respondents were married, 51 percent either divorced or separated, and the remaining 8 percent either single or widowed. Over the course of their lives, however, a full 79 percent had experienced a divorce. Most had been divorced once or twice; the maximum number of divorces experienced by one respondent was six. These divorces took place as recently as 2003 and as early as 1973. In terms of race, 87 percent of all respondents were white, and only 8 percent were black, 2 percent Hispanic, and 1 percent Asian. Fewer than 1 percent described themselves as being of multiple races or another race, and only 1 percent of all respondents refused to disclose their race.

The socioeconomic backgrounds of these respondents were also mixed, but most leaned toward a more advantaged status. Although respondents were not asked directly about their incomes, they did report their level of educational achievement as well as their occupation.

---

1. One individual chose not to report his age.

TABLE 3.1.
Sociodemographic Characteristics of Fathers' Rights Members

Mean age	46
Mean number of biological children	2
Current marital status	
Married	41%
Divorced/Separated	51%
Widowed/Single	8%
Race	
Caucasian	87%
Black	8%
Hispanic	2%
Asian	1%
Multiple/unspecified	1%
Refuse	1%
Education	
High school diploma/GED	9%
Associate's degree/some college/vocational training	31%
Bachelor's degree	30%
Graduate degree (master's, doctorate, or professional)	30%
Employment	
White collar	78%
Blue collar	13%
Retired	6%
Unemployed/student/volunteer	3%
Political party identification	
Republican	38%
Democrat	24%
Independent	34%
Other/no response	4%
Voting behavior	
Vote in every election	76%
Occasional voter	17%
Do not vote by choice	6%
Do not vote because not a citizen	1%
Gender	
Male	85%
Female	15%
Sample size	158

Overall, the sample was highly educated. Those who had a high school diploma or a GED comprised 9 percent of the sample, and those who had an associate's degree, some college credits, or some other type of post-high school vocational training made up 31 percent of all respondents in the study. Respondents with either a bachelor's degree or a bachelor's degree plus some other graduate training composed 30 percent of the sample, and the remaining 30 percent possessed doctorates, master's degrees, or professional degrees (law, medical, or dental degrees). Corresponding to these high levels of educational achievement, fully 78 percent of all respondents held white collar jobs, and only 13 percent had blue-collar jobs. About six percent were retired, and the remainder were either unemployed, students, or volunteers. Not a single respondent who discussed a child in these interviews reported that the child was currently receiving Temporary Assistance for Needy Families benefits.

The respondents were also highly politically motivated. Slightly over half—52 percent—asserted that they had worked on a political campaign at some point in their lives, 45 percent had not, and about 3 percent did not answer. In terms of ideological leanings, members and leaders tend to be conservative, but not overwhelmingly so. Fully 38 percent of respondents were self-identified Republicans, 34 percent reported being independents, and 24 percent labeled themselves as Democrats. Fewer than 4 percent identified themselves with other parties or did not respond to this question. Interestingly, the overwhelming majority of respondents, 76 percent, characterized themselves as strong voters and claimed to vote in every election for which they are eligible. Approximately 17 percent just vote occasionally, and only 6 percent never vote. Fewer than 1 percent do not vote at all because they are not citizens.

These party identifications, however, might overstate the conservative leanings of these respondents. A little less than half of the respondents in the sample—about 48 percent—engaged in the past or continue to engage in other types of political activity beyond their work in fathers' rights groups in the form of other affiliations or causes supported. Table 3.2 provides a comprehensive list of these affiliations and causes for which members claimed to advocate or participate at some point in their lives. As this list demonstrates, many of these respondents were active in a wide range of liberal, conservative, and more "neutral" issues.

Finally, it is important to return to the gender composition of these groups: as noted, 15 percent, or a total of twenty-three respondents, were women. Table 3.3 provides a snapshot of these women. Like their male counterparts, women who join fathers' rights groups tend to be from socioeconomically advantaged backgrounds. Of the twenty-three respondents, twenty-two were white and only one was black. In addition,

TABLE 3.2.
Other Affiliations or Causes Supported, Past and Present, of Fathers' Rights Group
Members and Leaders

Conservative	Moderate/Neutral	Liberal
Probusiness	Anti-sexual trafficking in women and children	Pro-affirmative action
Profamily-values local radio	Blind advocacy	Pro-extension of unemployment benefits
Keeping the Ten Commandments in school	Pro-campaign finance reform	Pro-animal rights
Supporting the troops in Vietnam	Ethnic group advocacy	Anti-Rockefeller drug laws
Anti-Equal Rights Amendment	Tougher laws against child molesters	Antiwar movement
Anti-affirmative action	More money for community colleges	Pro-African-Americans in journalism
Law enforcement advocacy	Campaign for public sewer systems	Pro-civil rights
Men's rights	Anti-domestic violence work	Chinese human rights
Pro-National Rifle Association	Suicide prevention	Education reform
Pro-life	American Legion	Environmental protection
Promise Keepers	University reform	Farmers' rights
Tax reform	Anti-drug campaigns	Health care reform
	Boy Scouts of America	Hunger prevention
	Various cancer societies	Educational opportunity for disadvantaged students
	Children's advocacy groups	National Education Association
	Temple/church activism	Anti-nuclear testing
	Community problem-solving	Public Interest Research Groups (PIRGS)
	Disability advocacy	Pro-music and arts education
	Elderly advocacy	Pro-union
	Anti-overmedication of children	Peace Corps
	Space exploration	Planned Parenthood
	Rape awareness	Poor people's campaigns
	School board	Voters' rights
	Students Against Drunk Driving (SADD)	Women's rights
	Professional associations	Pro-public transportation issues
		Amnesty International

TABLE 3.3.
Female Respondent Characteristics in Fathers' Rights Groups

Race	
Caucasian	22
Black	1
Education	
High school diploma/GED	4
Associate's degree/some college/vocational training	12
Bachelor's degree	2
Graduate degree (master's, doctorate, or professional)	5
Political party identification	
Republican	5
Democrat	9
Independent	8
Other/no response	1
Mean age	46
Reason for joining	
Relationship-based affiliation with focal men	
New wife	13
Sister/sister-in-law	2
Grandmother	2
Mother	1
Independent-based affiliation	
Non-custodial mother	3
Activist	2
Total sample size	23

all of these respondents had graduated from high school, with a total of nineteen pursuing higher education in the form of an associate's degree or further training (twelve respondents), a bachelor's degree (two respondents), or a graduate degree (five respondents). Interestingly, these women also spanned the range of political identifications, with five reporting a Republican affiliation, nine self-identifying as Democrats, eight labeling themselves as independents, and just one not providing a party membership. The mean age for the women in this sample was forty-six.

Why would women join fathers' rights groups? Respondents in this study reported two types of affiliations: (1) a relationship-based affiliation, due to a significant, positive bond with a man who was experiencing some type of hardship in his own life as a result of a family breakdown, and (2) an independent affiliation, including noncustodial mothers and child advocates (Crowley 2006b). As Table 3.3 indicates, the majority had a relationship-based affiliation with their groups, with thirteen as new wives, two as sisters/sisters-in-law, two as mothers, and one as a grandmother of a man who was undergoing difficulties related to child support and child custody issues. The remaining five had independent affiliations; three were noncustodial mothers, and two joined because they considered themselves to be child advocates.

Generally speaking, those with a relationship-based affiliation with their local fathers' rights group tended to be the most ardent supporters of the fathers' rights cause, with new wives in particular often becoming more vocal on these issues than their new husbands. At times they also reported a "conversion" experience that ended their prior memberships in progressive women's groups or pro-child-support groups in order to dedicate their efforts to the fight for "true equality," a mission they found in their fathers' rights group. Those with independent affiliations, on the other hand, supported their local fathers' rights group but did so with less militancy. They were more likely to remark on the gender-based discrimination that they experienced within the group and on their disagreements with their male counterparts regarding the organization's strategies, tactics, and goals than those with relationship-based affiliations. Moreover, those with independent affiliations were also more likely to retain their simultaneous memberships in progressive women's organizations or even pro-child-support organizations. Those who were concurrently involved in both pro-child-support and fathers' rights groups reconciled their dual memberships by arguing that they quite consistently believe in a strong child support system *and* a viable custody system that promotes sustainable relationships between children and both parents over time.

Reasons for Joining

Members come to fathers' rights groups in a variety of different ways. These paths can be broken down into three major categories of engagement: active, passive, or crisis. In some cases, fathers discovered their local fathers' rights group by actively seeking out more information about the problems that were afflicting them at the time. Typical of this approach would be searching the Internet or the phone book for possible appropriate groups to help them manage their family situation. In a similarly proactive way, these members would also often hear about the group after peppering similarly situated individuals about their strategies for coping with the ups and downs of family dissolution. Some even went so far as to contact their state representatives about the family law system and in the context of these discussions with these local politicians would learn about the group. When no organization was available in their particular community, the most extreme proactive approach was to start a new group.

In the passive approach, information about the group came to potential members through a variety of sources, including books, newspapers, billboards, local fairs, flyers at the local library, radio shows, and bumper stickers. Others heard about the group from current spouses or girlfriends or even through coworkers. For these men, the experience of separation from their families was heart-wrenching emotionally and challenging in terms of managing the legalities involved. Nevertheless, because they had never sought out a group to assist them in some part of their lives before, they were not aware of the organizational opportunities available to them in their communities. At some point information about the group had to come to them; and only then did they become interested in joining.

Finally, some individuals became aware of a fathers' rights group through a crisis situation. In these cases, a father frequently began his journey to organizational participation by experiencing severe emotional turbulence as a result of his family's breakdown. This breakdown then led to further problems in completing day-to-day tasks. For example, sometimes this personal devastation prevented a father from adequately doing his job. As a result, a psychologist, a representative from the human resources department, or personnel from an employee assistance plan might notify the individual in question about the services available to him through a local fathers' rights group. Private attorneys who perceived that their clients were facing powerful barriers to accomplishing the duties required of them would also refer these men to a local fathers' rights groups. Those fathers who wanted to retain their jobs and experience life in more fulfilling ways would then start attending meetings on their own.

Personal Case Management

Regardless of how they first came to hear about the group, the most common reason fathers offered—49 percent of the sample—in explaining their decision to join the organization was to secure assistance with their own particular family dissolution case. Most of them had specific questions about how the judicial system would handle their concerns and sought out the group to provide them with guidance. One father, Bart, had a particularly complex case that made his quest for information from his group extremely urgent. About four years previously, his girlfriend had given birth to his son, who was eventually diagnosed as a special needs child. After the couple broke up, the mother returned to live in Jamaica. Although he retained custody of his son, the fact that his son's mother lived so far away created many hardships on the family that he hoped the group could help him manage.

> I chose to join [the group] because my son is developmentally delayed and the experts here have voiced their opinions in terms of how [he should be raised], the things we should do to modify the behavior and things like that....I had a disagreement with his mother about his [living] arrangements. She wanted a stranger to pick him up [here] to take him to Jamaica for a visit without certainty that the person would return him....The experts didn't feel it was appropriate at this time for him to go back...to Jamaica and the Caribbean. Not that it's hostile or anything, but it could set him back emotionally..., and in conjunction with that to have a stranger to take him down and all of that when he has gone through a lot emotionally. So I decided not to [let him go], and she was threatening that she was going to come up and grab him, which I discovered she could do under the law....That's when I first went to the fathers' rights group.   BART

For others who joined for reasons related to their personal cases, the group provided not only much-desired information but also much-needed financial relief. Valuable knowledge passed from member to member enabled them to rid themselves of their expensive lawyers once and for all and fight their case *pro se,* as the following father named Samuel described.

Well, I joined the organization in hopes of obtaining help and finally getting my case righted. I thought I would have maybe resources within that group or information that would aid or assist me....I made up my mind shortly after I joined that group [to] get rid of my attorney and I basically now I am operating on my own....[I wanted] helpful advice, support, [and] information that would be pertinent...to help me in my case and, in a way, to maybe educate myself in the endeavors of domestic law and family court situations that I wasn't [yet] utilizing. SAMUEL

Men like Bart and Samuel, then, found their groups invaluable during their time of need.

For some members seeking court-related information for their own cases, the process of joining a group was challenging at first but ultimately well worth the effort. Recall that slightly over half of all respondents in the sample had never been involved in any type of organization prior to joining their local fathers' group. These members had trepidation about joining *any* type of group, much less a group about which they had little knowledge. Who would be involved? How would they be treated? Would they gain anything by attending? These questions were all foremost in their minds and created a substantial amount of apprehension prior to attending. However, as time went on, the group became an essential part of their lives. According to a father named Basilio,

The first meeting I went to—it was unusual. Well, when you think of a meeting, you think of—and not that I've been in AA [Alcoholics Anonymous] or any meeting like that—you think of a structured, boring [event where someone says] "I am the president, this is how things work, blah, blah, blah." [You go] to the thing and you look and it is different....I wasn't sure what to think....I wasn't sure if they were legitimate. I wasn't sure if I was wasting my time. They looked like a bunch of ragamuffins....You don't know if you're in the right place, I guess, because of the clientele almost....An example would be if you go to a biker bar. You know you are in the wrong place and that is not where you want to hang out for the night....That would be the type of feeling I kind of got. It's a bad analogy, but you get the point....I mean, you [think], "But my case is different [than the others presented at the meeting]: Why am I here? These guys have to be pretty bad, because, I mean, look at them!" It's judging by appearance. Then I go home and I discuss it with myself and I'm like, "Do I really want to go back?" Yes, because they did have information....I make the decision to go to the second meeting. Is it better? No, not really. You are still getting the same type of information. You have more questions, you go back, you ask those questions and you get answers that you don't like. Most of those answers are [like], "it doesn't end tomorrow," "it doesn't end the next month," [and] "it doesn't end the next time you go to court." For some people maybe, for most people, no.... The third meeting, fourth meeting, fifth meeting [are] almost the same, but it is getting a little better because you are getting to know the people. You are feeling a little more comfortable with them; you are feeling a little more [like] they are on the level [and] they are legitimate. You [start to become more confident]. A perfect example would be one day in [a] phone conversation with my ex when I had my son [with me], she would say, "I'll just take him when I get him, I am taking your rights away," blah, blah, blah, [and] "Your mother will never see him," blah, blah, blah, blah. [But] by this time I know my rights because I [have] see[n] them in the law books. There are law books [for the group]. I know what the [state] law says; I know what my rights are. So, in one conversation...I told her right off the bat, "What are you talking about, I have every right to my son. My mother has rights, [and they are] called grandparental rights." The conversation went on and now I am starting to feel a little more confident....By this time I picked up a new attorney by the way—through [the organization]. She was an excellent attorney. So I am feeling very comfortable with her because of her being an attorney through the organization—she likes the organization, the attorney that is—[and] she allows me to express myself and she just fine-tunes it in the custody orders.   BASILIO

Fathers also came to the group when they had nowhere else to turn. Exhausting legal remedies for change, these respondents turned to the group to provide them with a source of hope in their seemingly hopeless cases. In a variety of ways, these fathers sensed that the "system" had failed them and the only institution interested in providing them with any aid was their local fathers' rights group. James explained his reasons for joining in exactly these terms.

[I joined the group because I was experiencing] total frustration. Because absolutely nothing was happening in, through, or by the courts... allowing me to see my children, be with my children, participate in rearing my children, etc. To make a statement bluntly, I didn't ask for the divorce, didn't want the divorce, didn't see it coming.... I was blind-sided. My wife was having an affair and she ran off with a guy. [Then] she filed a restraining order against me and as luck would have it, I happen to own a sporting goods shop that sells guns. That was on October 6, 2000, and what happened was, in effect, I was put out of business because you can't have guns if you have a restraining order against you, at least in this state and in most actually. In essence, the police [who, by the way, were all friends of mine] came to my shop, I was escorted out of my shop, [and] I was not allowed to go home. I had the clothes on my back and the vehicle I was in. I asked where I could go and they said a homeless shelter. [This is what they told me even though] I have a $200,000 home, [and] I have three businesses. So it was a bit of a drag. So three days later, on a hearsay tip from a girlfriend [of my wife's] who thought she saw me parked a block away from my home, I was arrested. It was on a Friday....[The charges were] essentially fabricated and, unfortunately, I was thrown in jail on a Friday. There are no magistrates available on the weekend and I was in jail until Monday. That happened four times....[It was] always on a Friday and always not being able to get an arraignment until Monday. It was getting a little old and the police department was getting a little miffed with it. But nothing was happening. I kept bringing her to court and doing what I was supposed to do, and eventually everything was thrown out of court. I was able to open my business back up. Unfortunately, something came up. I had a nervous break down. I just lost it. I was seeking counseling, and I got counseling. And during that period of time, I was not allowed to see my children until this was all sorted out essentially. That's where it ended up. So then we get the final order, fast forward a year, and I was allowed to get my children, have my children on certain days and times. That never happened. It just got progressively worse. I was threatened by her boyfriend at one point where he was going to kill me. This went on and has been documented over the last year and a half or two years now. So it just went on and on. So I got frustrated with the police department not doing anything, attorneys not being able to do anything, the courts not doing anything, the guardian ad litem not being able to act, [and] the list goes on. That's the long answer [as to why I joined]. JAMES

Overall, fathers who sought out the group for help with their own personal cases expressed shock and dismay over their treatment in the court system. They reported never having been subject to the level of discrimination directed at them as they were by representatives of the judicial system. Searching for answers, they joined their local fathers' rights group as a way to manage their own cases more effectively in these difficult periods of distress.

Emotional Support

The second most common reason cited for joining fathers' rights groups—voiced by 17 percent of the sample—was the potential for the group to offer emotional support. Undoubtedly, separation and divorce are traumatic experiences that both partners in a relationship must come to terms with in their own ways. However, because of their disproportional role in most families as primary emotional caregivers, women may be more likely to have developed the tools necessary to help them cope with feelings of loss. In addition, although men might only have their partners as potential confidantes when discussing sensitive issues, women are more likely to have strong networks of friends and family to help them recover from difficult life circumstances. Indeed, in numerous interviews in this study, respondents complained that in American society women have many outlets to express their emotions and men have relatively few. Representative in his expression of this view was Michael, who explained that joining a group with individuals who have experienced similar circumstances provided him with a chance to discuss his complex feelings without being self-conscious.

One [reason I joined is that] I guess there really isn't much support—social, institutional, or cultural support—for single parents, especially for fathers, noncustodial fathers. This was one of the groups that seemed like it offered support and understood a lot of the problems that I was going through. No one else really seemed to listen or care....It was pretty bad.   MICHAEL

Other fathers such as Pablo indicated the enormity of this need for emotional support in the context of not having the financial resources to pay a licensed therapist for assistance.

Sitting in courtrooms waiting for my case, listening to other fathers, talking with them out in the hallways, and attending a few other fathers' support groups [made me] realize [that] men are just not real good networkers. We are not very good at talking about our problems and asking for support. A lot of us don't have money to pay for professionals. So that's what motivated me to get "elder statesmen" together with people just starting in the process, [so that] we could support and coach each other.   PABLO

In each of these instances, fathers reported feeling very isolated and alone. Without close friends and family with whom they could share their experiences, they turned to the group for emotional assistance that would help them heal from their experiences more quickly. Finding other men going through the same difficulties provided immense relief for these men as they adjusted to the challenging changes that were then emerging in their lives.

Changing Public Policy

Fathers also joined because of their desire to improve public policy for the generation of fathers following them. Interestingly, however, only 17 percent of members offered this reason for joining. Yet, despite its relative infrequency, this particular motivation inspired significant passion within those who reported it as central in their lives. At times, this enthusiastic drive came in the form of a desire to help others when "the time for change" had already passed in their own cases. Christian explained his motivation in the following way:

[I joined for] two reasons: one is sort of selfish, and one is sort of lacking any self-interest. The selfish reason is because I thought maybe

I could get some information from this group that would help me in my ongoing conflicts with my ex and with the courts. But having already been through it, [I] sort of missed out on the opportunity to really know what I now know prior to going into court. I guess my larger motivation was to be able to help others so they didn't have to go through the same sort of crap I've gone through....I also work as a hotline telephone counselor and I find there are a lot of people out there who feel the same way. [There are people] who have been through so much stuff that if they can make the world a little bit better place for the people coming after them, they'll feel like they've accomplished something. CHRISTIAN

Other fathers who joined the group for political purposes recognized the importance of high membership numbers in translating their claims into reality. In other words, by himself, a lone father might not get far in terms of reforming public policy. However, if like-minded fathers formed a group, elected officials might be more inclined to speak with them and give their cause a hearing. One fathers' rights activist named Shaun learned this critical lesson through trial and error.

Well, I guess there is no one specific reason [why I joined the group]. It's multifaceted, but the main reason that led me towards this is just the way that the system is set up in [this state]....When I began this process, I guess prior to going into the divorce [process], I always knew that in [this state] fathers were pretty much victimized. But, you know, it never really hit home until I became one of these victims. [I] talked to so many other fathers and saw the pain [that] they were going through that my first step was to attempt to ...change legislation through contacting senators and what not....And I quickly learned [that] this is not a one man fight. And the senators' main concern was, you know, their overall constituencies....One thing that was consistent with each senator I spoke to is the fact [that] they [each] wanted to know how many fathers were going through this, how many fathers felt the same way I did, and how many relatives and friends supported these types of fathers. These were [the] types of statistics and answers I could not provide them with, although I knew the numbers were great. And they were not interested in hearing from one person or individual people on a regular basis, but they seemed to want to have mass numbers laid before them on a red carpet....I guess that was one of the main reasons that I started this group....The senators all told me when I spoke to them [that] they were very surprised that nobody had started a fathers' initiative type group in the past since...no fault divorces became common in the 1970s. SHAUN

Shaun, like other fathers in his predicament, learned that political reform was most probable if men like him could rally together.

Fathers motivated to change public policy understood that in addition to joining groups with high membership levels, they also had to be concerned with a group's prospects for longevity. Several fathers reported that these groups often suffer from high levels of infighting about goals and tactics. As a result, organizations tend to splinter into smaller groups led by the disaffected leaders from the once-larger groups. This splintering, in turn, leads to a decrease in perceived effectiveness by lawmakers and other decision-makers. To avoid being associated with this type of disarray, fathers such as Irving actively sought out groups that were already established in the public eye in terms of making their appeals for change.

As I said, I didn't want to reinvent the wheel [when deciding to become active with other fathers]. I didn't want to compete with [another group] and try to draw members away from the group. I believe that there is strength in numbers. I believe that there is a need for unity in all of the groups. I believe that all of the fathers who have gone through a modern divorce [should] be united under one banner so [that] their voices would be combined and therefore heard better.   IRVING

Still other fathers were mobilized to join in order to provide what they viewed as a necessary counterweight to their political opposition (i.e., mothers). Simply put, women's groups have been active in the politics of family dissolution for years, whereas men's groups, although recently becoming more visible as described in chapters 1 and 2, have not yet become truly heavyweight policy advocates in the legislative arena (Crowley 2003). Fathers' rights groups, according to men like Jules, need to reverse this perception of "paternal apathy" through widespread collective action.

> I feel like in order for child support laws and custody/visitation laws to be more fair and reasonable to both parents, and especially the children, changes have to be made. Without numbers, the changes won't be made. Also, [I think] that women's groups throughout the country have had an upper hand in this process and men have not been, in my opinion, realizing what has been going on. Women have had an upper hand in this because they made the most noise. I feel like in order for things to be equal in any situation, both sides need to be heard loudly. JULES

Here Jules verbalized a theme of optimism that was common throughout the membership of these organizations. If women could be successful in influencing legislators on issues of importance to them, then men could be successful lobbyists as well. Fathers simply need to come together under a common banner in order to be taken seriously by those in power.

The remaining 17 percent of sample respondents articulated a variety of other reasons for joining fathers' rights groups, including support for friends and family members, a desire to learn about these family issues, and altruistic motivations toward children going through the family dissolution process. In addition, it is important to note that the reasons listed for joining represent only the initial explanations members offered for getting involved. Over time, as members experienced the dynamics of the group, they became exposed to all of the organizational activities and frequently became involved in them as well.

Recruitment Strategies

The key to any group's long-term success is its ability to recruit new activists. Within fathers' rights activism, the key variable determining which recruitment path a group undertakes is the extent to which a group is made up entirely of volunteers or instead relies, at least in part, on a paid, professionalized staff to conduct its business, like Bruce's

group detailed at the beginning of this chapter. Out of the twenty-six organizations in this study, only one (Bruce's group) was professionalized.[2]
First, then, let us consider recruitment in all-volunteer groups.

Most all-volunteer fathers' groups reported slow but steady progress
in designing a marketing strategy to appeal to the greatest number of
fathers. These groups would typically place small classified ads in the
newspaper or write letters to the editor of their local papers to spot-
light their cause. These actions would often result in local television
or radio coverage of their group. Discussions with family court judges
and state legislators would then follow. At each stage in this process,
groups aimed to attract new members; however, overall these efforts
were largely arbitrary and uneven. Indeed, some leaders did not even
mention the opportunity to join the group *at all* during publicly open
informational meetings. To the extent that membership appeals were
made, leaders quickly described the option of joining to all attendees
at the end of the meeting; these sales pitches lasted one minute or less.
Even though the annual fee to participate was frequently less than $100,
it was often unclear how many of the regular attendees actually paid
these dues in order to become official members. Remarkably, for these
groups no high wall differentiated the services offered to paying members versus those offered to nonmembers.

In addition to the efforts of leaders of all-volunteer groups to recruit
at the organizational level, members themselves were responsible for attracting new participants. At this grassroots level, for all of the reasons
described above, numerical strength is an important factor motivating
individuals to join these groups in the first place. Fathers are looking
for help with their individual cases; they are also seeking emotional
support. The larger the group at meetings, the more experience and empathy will be offered to those in need. Numbers matter most, however,
in efforts to change public policy. Yet transforming public policy was
only the second most common reason given by respondents for joining
(tied with emotional support and far behind personal case management).
Given this lower ranking, it is not surprising that most activists described their recruitment strategies in "convenience" terms; "intense"

2. Some of the groups in this study had paid staff members at higher levels of the
organization, but not at the level studied here (i.e., there were paid staff members at
the national level, but not at the state-level).

strategies were less common, although some members used both. The next section describes the convenience and intense strategies of members involved in all-volunteer groups in more detail and outlines the motivation behind the decision of some members not to recruit at all.

Convenience Strategies

The majority of respondents—about 89 percent of the sample—described their recruitment strategies in terms of convenience. The modus operandi in recruitment strategies for these activists was to be open as opportunities arose to talking to other individuals who might be experiencing difficulties in their family situations. This could occur in a variety of circumstances; the key was recognizing these critical opportunities to publicize the work of the group. Juan described the process in the following way:

> What we share [about recruitment] with our members is this. Someone in your place of employment or where you live is going through what you're going through. And you need to reach out to the person and tell him [that] there is a place you can go to where you can be safe and express your feelings and can get help. That happens in places as simple as a soccer game, grocery store line, barber shop, library, [or] church. We just start a dialogue, [like] "Oh, are those your kids? Do you live with them? Oh, you're divorced?" And it progresses from there.   JUAN

For others, persuading outsiders to join was much more of an internal decision rather than one encouraged by other activists, like Juan. For instance, one father named Marco made recruiting others through convenience strategies a personal mission that he insisted he would only stop when all fathers obtained true equal rights with mothers. He likened the struggles of fathers to the gay rights activism of the 1960s and 1970s; many people, he reasoned, are negatively affected by these issues, but for change to occur, people first have to become more comfortable talking about them.

> Back in 1994, I made a vow that I would tell two people a day. I said, I'm going to tell two people every day about the horror that our social infrastructure is doing to the American family. And I don't always do

that, but you're the second person I talked to today.... It's almost like the gays from eight years ago or nine years ago. Until you come out of the closet and until people have a social dialogue about it, it's not going to change.... I was in an airport in Memphis and I was talking to a guy, talking about where his work was, and then he brought it up by saying, "Well, I'm trying to see my daughter."... I said, "By the way, are you paying child support? Are you paying it in two states? Do you get a chance to see your daughter? Does your ex prevent you from seeing your kids?" And I can tell you that I have yet to find someone who is not directly affected by this issue or has an immediate relative that's affected by the issue.   MARCO

Marco, like many others in fathers' rights groups, believed he could foment large change through small actions.

For members using the convenience strategy, however, recruiting others to the "cause" was typically much more about proximity to potential participants in normal, everyday interactions than a committed decision to provoke a rights revolution. For example, certain members reported going out of their way to talk to likely members at "male-dominated" locations like the local lumberyard. Others, such as Brandon, met potential members while commuting.

I was waiting for a train and I started talking to somebody and said, "You've got to join the group." His situation was that he is from Africa. He was a wealthy landowner in Africa, married twenty years, and had four children. His wife wanted to see the United States. They moved to the United States and within a few months, he was divorced, out of the house, and doesn't see his kids. I was like, oh my God! He got screwed.   BRANDON

The key for Brandon's recruitment efforts was paying attention to his surroundings in the search for new members. Reed followed the same philosophy while at a nearby gas station.

I even met a guy at the local gas station [while I was] copying some things for my trial on my divorce.... I am making copies, this guy comes in, and he wanted to copy his license. I said, "I am almost done

buddy; I'll be done in a minute." He goes, "What are you doing?"
I said, "Just something for a divorce." He goes, "Oh my goodness, my
wife left me [after] she met a guy on the Internet." He is going on and
on. I said, "Here, here is the number of this group. Contact them, and
they can help you." That is how simply I meet people.   REED

Several additional respondents spoke about the special nature of Wednesday nights as a significant time to recruit new members. In many states,
fathers who are noncustodial parents often receive "boilerplate" parenting time in the form of every other weekend plus Wednesday evenings.
Members seeking to attract new individuals to their groups were therefore
on heightened alert to look out for fathers who might be out with their
children on Wednesdays. Blayne explained this approach in great detail:

I mean, I don't just walk up to someone. But if I see someone holding a child's hand and they don't have on a wedding ring and it happens to be Wednesday night, chances are, if that guy's not married
and he has a son or daughter and it's Wednesday night, probably that's
the only day he gets [him or her]....I take my daughter out to eat
on Wednesday nights when I have her and Burger King and McDon-
ald's are full of unwed, divorced, or never-married fathers. That's their
night.   BLAYNE

Once these potential recruits were identified through their public visibility on Wednesday nights, members would then solicit them to speak
about their family lives and the possibility of joining their group.

Still other group participants invited potential members to join
through fortuitous business contacts. Sales and marketing jobs were
particularly helpful in reaching out to new members because they provided numerous opportunities to speak to many different people on a
consistent basis. Sean, a loan officer for a mortgage company, described
his recruitment tactics as follows:

I had a client that I called yesterday to talk about mortgages, and
he started telling me about his domestic situation. I just said, well,
maybe you ought to check out this group. It is not just for fathers,
although 90 percent of the people there probably are fathers. He is

not divorced yet, but the conversation was leading to the fact that he was looking toward being that way. I gave him the Web site address and talked to him the next day. I couldn't help him financially, but he said he checked out the Web site. He was interested and [said] I would probably see him at a meeting.   SEAN

Notably as well, some members used their faith to reach potential members. Interestingly, activists focused on these types of efforts especially when fathers were experiencing a significant amount of pain and were "acting out" in ways that were harmful either to their ex-partners, their children, or themselves. One particularly devout member named Stephan used his religious beliefs both to promote a sense of calm among desperate fathers and to give them an opportunity to change their own lives by joining the group.

It was at church [where] I tried to explain to many gentlemen that you don't have to go through it alone first off. Then I relate my own situation and then the next thing I point out is...we try to stop this from happening to other guys. How do you say [it], the cow is already out of the barn now, but we have to stop this from happening to the other guy. Basically, I also tell them that their situation is going to be all right. I always say that to people. I guess briefly as I tell them it's going to be all right, I use, as a Christian,...a lot of biblical references. Because you get a lot of real hard language out there a lot of times and I try to remove the bitterness from people and also from [the organization] itself, believe it or not.... What happens is people will be talking or people will write certain things. I do almost 90 percent of my correspondence by e-mail. I will get an e-mail...about somebody's personal situation and I always e-mail back. I try to explain you can't be bitter about this because the [e-mail correspondents] will start going into the mother has the upper hand, because blah, blah. They'll go on. I say, it's all true, but what you have to understand is things have a way of changing later on.... Things changed for me. What I can say briefly [about my situation is that] tomorrow I will fly to [another city] to get my son and I will get on a plane with him and fly back here.... He is going to be here for two weeks. As you can tell, [this arrangement] is over and above the visitation agreement, so some things have changed. That's what I try to explain to the guys. Things have a way of changing—you don't have to do anything. I mean, yeah, the courts are good and everything, but on your own if you're a certain kind of person, if you have a certain kind of dedication to your children and if you're prayerful, then things will just change.... That's how I try to recruit people.   STEPHAN

In sum, the great majority of respondents in this study argued that they had a responsibility to recruit new members to their cause. However, most did not make special efforts to attract new members. Instead, they relied on proximity and circumstance to make their pitch about the benefits of joining.

Intense Strategies

Although strategies of convenience were the most popular form of recruitment for most activists, a significant majority—73 percent of the sample—also pursued new members quite vigorously as well through methods beyond mere talking about their groups at an opportune time.[3] For these individuals, the key to achieving equality for fathers was publicizing their cause at every opportunity. These members would not wait for others to cross their paths to promote the group; instead, they would actively try to cross well-trodden paths of similarly situated fathers. By far, as Aaron described, the most popular method to recruit others in this more intense way was through the Internet.

Well, things have changed since 1995. Now it has actually become somewhat easier to channel [our communications] with the rise of the Internet. For example, we have created a kind of cyber-virtual community out there which you can tap into any given time. Dissemination of information is much more rapid. It has been a boom, in my opinion, to a lot of small, grassroots types of organizations, which we remain to this date.   AARON

Group members and leaders used group Web sites as active recruiting tools by posting information about the organization as well as other

---

3. Some members reported using both convenience and intense recruitment strategies.

important reference materials for parents in need. These participants also listed calendars of upcoming events and meetings to draw people to their cause. In addition, most of the groups utilized an active List-serv and message board where members as well as the general public could post their questions concerning child support and child custody and receive knowledgeable answers from longstanding group partici-pants. When nonmembers would post a query, members would re-spond to the question and end with strong encouragement to join the group.

Other respondents engaging in intense strategies reported using more traditional mechanisms than the Internet for recruiting new members. For members such as Jake, for example, this simply meant wearing the group's button on his jacket and generating conversation from that starting point.

> I focus on my recruitment [efforts] with friends, family, and neigh-bors. I don't hide that I am a fathers' rights activist....I wear a but-ton on my coat. Anytime someone gives me an opening to bring up a political issue, I bring it up and I talk about fathers' rights....So frequently I'll talk to them about some of the challenges and the value of getting involved; not only the value you get for your personal case—just learning more about the law and situations other fathers have been in—but also in trying to change public policy.   JAKE

In addition to buttons, other important forms of popularizing the fa-thers' rights cause included the use of bumper stickers. Frequently these stickers serve to attract the attention of those who might be inclined to support the goals of fathers' rights groups but have yet to take any concrete action. Vince was one member who aimed to start a dialogue on these issues whenever he was traveling or simply walking to his car in a public place.

> [Recently] I was at Costco in the parking lot. I have these bumper stickers on my van from [my fathers' group]. This guy came up [to me] and I couldn't understand why he was just standing there. I was talking on my cell phone, and I said to him "Can I help you?" He said, "I was just looking at your bumper sticker." ...I gave the guy my card

and I said to call me. He said, "I think it is too late." I said, "It is never too late, call me."   Vince

Other techniques included posting handmade signs across activists' local neighborhoods. For fathers like Allen, this strategy became the springboard to much more ambitious forms of marketing for his group's cause.

> When we first started, I built homemade billboards and stuck them on properties of my friends that live on highways and stuff. That's what really got it going. Once we had our first couple of meetings... I told these people, "It's your responsibility to help get this group going."...I set goals for them and said, "Do you want to change the system or do you want to let it go the way it is?" I also made it clear that it is going to take some time. It could take ten years. If it takes ten years, that means your child doesn't have to go through what you are going through. ALLEN

Allen was able to take his simple action of putting up homemade signs and transform it into a powerful recruiting tool by asking others to do the same. Signs spread like wildfire throughout his community, and increasing numbers of people came to the group's meetings. Displaying some symbol of the group, either on the Internet, buttons, bumper stickers, or signs, were all common ways of attracting support for the group. Producing radio or television ads, as well as designing phonebook ads, were also typical strategies, although groups had to rely on donated air time or publication space in order to be able to afford this type of publicity. As the above examples demonstrate, these techniques were compelling enough to start many new conversations between long-time members and potential new recruits.

Fathers' rights groups also used other ways to attract new members, including participating in more structured forms of political action. Rather than simply posting a visual message to garner publicity, members pursuing intense recruitment strategies expended valuable personal time to spread the word. Some members, for example, volunteered to answer the group's public telephone hotline, which some groups offer to *any* father "in-crisis"—whether that crisis be emotional or legal.

Typically fathers would call with difficulties regarding seeing their children on a regular basis; this conversation would serve as an opening to discuss public policy in greater detail and the benefits of joining the group. Another widespread technique embraced by committed activists like Amy was to attend local fairs, parades, and rallies to represent their local fathers' rights group.

> We have a booth at [our state fair] and we do try to get signatures.... We pass out brochures and we let the public know what we are about and what we are trying to do.... This spring we had... I don't know if you'd call it a rally.... There was like an Easter parade in [our town], I believe it was the Saturday before Easter, and we marched in the street with the other participants.... We carried our banners and just tried to get information out there that [something needs to be done].... Then we had a parade in the little town where we live and that was the Saturday before Mother's Day.... We carried our signs and we walked and passed out brochures just trying to make the public aware that something needs to be done.   AMY

One of the most extreme strategies was to recruit new members right at the local courthouse where judges heard cases related to child support and custody. For certain members, this meant leaving organizational business cards in the court offices where fathers filed paperwork. For others, it involved participating in an active "court-watching program." In these efforts, members would sit in on public court sessions related to child support and custody in order to monitor the proceedings in terms of their fairness to fathers. Basilio engaged in this strategy and found it to be extremely important in energizing a new membership pool for the group.

> Well, at one point in time we adopted a program where some of us would go up to the court house and, you know, you sit. When you walk into the court house and you sit and watch some of the antics that go on in the waiting room... the antics are incredible.... When you really stop and you look at it, it's a shame, it really is a shame because a lot of these [lawyers] are not advising the correct way, they are just advising the quick way. Let's get in, let's get out, and this is what is going to be done.   BASILIO

Programs like Basilio's attempt to engage fathers at court in conversations about the group at moments when they are likely to be very open to assistance. This aggressiveness, Basilio hoped, would pay off in a higher membership success rate down the road.

Avoidance Strategies

Although most members engaged in at least some form of recruitment, either through convenience or more intense strategies, a small handful of respondents—about 11 percent—did not participate in any recruitment activities at all. Their reasons for avoiding this task were varied. Some reported that they simply did not have friends or acquaintances who were in similar familial circumstances. Others feared that the group did not have a politically acceptable message and did not want to be personally labeled as somehow out of the mainstream with respect to family policy. Patrick explained his apprehension in the following way:

> In society there seems to be that same, chivalrous attitude towards moms. Not a lot of people really want to go against that....[The mistaken belief is that] we're just whiners and criers and mom beater-uppers and that kind of stuff.   PATRICK

Casey echoed a similar view, arguing that by recruiting individuals to his group, he risked being pigeonholed as a father who does not want to support his children.

> That's an interesting question [about my involvement in recruitment] because, you know, I was looking through the newspaper the other day and there was a women's seminar [taking place] on going through divorce. There was also a meeting on women and divorce, yet when it comes to men and divorce, I feel like there is some sort of stigma attached...that if we are seeking help to do better in our divorce, then we are somehow depriving our children or depriving our ex-wife because we are supposed to be paying for it, we are supposed to be doing things that will help them....I think that a couple of people, maybe one person I talked to, thought that I joined that group because I was going to stick it to my ex-wife or that I wanted to really beat her

badly in court. Really, it wasn't for that reason; it was just because I was frustrated. CASEY

Others reported that they did not try to get others involved simply because it is difficult to entice men into joining *any* type of organization. One father named Jackson explained that this was a longstanding problem for men who want to come together to effect change under any circumstances.

> I've talked to others, but it's hard to recruit men actually. I find it hard to get men involved....I think [that] there is basically one reason [that more people do not get involved with these groups]. They are too damn busy trying to earn an income to live decently and pay their child support..., or else they would rather cry about it than get involved. JACKSON

Finally, others, such as Louis, did not participate in recruitment efforts because of a belief that most men would be frustrated with the slow pace of these types of organizations in advancing reform.

> To be honest, the group is so slow-moving to get anything to happen; it's very demoralizing for people to go to the meetings and be told we are making progress. People are in much worse financial conditions than I am. You just can't wait years for things to happen. To me, [the group] is not as proactive as it needs to be....If somebody tells me that he is having a problem, I will direct him in that direction, but that is as far as it goes. LOUIS

As Louis and others document, fathers' rights groups face difficult recruitment challenges. Members stay in the group because they receive some benefit from doing so; even so, they are not completely comfortable with the group's reputation, their own capacity to attract other members due to competing pressures on everyone's time, and their own group's track record in generating change. For members, organizational maintenance and growth are serious concerns that they, at least at the time of this study, felt powerless or unwilling to address.

Recruitment in Professionalized Groups: An Exception

In contrast to all-volunteer groups, professionalized groups, which are far less common than all-volunteer groups and rely on at least one partially paid staff person, took a much different tack in securing new members. To meet their payroll, these groups not only had to apply for grants, but also were heavily reliant on membership fees to support their activities. In fact, memberships in these groups were comparatively expensive, frequently costing more than $100 per person per year. And in order to survive, these groups had to aggressively "sell" membership in their organization at every opportunity. Bruce's aggressive sales pitch at the beginning of this chapter is an example of how recruitment is pursued in these professionalized groups. Unlike in all-volunteer groups, leaders do all of the recruitment work; there is little one-on-one membership-based recruitment.

The most important recruitment principle for professionalized groups involves offering services to members that are exclusive and of a high quality at a reasonable price so that members feel like they are getting their money's worth. Toward this end, services provided to members compared to nonmembers first must be highly segregated. Recall that in Bruce's group, only those individuals who joined the group were able to meet with the organization's attorneys. Bruce quickly escorted the person who did not join to the door at the end of his introductory comments. Second, the organization must be run efficiently, like a business. Because this strategy was very rare among fathers' rights groups yet so interesting, it is worth quoting Bruce on these points in fuller detail.

> Well, one of the things I decided to do when I got here is...my background is building and designing restaurants and nightclubs...One of the things that restaurants and nightclubs have is lots and lots of staff to do things. You have to have your chefs and your cooks and you have to have waiters and waitresses, and your door hosts and your bouncers, your bartenders and all that. One of the things that this organization did not have when I got here was any tools or services that somebody could really tap into. They had one individual with a high school education running the organization; they had a gay gentleman who lived in the building where the office was that would come down

here...he had some computer skills and he would help type up documents once in a while. They had two attorneys and that was it. They were signing up about five to ten people a week. Last week we did about forty-five people. Their average was about 400–500 members a year; now we average about 1,600 members a year.

When I looked at the organization, I said two things have to be done. Number one, we have to get the tools available for people to use....So I started looking at developing a law library with all the codebooks and all the research materials you could possibly need and we started pumping that up. We started putting the word out through the community, basically through the attorneys we already had and people whom I met, that we wanted more attorneys. We now have sixteen attorneys that we work with. I needed some paralegals to prepare paperwork, so we brought in two paralegals right away. We brought in our own process servers, we brought in our own counselors in many different fields, and we are still building that up. In fact, we are in what I call phase three of our development right now. We are developing some anger management counseling, some stress management counseling, financial counseling, drug and alcohol counseling, and a batterers' intervention program. All of that is being done in the next phase. That alone or just simple word of mouth...creates the momentum. Each person that came in was given a flyer, a business card, and a follow-up letter just like any salesman would do in the insurance business or car business to get some referrals....We are a 501(c)3—a nonprofit organization—so I went to a lot of the newspapers and radio stations and said, you know,..."Would you give us some free advertising in exchange for things that we buy?"—and they did that. We developed a relationship with a billboard company that would put a billboard up for a couple thousand, which is the average cost per month, but we'd leave that thing up there for six or seven months as long as they hadn't sold that space....We developed an award-winning TV commercial which is a beautiful commercial. Every time I look at it, I start crying; it is a wonderful, very heart-pulling commercial. Anyway, we did our own TV commercial and we have several TV stations here that would put that out. If we spend $2,000–$3,000 with them, they'll give us $4,000–$5,000 in return in free advertising. So we developed that. It was a donation to the organization.

We made contacts with all of the other legal aid type of services throughout the [area] as well as with all of the law libraries and all the counties. We went to all the counties and most of them agreed to allow us to put our flyers up [in their administrative buildings]. We developed some very professional flyers and so we are connected with almost all the contiguous counties of [this city], and we'll get referrals from them. I developed a relationship with all of the senior managing attorneys with our [state's child support agency]....I put a suit and tie on and went and shook everybody's hands and introduced myself and developed a partnership with them. The [child support] agency can enforce and collect child support, but they can't enforce visitation. So now we get about 400 referrals a year from the [child support] agency for enforcement of visitation, so that pumped up our membership....We are, by far, the biggest organization in the country that at least does the type of hands-on casework that we do.   BRUCE

Bruce was clearly an ambitious man with a proactive membership agenda for his organization that seemed, on its surface, to be very successful. However, even with this relative success, the pressure to pay the operational bills on time often seemed to be quite daunting for the organization, which was open during normal business hours throughout the week. Compounding this stress, Bruce's group had recently opened up a second branch in a different part of the state. During the time that his group was being observed in this study, he expressed concern that the new office was not "bringing in the membership numbers" that are necessary for the organization to survive. At his own office, Bruce often wandered around to see how many people were in the reception area waiting to be signed up with a new membership package.

However, despite these financial worries, Bruce did not invite all potential members to join; the group typically engaged in a minimal level of screening to ensure that new members "represent" the organization well. For example, while his group was being observed, one man stepped into Bruce's office and described his concern over his partner's mental health. He claimed that his wife, from whom he was then separated, was making outrageous claims against him, accusing him of drug usage and verbal abuse. She even issued a temporary restraining order against him. Bruce listened to this story dispassionately and made several concrete recommendations. He advised the man to try and re-move his case from what he viewed as an unfriendly court jurisdiction. As he continued to discuss his case, the potential client also indicated that he did not necessarily want a divorce, but rather was most con-cerned about his children's safety. Bruce pushed his own chair back and suggested that this man consider marriage counseling. Throughout the entire discussion, Bruce seemed aloof and disengaged.

After the man left his office, Bruce explained his standoffish attitude to me directly. He pointed out that the man put a large coat on Bruce's desk while he was talking. Bruce then stated that he felt uncomfortable with this man and suspected that under the coat was a tape recorder. Although not 100 percent sure that this was the case, Bruce clearly was ill-at-ease with this man. Because he is not a lawyer, Bruce has to make sure that he never dispenses legal advice, which would make him guilty of engaging in the unauthorized practice of law. Someone who disagrees with the goals of the group might try to "slip him up" by tape-recording him saying something inappropriate. Bruce remarked that it is much better in these instances to avoid further discussions with these suspi-cious individuals than to invite them to be full-fledged members.

Gerard, who works with Bruce, demonstrated a similar capacity to reject potential members who did not satisfy the requirements of the group's concerns about reputation and overall philosophy. While he was being observed as part of this study, Gerard interviewed a man who came to the group's office with his new girlfriend. This man explained his desire to divorce his wife, from whom he had been separated for close to a decade. He further elaborated that he was only with his wife for three days after they got married, and he only recently discovered that he has a nine-year-old daughter with her whom he has never met. He asked Gerard to help him obtain a quick divorce and indicated that he wanted nothing to do with his daughter. With his face deepening in color, Gerard warned, "You realize that by saying that you never want to meet your daughter that you are teaching her that all men are scum." The man responded with equal anger that he simply was looking for help with his divorce. Gerard replied, "We can help you with your di-vorce, but you have to understand that our primary purpose is to help fa-thers see their kids." After Gerard made this remark, the man abruptly walked out with his girlfriend, declaring that he wanted no part of this group. Gerard freely let the couple leave and indicated his sadness over the father's attitude. To Gerard, fathers like that man unfortunately give *all* fathers a bad name and, within this context, forfeiting those potential membership dues was an easy concession to make.

The Magnetism of Membership

All organizations that operate within the American political system face challenges regarding their operational future. At the heart of these concerns are questions of membership attraction, retention, and growth. For groups to be effective over the long run, individuals must be strongly drawn to the cause or philosophy that is being advocated. Groups also must be able to retain the members that they acquire and actively strategize as to the best means of drawing new faces into the fold. In all of these ways, fathers' rights groups are no different than any other set of organizations seeking to promote social or economic change in the twenty-first century.

Where fathers' rights groups *do* differ is in their choice to retain an operational form that is somewhat at odds with notions of what groups *should* look like at this moment in history. Unlike their contemporaries, they have not become completely professionalized organizations with mailing lists of members who do not know one another. Instead, they are largely of the "old-school" character, organizing at the grassroots level and bringing together—in-person—members from different walks of life to fight on behalf of a common cause. Although a diverse set of motivations attracts members to the groups in the first place, once they are involved, most activists find the organizations compelling enough to at least discuss their goals with potentially interested recruits. It then becomes the task of leaders, as examined in the next chapter, to move the group to a higher level of political and interpersonal effectiveness over time.

4

Becoming the Chief

Patterns of Leadership and Governance in Fathers' Rights Groups

The setting is a donated space provided by a Protestant church in the Southwest. Even though the room is currently being used by the fathers' rights group Proud Parents for Justice, an atmosphere of religiosity remains in the air. The chairs, on which twenty men, three women (one of whom has brought her children), and the leader sit, are arranged in neat rows, as if a church service were about to begin. All attendees are white. They sit facing the piano and the organ in front of the room, which are right behind the altar. The cross on the altar bears the words, "Do This in Memory of Me."

Proud Parents for Justice's leader, Carlos, starts the meeting about ten minutes late. He introduces himself to the group, although many of the attendees seem to have been coming for long periods of time. A commanding presence in a tie and a jacket, Carlos explains that his group has two main goals: child support reform and child custody reform. He then outlines the three dominant themes he considers most important to the group's success.

CARLOS: We have many purposes here, but I want you all to know our principles. First, be the best parent that you can be. Even if you only have one hour of supervised visitation per month, make the most out of it. Second, work to make your situation the best it can be. This organization can help you in realizing that goal. Third, spend time changing the system. It is easiest for the court to divide child support and child custody in traditional ways. You all should try to change the system, but remember that the first two points that I mentioned are more important than point number three.

(Some discussion ensues of legislative developments in the state and of other fathers' rights groups making news across the globe. The dialogue then turns to the issue of Carlos as a great leader for Proud Parents for Justice. Because the members are comfortable with one another and with Carlos, they are able to point out his strengths and weaknesses without making him feel bad.)

PROUD PARENTS FOR JUSTICE MEMBER 1: Carlos is a great leader. Why? Two Reasons. First, he is clear-thinking and logical. He speaks well in front of a group. Second, he is also very objective. His emotions do not play into his answers.

PROUD PARENTS FOR JUSTICE MEMBER 2: He is an excellent researcher and has great speaking credentials.

PROUD PARENTS FOR JUSTICE MEMBER 3: These things are true, but I do believe that he has one weakness. The ability to raise money on behalf of our issues is key. This is where Carlos has a weakness.

PROUD PARENTS FOR JUSTICE MEMBER 4: Well, I really appreciate Carlos. I am really aggressive, and Carlos is a calming presence.

PROUD PARENTS FOR JUSTICE MEMBER 5: I agree. He has a great intellectual ability to understand the issues, and takes a moderate approach. We all respect him here.

PROUD PARENTS FOR JUSTICE MEMBER 6: I appreciate that Carlos treats all of us as we are, as individuals.

PROUD PARENTS FOR JUSTICE MEMBER 7: Carlos is terrific. He has an intense knowledge of what is going on in other states. Prior to Carlos, we had another leader who was not so positive for the group. Members were really angry then, and the group was perceived as "angry." Carlos has made the group more respectable.

Arguably one of the most important changes in American family politics from the 1970s to the present day is the almost complete replacement of mother-oriented advocacy groups concerned primarily with child support reform with father-oriented advocacy groups dedicated to reform in the areas of both child support and child custody. Before the revolutionary legislative initiatives enacted in the 1970s and 1980s to strengthen the child support system, mother-oriented interest groups proliferated throughout the country. These were grassroots-based groups started by local, middle-class mothers who took politics into their own hands when confronted with the dual injustices of abandonment by their husbands and financial destitution. Through their efforts, they truly defined the scope of community-based activism that would shape family law in the years to come.

For example, For Our Children's Unpaid Support (FOCUS), founded in 1981 by Bettianne Welch in Virginia, began its work by collecting thousands of signatures of outraged taxpayers who protested against the use of welfare dollars to support children whose financially se-cure fathers had simply abandoned them.[1] Welch was one such victim, and she succeeded in lobbying the Virginia state legislature to enact an automatic wage withholding bill—which deducted a father's sup-port payments directly from his paycheck and channeled them back to the mother. Another group with the same acronym of FOCUS— with the acronym this time standing for For Our Children and Us, Incorporated—began as a result of Fran Mattera's picketing against the layers of governmental red tape that prevented her from receiving timely child support payments. She began her demonstrations outside a Long Island family courthouse in 1972, and by 1978 had built up her organization to include numerous paralegals to help women navigate their way through the support system. Echoing this experience, Elaine M. Fromm, left penniless by her husband when she was pregnant and already a mother of three in 1961, started her own group, the Organiza-tion for the Enforcement of Child Support (OECS), also as a means to call both citizens' and policymakers' attention to the economic plight of mother-headed families.

Perhaps most well-known was Geraldine Jensen's group, the Asso-ciation for Children for Enforcement of Support (ACES). In 1977 when Jensen divorced her husband, she became the primary caretaker of her

---

1. The discussion presented in this and the following two paragraphs is based on Crowley 2003, chap. 6.

two young boys. Within the year, her ex-husband had stopped making child support payments. In 1983 Jensen began ACES in Toledo, Ohio, by placing an ad in a local paper asking women to contact her if they too were experiencing child support difficulties. She was flooded with responses. Working in conjunction with more broad-based groups such as the National Organization for Women (NOW), the Displaced Home-makers Network, and the National Council of Negro Women, ACES tapped Congresswomen Barbara Kennelly (D-CT), Patricia Schroeder (D-CO), and Marge Roukema (R-NJ) to make enhanced child support enforcement an important federal priority. Indeed, the passage of the Child Support Enforcement Amendments of 1984 and the Family Support Act of 1988, which toughened penalties against fathers who economically abandoned their children, did much to alleviate the pressing financial strain under which many similarly situated women were operating at the time.

But carefully observing this activity in the background were many men's divorce reform groups and men's rights advocacy groups, the precursors to modern fathers' rights organizations, as described in chapter 2. These groups suggested that women were primarily to blame for their economic problems in cases of family breakdown because they were largely "gold diggers" and financially irresponsible. During the 1980s Congress restricted their testimony on pending legislation to written submissions due to the misogynistic nature of many of their arguments. However, women's grassroots activism during the 1980s did provide the more astute fathers' rights sympathizers with insight into how to construct their own, more effective mobilization campaigns in the future. This learning period soon paid enormous political dividends. Indeed, once these women-led groups who advocated solely on behalf of child support reform won passage of many of their policy proposals, they quickly disbanded (the only major exception was ACES). Fathers' rights groups, on the other hand, organized under the direction of an evolving set of leaders who were now more sophisticated than ever before in making their political claims and were ready to methodically take these women's groups' place.

Who, then, has risen to the top of fathers' rights organizations today? We know that they are individuals who shoulder a disproportionate share of the costs of organizing. In addition, scholars have also pointed to three other attributes that define successful leaders. First, skilled leaders are those individuals who are alert to new possibilities for political action (Kingdon 1984; Rickets 1987; Schneider and Teske 1995). They are constantly scanning the political scene for the best time to make their policy pitch to chief decision-makers and the public alike. Second, successful leaders are those who are able to use rhetorical ingenuity to make the best possible case for their claims (Baumgartner and Jones 1993; Riker 1986). In other words, they are incredibly verbally adept at presenting their view of a better world to others in advocating for change. Finally, successful leaders are persistent (Mintrom 1997; Polsby 1994; Weissert 1991), meaning that through good times and bad, they never waver in their drive to fulfill their policy mission. On the surface, then, leaders should distinguish themselves from the rank-and-file membership across a wide range of notable characteristics.

However, as pointed out in chapter 3, fathers' rights groups operate in ways that are very different than the majority of organizations in the twenty-first century. Their most striking characteristic is that they continue to have in-person meetings in an effort to fulfill their organizational goals. In an era dominated by groups that primarily only ask that their supporters send in checks as signals of their support, fathers' rights groups face unique challenges in retaining the energized spirit and interest of their members. These challenges can, at times, be overwhelming and diminish the enthusiasm of even the most charismatic leaders. As a result, leaders are not necessarily the most dynamic personalities involved in these groups nor possess *all* of the optimal leadership traits described above; instead, they may simply possess the third characteristic in abundance: resiliency. Being the last one standing in the face of constant turnover—and without pay in the case of the all-volunteer groups—also means that institutionalized power within the organization is always subject to contestation. Each day, in fact, leaders must work to earn the respect of their followers. This precarious position also influences the scope of their decision-making authority, their ability to determine which members to retain or expel from the organization, and their capacity to effectively plan for leadership transitions when they desire to move on to other opportunities in their lives.

Becoming a Leader

How did the current set of fathers' rights group leaders come to head their particular organizations? Did they simply rise through the ranks of the membership, or were they the original organizers of the group? The process of becoming a leader of a fathers' rights group is specific to each organization, but definitely not restricted by gender. In fact, 19 percent of the leaders in this study were women.[2] To help explicate the process of presidential selection, each leader in the process of forming their group helped generate a set of written organizational bylaws, from which a description of the leader identification procedures could be derived. On paper, selection procedures were fairly straightforward. Individuals could become leaders in one of two ways: the rank-and-file membership could elect them, or far more commonly, the board of directors could elect or appoint them. Recall that the majority of these leaders were volunteers, donating their time and experience to their groups due to their commitment to the cause.

There is a marked difference, however, between the ways in which a leader is supposed to be chosen according to the bylaws and how a leader is actually chosen in the "real world" of activism. Large, well-established organizations may need firm procedures of governance in place in order to maintain legitimacy among their membership bases. Under these circumstances, carefully developed and followed rules for selecting leaders promote the ideal that all rank-and-file members have the opportunity to be heard through a spectrum of democratic processes. Over time, however, these rules may harden, producing organizations that are highly bureaucratic in nature. In contrast, fathers' rights groups are in their infancy, which provides them with a degree of flexibility—some would say haphazardness—in terms of how they actually go about selecting the individuals who will guide them in obtaining their multiple objectives. How exactly—and perhaps distinct from the bylaws—do leaders emerge to take the reins of power in these groups?

2. Note that several of the twenty-six groups included in this study had co-coordinators or copresidents, generating a total of thirty-one leaders considered in this chapter.

By Interest

The majority of leaders in this study—61 percent of the sample—took control of their organizations out of sheer passion and interest in the cause. These leaders perceived themselves as "natural activists" who are more intrinsically inclined than the rank-and-file membership to assume the top position in these organizations. As the workhorses of the organizations, they seized the opportunity to provide future direction to their groups. Lawrence described how his dedication translated into his rapid promotion to the top of his organization.

> Well, when I first became involved in [this organization], I went to all of the meetings. I spoke a lot. I organized activities and did a lot of research. I am very tuned into what's being done with family research, and after a year of doing that, I was asked [to become president]. It wasn't voted on; I was just asked to assume the leadership position. LAWRENCE

Once asked, Lawrence harnessed this chance to move the group in his preferred direction. This type of leader recognizes that it is always difficult to motivate people into action—especially volunteers—but believes that he or she has a special talent in this area. Another leader, Henry, saw this skill within himself and reaped the rewards of leadership when others saw it in him as well.

> I think [that] to a great degree, the organization exists based on people's ability to do things. I guess I had done a lot of things in terms of…coordinating projects and I think one law [governing most] people is that people who are willing to work and do things are likely to become the leaders of the group. The trouble is most people might agree with our feelings, but most people can't get themselves motivated to get off their butt and do [anything] about it. To a great degree, I was probably a doer [in terms of] initiating a lot of things and getting things done; because of that, I believe I was chosen to be a leader of the group. HENRY

Other leaders did not necessarily know that these types of organizations existed prior to some pivotal event in their lives, which then prompted them to work on behalf of these issues more seriously than their counterparts. For example, a leader named Allen wrote a letter to a newspaper editor about local fathers' issues, and a grandmother living in a nearby city who read the piece reached out to him and asked him to do more. From this small initial action, Allen found his calling by starting his own fathers' rights group.

> I got a call from a grandmother [after she read my letter] and she called actually from my hometown. She said, "You've got to do something; you've got to get a group going." She really pushed it, [and] at that point I had actually thought about doing something like that. At that point is when I said, okay, I am going to do it, and that's when I got hold of [another fathers' rights activist]. It was a grandmother that did it.... I just called this other activist up and said, "I am interested in starting up a chapter of your organization." I said, "I'd like to meet with you." I drove out there; it is about a three hour drive to [this city]. I took a day off work, met with him, and I asked him if he was interested in building a Web site. He said sure. I said, "Okay, it's on me, I'll do it." ALLEN

Others, like Kyan, were "baptized by fire" into a leadership position by attending a state-wide drive to educate legislators on fathers' rights issues.

> I saw an ad in the paper about a fathers' rights type...group going to the capital [that invited people to go] if you wanted to lobby for a bill that the [group] had going. I called and met [a leader] down there at the capital, and he asked if I wanted to have a chapter in [my city]. I said, "Sure, fine," and then I talked to him on the phone quite a bit. KYAN

As Kyan indicated in his interview, he clearly had an above-average interest in becoming involved in this type of cause. He had already distinguished himself by his willingness to engage in time-consuming legislative education efforts for no remuneration. This level of commitment was so unique that by simply taking this action, he was instantly given a leadership position in a new chapter. Notably here again, Kyan viewed this opportunity as a "reward." Unlike those leaders who assumed their positions by default, as we shall see, leaders who came to head their organizations because of interest brought an unparalleled level of energy to the cause overall.

By Default

In contrast to simply having a passionate interest in the cause, the other 39 percent of the sample took on the job of leader "by default." That is, these respondents asserted, no one else wanted to do the job, so they assumed the responsibility themselves. In other cases, a small collective within the group simply "dropped" the job in their laps. There might have been some type of vote or appointment process once this happened, but clearly it was a symbolic action. As one leader named Eli described, when he was chosen there literally was no one else to guide the group unless he took on the job himself.

> At the point that I took over, there were actually 300 people listed as active members, but the board of directors consisted of three. The president asked the other person in charge what he thought, [and] he said, "I am swamped; I don't want [the presidency], [and] don't even consider thinking about it." Like I said, [then the current president] showed up at my door and said, "You're the only one left," and that's how it happened.   ELI

In circumstances like Eli's, the job came to the person in question rather than the other way around. Once presented with this opportunity, however, these leaders assumed the position out of a sense of duty to fathers' issues.

In some cases, however, this forced "choice" to become a leader produced strong, negative feelings among those who were "chosen." In fact, several leaders, such as Aaron, expressed bitterness because they came to believe that they were the only ones willing to do the hard work on behalf of the organization.

> Well, I was almost tempted to say [that I became the leader] by default. It's a thankless job that you receive no pay for. You sacrifice a lot of time and a lot of out-of-pocket expenses that you never get

reimbursed for. I am trying to think back. We have a formal board and we have board meetings. I guess I just was chosen at some point; I mean, that's actually what happened. I was chosen and elected. I first joined as a board member and then I was elected president at some point.   AARON

Amplifying Aaron's point, another leader named William described himself as the "scapegoat" when he argued that "everybody wants to see me on the front line. They don't want to go forward themselves [and run the organization]." William too felt that he was a scapegoat in the sense that if he could not achieve results for the group, the membership blamed him without respecting the fact that he at least tried to effect change. Another leader named Juan echoed this concern by stating, "No one wants to do the nuts and bolts—the paper work, the treasury, the counting of the money, [and] the sending of the transmittals—so I took it." Notably, even a female leader described her wish to vacate her post, but could not do so due to the lack of interest among the rank-and-file of becoming her replacement.

The guy who was previously the coordinator left with the past president, which kind of left a void and I stepped up. . . . Every year or so . . . I say, "Listen guys, I have had it, will somebody like to take this over?" And nobody has stepped up.   SARAH

Other leaders who assumed this position "by default" did so because they sensed that without their leadership, the group would move in a negative direction. For example, one leader named Justin astutely noted that his group was quickly heading toward a crisis in focus. Several outspoken individuals in his organization wanted to dedicate the group's resources toward child support reform, but Justin wanted to continue working on custody issues. At the time, his faction was simply the more powerful one in terms of choosing the leadership of the group.

I try to stay away from the child support issue with my group. As time went on, [the board] began to develop an understanding of what I was trying to say versus others who were in the leadership positions [on the board] at that point. Eventually we had a board election, and I was nominated and elected as president. Like I said, there was already a big rift developing at that point. There were two opposing camps: one was pushing the presumption of joint physical and legal [custody] and didn't want to argue this child support thing at all....[The other camp's argument] is all about [our state's child support guidelines]....I am supposed to be [elected], but the way the bylaws got put up, we are really supposed to [leave] every couple of years. The last time around everybody said [not to leave]. I offered to [leave],...because I said I am getting tired here between work, kids, and everything else, [but I took on another term].   JUSTIN

Justin believed that if the group were to stress child support reform, lawmakers and the public alike would not take the organization seriously. He felt compelled at this critical juncture to assume power within the group and lead it toward what he believed to be a more productive direction: custody reform. Yet even with this sense of responsibility to the group, at the end of several years Justin was looking for a way out of his duties. The right person simply needed to come along to take his place.

As a final note, it is important to point out that although some individuals became leaders by default, once they assumed this position, they developed a passion for it. In this sense, they became very different from the leaders described above who continued to be reluctant holders of power. Recall that Bruce was the head of a professionalized fathers' rights group. He also was one such leader who initially hesitated heading his local fathers' rights group but then gradually saw it as a unique opportunity for him to direct the organization into the twenty-first century.

I think [I became the leader] by default....The board of directors were some very professional people...and I was the first one that had come along to want to do certain things with the organization that were on that professional level. Like I said, the gentleman prior to me had a high school education—a very hard working guy and a good guy—but didn't have the sense to take this [organization] to the next level. I presented to the board [my] marketing [plan] and actually when the director's position opened, they asked me to be the director. I didn't apply for it. They said, "Why don't you just take over and run with it as long as you want to?" I said, "Okay fine, whatever," so it really was by default. I know [I got backed] because I run this thing a little bit different, and I think that is what makes this organization successful. Most men's rights organizations fall apart. They get somebody with a passion to create change and to be part of the movement, but they forget in order to do this you've got to run it like a business. You've got to provide the tools to people that come to you for help [so they] can actually get some help rather than a bunch of rhetoric. I am the kind of guy that will go to the court house in a suit and tie, shake hands with the judges, [be on a] first name basis with most of the judges and a lot of state representatives, shake their hands and pick their pockets at the same time. I am going to promote [one of our] programs to them, or a parenting class or an anger management class, and get the judges to order it [so that men] come over to us. We actually are very close to getting a contract with [an airline company] through a new program...[that] will be part of its employee package, when an employee goes through a divorce or paternity suit. [He] is going to get referred by his human resources department to us and [the airline] is going to pay for the entire cost of [its] employee having to go through [us], which is a lot cheaper than the cost the company [would have to] incur due to turnover if [he] has productivity problems. We've gotten to that point where we can actually take this organization and franchise it state-wide. BRUCE

Bruce's level of commitment was rare, and could partially be explained by the fact that he was one of a handful of paid leaders in fathers' rights groups across the United States. However, this passion was nonetheless expressed by a person who had come to this leadership position by default. Once he was secure in the director's chair, he was able to move fully forward with his plans for reworking and re-envisioning the organization.

Of course, it is only once an individual becomes a leader that the true hard work of running the organization begins. Decisions must be made on a frequent basis; the challenge facing these leaders is how to best go about moving their organizations forward without losing the support of the rank-and-file membership. As we shall see, leaders approach this question of responsible group stewardship quite differently.

Making Decisions

Leaders are, in essence, tightly wedded to a group's prospects for survival. Part of their duties involves laying out the overall direction of the group, as well as making more minor choices regarding the group's day-to-day operations. Both types of decisions are clearly important and must be treated with care. After all, successful decisions will encourage not only growth in membership, but also increased confidence among those individuals who are already established members. Conversely, unpopular decisions will inhibit further membership growth and decrease feelings of efficacy among those already involved in the group. Of course, the *content* of these decisions is not the only factor that matters. *Process* also matters. Members who actively engage in decision-making may be more supportive of the organization over time. In contrast, strong-armed or otherwise top-down directives and negative tactics might hasten a group's demise by signaling that the opinions of the rank-and-file membership are of no importance to the group's evolution.

With the stakes so high, how do these leaders formulate a plan of action for their group? As described earlier, fathers' rights groups have a formal set of rules that govern their organizations. These rules include the rights and responsibilities of both members and leaders to map out the future of the group. However, despite these formal procedures, the fathers' rights groups involved in this study were governed extremely informally. In other words, the groups tended to "fly by the seat of their pants," as indicated by several fathers' rights activists. Yet even within this environment of informality, there is significant variation in the power of leaders to shape decisions that affect their organizations. Some work largely by building or tapping into a consensus view on a particular topic, and others work closely with their board of directors in crafting recruitment, marketing, and political strategies. Still others govern more autonomously, operating in isolation in ways that they believe are vital to each group's prospects for eventual success in meeting their goals.

Governing by Consensus

Approximately 32 percent of the leaders claimed that they make decisions by consensus in their groups, because on the major issues facing them in the current policy environment, there simply is very little disagreement. Where consensus dominates, voting on specific issues may then become inconsequential. As Juan pointed out, voting may only matter when money is being spent. Then voting creates a record of accountability for potential audits in the future.

> Consensus and voting are almost the same [for us]. But we don't really have major [contentious] issues. We [might] have issues concerning our Web site; we have issues about a publication we put out....When it comes to additions, deletions, or updates, it's a consensus, we think, do we put this in [the publication] or not? We [only] have votes specifically on expenditures....We're all in this and are volunteers in this. Nobody gets paid. [Decision-making] is usually done by a consensus. JUAN

Other leaders looked to past presidents for guidance before presenting an issue for discussion within the group. Lawrence, another leader, argued that clearing an issue with the "elder statesmen" of his group made his judgment on a specific topic carry substantial weight with the membership at large.

> We don't take votes. I don't make the decisions. It's consensus. A lot of the decisions get made in consultation with [the founders of the group]. They originally...formed [this group] back 10–12 years ago. They are old and wise. Their technical position is "coordinator" and they have been there, done that, and they know a lot of people, a lot of politicians, and policymakers in [our state]. So I personally run a lot of things by [them] and consult with them before we do anything. LAWRENCE

In many ways, the level of consensus within a specific group can be taken as a barometer of how effectively the organization is operating in meeting its goals. Leaders like Jaime, for example, took pride in the fact that his group's membership up until the point of his interview had resisted being consumed by debates over what he regarded as the tedious "details" of organizational direction, like specific tactics in promoting public policy reform. He saw himself as committed to a cause like all other members and viewed disagreements within his ranks as a distraction.

> It's unusual that we don't agree.... Some of these [other fathers' rights] groups have [become] like debating societies.... [They] have these ferocious debates and get divided, [and as a result] people...leave the organization. They become debating societies. They get together for the purpose of arguing. Our organization is very much different. The policy is a means to the end. The end is helping the parents...with the counseling [that] I do, the drop-offs [of children from one parent's house to the other parent's house that] I do, with what we get to the legislature. Really, a question is, what is there to disagree about and what is the goal?   JAMIE

In this case, Jaime made the important point that he does not want his group to deteriorate into a "debating society," which he viewed quite negatively. Like other leaders in this study, Jaime valued input from the rank-and-file membership as long as the dialogue did not detract from the group's overall mission to help families experiencing the dissolution process.

Governing by Board Cooperation

Other leaders—also 32 percent of the sample—expressed a strong preference that important decisions be made by the board of directors in conjunction with the president. In this model, leaders acknowledged that there would be some issues on which consensus among the membership would not materialize. This could be due to the opinionated personalities in the organization, the potential controversy regarding the matter at hand, or the introduction of some other destabilizing force within the group, such as the emergence of a related current event. In these cases, leaders looked toward those with the strongest stake in the organization—the board—for help in guiding the group in these important matters. A leader named Gilbert described this strategy as follows:

> Let's put it this way, I don't consider myself, even though I am the person who founded the group in [this state], as the person who is the leader. I have a board, which consists of probably about seven people, and we vote on what we think is [appropriate] for spending. . . . We vote for the best interest of our group. . . . At the board meeting, [which] we have two weeks after the regular meeting, we get together. We usually get together at a place where we get to eat and everything. We'll just sit down and I'll come up with some proposals. [I'll just say,] "What do you think about this? . . . We'll just discuss it and we'll ask everybody to vote.   GILBERT

As Gilbert indicates here, some group leaders hesitate to be too "powerful." Leaders who tended to defer to their boards expressed a sharp concern that no one in the group perceive them as having too much control over the organization's fate. Consider the perspective of Eli, who worried about this issue quite a bit.

> There are five of us who work in the group, I don't want to say on a daily basis, but at least on a weekly basis. Basically, . . . decisions are made by the five of us who are listed as board members. It is not a dictatorship and I get outvoted a lot.   ELI

Eli stressed that he frequently does not get the last word when it comes to determining group policy. Similar to other leaders who governed like him, Eli found a well-defined, collective wisdom in the board, which is composed of individuals who are disproportionately committed to the cause of fathers' rights. Acquiring a sense of how board members perceived a particular issue positively contributed to group leaders' own thought processes and made the group more resilient over the long run.

Governing Autonomously

A final set of leaders—36 percent of the sample—reported little or no compunction about making major decisions affecting the organization without consulting the rank-and-file membership *or* the board. Part of this motivation came from experience and the belief that they, as presidents, had acquired the sense to know what is best for their organization. Simona expressed this view succinctly by arguing that even though her board was populated by well-respected individuals, she had amassed the skills necessary to do her job effectively on her own.

> They pretty well leave the day-to-day operations and decisions up to me because I've been in this for nine years. Most of my board of directors are professionals. One of them is a former supreme court justice here [in this state]. None of our board of directors live in [this] area; they are from all over the state, so all [of] our board of directors meetings are done by conference calls or e-mails.   SIMONA

With this expertise, these leaders described themselves as confident in moving the group forward, although sometimes they had to disguise their own self-perceived competency with the trappings of respect for consensus. Leaders like William, for example, believed that they had the authority to direct their group in a specific manner, but that others might not approve of this approach and might consider it to be heavy-handed.

> It's more informal and there are a lot of consensus kinds of things going on, but I try to be careful in that regard. I would be [careful, otherwise] I would be seen as kind of a one-man show. I do have a lot of influence because of the intensity of my involvement and the passion that I project with all of it....But I try to be careful to make sure that [any suggestion] is brought in the form of a motion by somebody and then [he or she] carefully asks for a vote to see if the majority would go along with it. Or anything I wish for, I try to sneak around and ask somebody to make a motion.   WILLIAM

Other leaders maintained that they assumed more control over the group not because they were more qualified than the other members but because of the hectic lives of the group's board members. Justin explained the situation in the following way:

> I'd say [that] half the time it is me making a decision. I usually try to get everybody on board. They kind of listen to me.... They are all trying to hold down jobs, pay their child support and run around and see their kids, so very few of them can spend hours on any one project. Of course, right in the middle of [one group project] they'd say I've got to do this, or I've got to do that, or something has come up at work, I can't do that.... Lately, like I said, in the last year, I've got a couple of guys here who did well, got turned on, believed in the movement, and have really become work horses.   JUSTIN

Finally, another set of leaders tried to balance the needs of the members with their personal inclination to make decisions on their own. Usually, these leaders discovered through trial and error that their judgment was better than that of the rank-and-file. More precisely, they feared that by not assuming the role of the final arbiter in terms of decision-making, the group's goals would be compromised. As Carey explained,

> The major decisions all come down on my shoulders. There is open discussion about some of the issues. I try to be as democratic as possible when doing this, but sometimes you have to rein people back in because they tend to let their own personal issues cloud the overall issue.   CAREY

Because Carey viewed himself as the central caretaker of the group due to his experience in the trenches of fathers' rights activism, he had learned to judge which types of appeals work with elected officials, and which do not. He worried that those members with overwhelming, desperate, or even tragic personal issues could become too emotional in strategizing for the group and ultimately, without his intervention, lead the organization in an unproductive and even dangerous direction.

In sum, the informal environment in which most fathers' rights groups operate translates into certain predictable outcomes when it comes to the decision-making roles assumed by leaders. Because these groups depend on the time and labor sacrificed by volunteers, about one-third of the leaders are most comfortable formulating decisions by consensus. They also prefer this option because, as they report, most of their members are "like-minded" when it comes to the multiplicity of issues facing contemporary fathers. Another third of the leaders governs by consultation with the board, a strategy assumed when stronger differences of opinion within the group are apparent or when the group is otherwise experiencing a period of flux. Finally, the remaining third of leaders prefers to govern more autonomously. These leaders often have a visionary sense of where they want the group to go and believe that their office gives them the authority to exercise a significant amount of power over daily and long-range decision-making.

Most decisions that leaders make are routine and uncontroversial. However, there are exceptions to this rule. One of the most difficult decisions a leader can face is whether or not to expel a member from the group. Some groups had experience in doing this, but others did not. Nevertheless, all leaders agreed that certain conditions existed under which such an action could and should be taken. It is to these decisions that this chapter now turns.

Expelling Members: The Good, the Bad, and the Ugly

As described in chapter 3, there is significant diversity among the membership of fathers' rights organizations. Variations in age, occupation, education, and religion among members are all important and give each group a unique identity. One factor, however, not captured in the descriptive analysis presented earlier relates to differences in members' *behavior*. All of the groups studied here had norms and expectations concerning how their members ought to comport themselves as representatives of the fathers' rights cause, and if their members failed to conform, leaders imposed consequences, from verbal reprimands to outright expulsions. These leaders, in other words, policed their own members in order to protect the reputations of their groups overall. What were these potential or actual offending behaviors? Was there convergence among these groups as to what constituted "bad" behavior, or were there particular rules of propriety for members instituted by each group on its own?

About 35 percent of fathers' rights group leaders expressed strong reluctance to actually expel members from the group. Members would often leave on their own if they came to believe that the organization could do nothing for them; in these cases, leaders reported refunding their membership fees on request. Groups also lost members through attrition over differences in ideology or preferred tactics. That is, groups naturally shed members who do not agree with the strategies that the organization uses to achieve its goals. For the most part, these disagreements occurred when some members did not view the activities of the group to be radical enough to stimulate needed change in public policy. Disgruntled individuals typically left the group to fight their battles on their own, or they departed to start a new group under the guidance of their own vision. This process, of course, dilutes the strength of the cause overall, as a once-strong group splinters into numerous, less-effective pieces. As a result, leaders argued that they must do everything in their power to foster cohesion among these various factions within their own organizations. However, in a variety of instances, no matter how hard leaders tried to foster unity, individuals behaved in ways that were intolerable to the group's core membership. Leaders then took an active role in removing these individuals as members.

Negative Representation of the Group

By far the most common reason, cited by 39 percent of leaders, to expel a member—either in fact or potentially—was the engagement by that member in specific activities that portrayed the group in a negative fashion.[3] In some cases, attitudes articulated within the group setting were enough of a cause for concern to ask a member to leave. Sarah detailed one incident which took place within the context of a highly combustible group meeting that resulted in an expulsion.

---

3. In an extreme example of the type of behavior that places the group in a "negative light," in the United Kingdom the group Fathers 4 Justice temporarily disbanded under accusations that some of its members were plotting the kidnapping of Prime Minister Tony Blair's son, Leo. It was, in other words, a mass expulsion of members (Pool 2007).

This guy actually sat in my house, with his arms crossed before his chest, and said, excuse my language, "I don't care about that bitch. I don't care about [those] kids. All I want to know is how to keep that house that I built with my own two hands." I told him [that] he could be excused because that was not our principle.   SARAH

For Sarah, even ideas expressed internally, only to other group members, had to conform to a certain level of respect for the group's core mission of helping families thrive in the postdissolution context. The same could be said for Gilbert's organization. Even though he had not yet experienced an expulsion, he could foresee the conditions under which such an event might occur.

The only way I could see that happening would be—and I always tell everybody—we are not a bashing organization. We are a fathers' rights organization. Even though we [are mostly concerned about] fathers' rights here, [there] are some women [who are] noncustodial parents, and we'll represent them just as much as we would a father. We also represent grandparents because we think grandparents deserve an active role in their grandchildren's lives. We tell people, "Whatever you do, don't step on people's toes." There are some scumbag fathers out there, believe it or not. [There are] some fathers [who] just don't really deserve their kids and [there are] some moms [who] really don't deserve their kids. We don't want to interpret ourselves as a biased organization. We are here to help people if we can. If we have mom and pop that can't get along, we could come between them both and come to a good solution, a good parenting program for them to get along for the best interest of the children. That's why we are here. As long as we see [that] the children are benefiting from it, that is what our goal is.   GILBERT

Similar to Sarah, Gilbert argued that even within the confines of the group setting, members had to demonstrate an acceptable level of comportment with respect to how they talked about differences with other family members in their lives.

Much more compelling, however, was a concern articulated by group leaders that members never act in ways detrimental to the organization in the public sphere. This was an especially sensitive issue when it came to cultivating the group as a positive voice for families in the halls of legislative power in the states. Carlos explained how this type of "acting out" could ruin the group's chances in obtaining its policy goals.

> One person, in fact, this very person I told you before I wish weren't in the organization, was in a leadership role. He was asked to step out of it because the effect of his involvement was very damaging to the organization. Part of it was just that he [often said public things like,] "You're screwed," [and] "Nothing is going to work." He didn't offer anyone hope in any way, but he's also very contentious. He's not someone who can work with legislators, judges, and magistrates, because his view is that they're all corrupt and stupid.   CARLOS

Worse than these negative public attitudes were inflammatory actions or threats of action taken against members of the judiciary or the legislature. As Justin detailed, even though his group was attempting to reform the legal system, which in his view is populated by professionals who did not treat fathers as fully capable parents, all group members had the responsibility of treating court officials with respect.

> Well, [we had to expel individuals] when they did something just totally inappropriate in the court. One was almost at the point of threats. In doing so, that person used [the name of our organization]. I said whoa, he had no business doing that, and we didn't endorse that.   JUSTIN

Another leader, Eli, reported a similar incident of unacceptable behavior that took place at court.

> One [person who we expelled] stormed the courthouse with one of our shirts and buttons on, and was militant in nature with picket signs, running up and down the halls of the courthouse. [Other members in the group] didn't feel that that [served] us well. Others [that we have expelled] have gone and made statements publicly that were nowhere near what the group thought.   ELI

One leader in particular, Raimondo, took what he viewed as outlandish behavior extremely personally. For years, Raimondo had worked to develop a professional reputation with his state legislators. He met with them on regular occasions, dressed appropriately, and was respectful of their time. "Loose cannons" threatened to squander this political capital that he had so meticulously cultivated in previous years.

> [The individual that we expelled] was really a militant hothead [who] took it upon himself to contact a number of state legislators. [He then] berated those legislators on the phone [and claimed to represent our group].... He's not a spokesman for [our group], and to use our reputation, to risk our reputation that we had established with his unprofessional [behavior] and tirades to state legislators [was unacceptable]. I'm talking about elected officials and their staff to the point where it reflects poorly back at us.... He's out of here. And we took board action to remove him and we have not allowed him to attend any of our meetings.   RAIMONDO

It is important to note that other leaders reported similar problems but chose to handle them in a different way. Ivan, for example, elected to actively isolate the problematic member by not keeping him informed of all of the group's activities. He also sought to physically contain him if certain important judicial personnel were going to be present at the group's meetings.

> We have another board meeting where the domestic relation judges are coming. I went around and told everybody when [the problem member] wasn't around [that] I don't even want him there at that meeting. Because the second he opens his mouth, he is radical and hateful, tearing apart [the] child support agency. He's right, there are problems, but you don't go about it in a radical way. So I talked about how to get rid of him or set him up. At the next board meeting, I am going to talk to him ahead of time and have two guys sit on either side of him.... When the judges are there, you don't want [them] to see us as a radical or hateful group.   IVAN

In this case, Ivan feared the way in which this particular member would represent the group to local judges. By placing "better behaving" members on either side of him, Ivan hoped to contain his negative influence.

Other leaders took an even milder approach to those who negatively represented the group. Rather than expel the offender, the leader would take that person aside and explain to him or her why a specific behavior was objectionable. But sometimes even these strategies would not work, and leaders had to subtly pressure these individuals to leave the group. This was difficult, however, because at times these offenders were dynamic personalities who attracted others to support their own personal agendas. Aaron recognized this dilemma within his own group, and he struggled to contend with it on a regular basis.

> We have one phenomenon...you have what I call the newbie or the shooting star....[The newbie is] someone who comes in there, who doesn't have a historical perspective, [and] who is personally obsessed by his own case, for example. [The newbie] thinks that the organization should stop [what] it's doing and rally around him because he is being dealt a grave injustice. Usually those individuals come in, and it could create problems for an organization because sometimes they are actually functional. They are not necessarily dysfunctional people, and they can be disruptive in that they operate [like] demagogues do, on an emotional level. So, to a certain degree, they can actually have a following, so to speak, and they can start to create seeds of discontent within an organization.... You have to kind of show [these] people the door. The smart way to do it is to do it gently, if you have to. I don't think we have [taken] anyone by the scruff of the neck and thrown [him] out. We didn't have to do that.   AARON

Management of the organization's reputation, then, was an important part of fathers' rights groups' overall strategy to become significant players in the field of family policy. Leaders dealt with threats to their organization extremely seriously, especially if they themselves were the ones who had spent significant resources in building the organization from the ground up.

Abuse of Power

An additional 16 percent of leaders cited the perceived abuse of power as a reason for asking individuals to leave the group. Both leaders and members were involved in these types of situations. Leaders could act in extremely authoritarian ways, demanding that the organization move in a direction that was against the will of the majority. In these cases, the membership collectively asked these leaders to exit the organization. Alternatively, the members themselves would be the troublemakers. In some cases, the infraction involved misuse of the group's e-mail list. Members in charge of marketing, recruitment, or publicity could gain access to organizational information and exploit it for their own purposes. Simona explained how this occurred in her own group.

> I've only had to expel one member....He gained access to our e-mail database, not only my personal database, but mine from my companies and [the organization]. Then he began sending astronomical amounts of e-mails out, so we asked him kindly [to stop]. He didn't listen so we expelled him. On top of that, we had him taken off five Internet service providers because he was continuing to do that. I had to apologize to many e-mail groups and beg for their forgiveness for his erratic behavior. SIMONA

It was unclear exactly what kind of information this former member was sending on behalf of Simona's group. In the cases described below, Allen explicitly described the nature of the offending messages; one involved the spreading of objectionable religious material and the other entailed disseminating a more radical message from an unaffiliated, antigovernment group.

> I had one guy who was extremely hateful and he was always sending me information, absurd things. He must have been from some kind of cult or something, I don't know. He sent me things I thought were just outrageous and I expelled him....[There was another time when I had to expel someone]. When I send out a mailing list, I send it out blind carbon copy so the people can't see the other people I've sent it to. One time I made a mistake and sent it out so that everybody could see everybody else's e-mail addresses. One person took the e-mail addresses and sent out some of his radical stuff to the group. That was absolutely uncalled for....He is part of a fathers' group, but he is also part of a militia group....He is very antigovernment; he is terrible. ALLEN

Other leaders described more extreme abuses of power that forced the group to expel individuals. One of these circumstances involved alleged embezzlement from the group's treasury, with the case ultimately ending up in court. These types of situations were rare, however, as the majority of cases of abuse of power did not involve actual lawbreaking.

Behind in Child Support Payments?

One of the most compelling debates within fathers' groups today is whether or not to expel members who are behind in their child support payments. Emblematic of the minority opinion—mentioned by 10 percent of the sample—was Shaun, who stated quite bluntly that all fathers should behave in a responsible manner with respect to child support. In other words, men should "earn" their right to participate in fathers' rights groups, and in addition to not being convicted of any type of abuse, paying child support on time was part of this process of "earning" respect.

> Well, in order to be a member you cannot have been convicted of domestic or child abuse. You have to pay your child support. We're strong proponents of paying your child support, providing for your children, and not abusing your children or spouses or ex-spouses. And right now that is the major criteria for [disqualifying yourself as] a member. SHAUN

To leaders like Shaun, one of the top priorities of fathers' rights organizations should be promoting a positive image in the public. Once this image is solidly instilled in every citizen's mind, then these groups could argue about the merits of the child support system with integrity. Consistent with this attitude is the idea expressed by these leaders that the law must be obeyed no matter how unjust and that fathers must work to change the system from within.

Other leaders, however, vehemently disagreed with Shaun's position. To them, fathers face enough discrimination and misunderstanding in society without having to confront hostility from a group that is supposed to be helping them. More important, the ease with which any father can fall into child support arrears makes this policy a self-defeating organizational strategy. Carey articulated this position in the following way:

> [Kicking someone out of the group because he is not up on his child support] is the biggest bunch of BS, and that does more to hurt the overall picture and hurt those parents than [you] could ever believe.... That is the biggest bunch of garbage I've ever heard. If I [were] ever participating in a group and [was] told that by a director, he probably would have a pretty good battle on his hands.... It is so easy, the way things are now, for you to be called "in arrears" because of the way the laws are written. That is a ridiculous requirement. The gentleman that I live with is going through his own custody battle right now. They are claiming [that he is] several thousands in arrears, yet there is no court order for child support. Okay, I should kick him out of my chapter? No, sorry. That is not going to happen.   CAREY

Another set of leaders echoed these same concerns by pointing out that administrative errors are not the only source of problems fathers have in keeping up with their support payments. Periods of unemployment, for example, can also wreak havoc on a man's ability to pay. Thus, a significant disagreement exists as to whether arrearages with respect to child support obligations was cause enough to expel a member from the group. Although a handful of leaders argued vehemently in the affirmative, the majority maintained that this policy erroneously punishes exactly those individuals whom the groups were designed to help.

In the cases described above, the leaders decided whether or not an individual member stayed or was forced to leave; only rarely was there a rebellion against a specific leader. In this particular way, leaders wielded enormous amounts of power over their membership, and in many cases groups became personality-driven enterprises guided by those at the top. Eventually, however, all groups have to experience a leadership change. Leaders may pass away, move, or simply turn to other interests. They then need to rely on the rank-and-file for assistance in securing their replacement. These changes, described below, were not methodic nor carefully scripted by any means. Instead, the process of passing the leadership baton from one individual to the next ranged from smooth to extremely bumpy.

Leadership Transitions

As described above, many leaders in the study assumed their position in fathers' rights organizations by default; that is, for a variety of reasons, not many rank-and-file members desired to rise to the top of the group. Those who finally accepted this position often did so begrudgingly. And even those who had moved into the position with more optimism and enthusiasm expressed an extraordinary amount of burnout within a short period of time. The problem for these current leaders was finding suitable members who would assume their important duties if asked. Although a small set of leaders chose to step away from the limelight of leadership and simply expected someone else to pick up where they had left off, other leaders, such as Justin, actively tried to groom their replacements. Justin felt compelled to provide training to those members who he believed were most likely to be skilled in the area of dealing with state legislators, but found this task to be challenging.

> [There is one man] who, I hope, one day will take over for me because I am getting battle-scarred here....I [also] had a couple of guys call me up and say we can't [take over the leadership position] right now. [Even so], I've been introducing these people to my contacts in the political arena, so they should be more and more involved in that, because eventually I've got to move on, too.   JUSTIN

Although the majority of leaders struggled with finding a successor, one leader was being forced out of his position at the time of this study. Raimondo detailed the unfortunate circumstances surrounding his departure, which gave him no authority whatsoever to control who occupied the leadership chair after him.

> Unfortunately, at this juncture, at least, I have a very difficult board of directors to work with. I have a faction on my board that I consider to be more radical. They certainly are slightly more militant than this organization should be. They want to take it in a different direction. We've had persistent irreconcilable differences, as I stated in my news release [explaining why I am quitting], and on top of that, they [have been exerting] their pressure on me....What you don't realize is since

I started this organization, I have never taken a dime of salary. I did this as what's known as an organizational missionary. I put probably $60,000 of my own money into this organization and I've raised another $50,000 or $60,000 on my own. My board has raised virtually nothing and yet they want to, they want to take things in a different direction. I got tired of having to deal with this. I'm considered a subject matter expert on child support and on paternity fraud, for example, and that's where you will see me here until four [o'clock] teaching, training fathers on being better fathers and working nationally on behalf of paternity fraud victims. . . . I'm resigning from both my position as executive director as well as on the board. I've totally had it with these guys. . . . Let me say this, I understand the frustration of these parents [in general], particularly fathers. They see three years and virtually, in their minds at least, they don't see the progress we [have] made, they don't see us reaching the goal they thought we would [have] at this particular time. [Certain members of the Board] want us to take additional steps [that in] my opinion damage or jeopardize the work that we've done, such as holding rallies and demonstrating and picketing and so forth. . . . I think [that] there is a place for that, but we've managed to make a lot of headway. Keep in mind that I've personally been serving on two state committees and councils appointed by the governor and the [top court]. So I'm there inside advocating where the power base is. In fact, the big to-do about [this state's] child support guidelines that has been in the papers here. . . in the last week or two was the result of [the work of] one of my committees. . . . That's how those recommendations are made, with some effort on my part. . . . Well, we got [to these] changes that would make it a little more equitable for all parents, we got there because of the efforts [of those] on this committee of nine members. But some of these guys don't see that. They see we haven't reached joint legal-joint physical rebuttable presumption in the law yet and as a result, they're getting impatient and antsy and they want to do something.[4] And, as a result [of this], these things [that] they want to do are not the correct

---

4. A rebuttable presumption in this context means that the courts would automatically presume both forms of joint custody in all cases unless there were a compelling reason to decide otherwise.

things for this organization. So when you reach a point like that, it's time. You have to decide what to do and how to do it. I've always been a professional, at least I considered myself that. I did all this as a missionary, remember. [The group] never paid me a dime [beyond the basics]. All I ask is [that] they pay me my expenses so I don't have to worry about where I'm going to get food or rent or clothing and the rest of it. I'll do it and work full time at this. That's the understanding we started off with. Now [the group is saying], we don't care about this anymore and we don't care about what you did. We want you to do this and this. I'm not prepared to do this.   RAIMONDO

In this particular case, Raimondo clearly had reached a breaking point. In his view, he had worked as a tireless advocate for change and had established himself as a powerbroker for fathers' rights within state-level politics. However, a new set of members disagreed with this "insider" strategy and pressed Raimondo for the implementation of a much more aggressive political campaign. Yet if he followed their advice, Raimondo faced ostracism from his friends and colleagues within government. Faced with this difficult choice, Raimondo decided that it was in his best interest to leave the group.

Committed but Fatigued Leaders

The single most important sentiments expressed by leaders involved in fathers' rights groups were dedication and weariness. Leaders in fathers' rights groups have a strong belief in their cause. They are often more informed on the plethora of complex family issues currently being debated in state and national politics than the average rank-and-file member, and they each aim to run efficient, high-profile organizations. Although most assumed their position quite proactively due to their commitment to the issues, others volunteered to be the group's leader because no one else would do the job. Once there, however, they took their position and the duties of their office quite seriously.

At the same time, group leaders expressed a strong sense of weariness. They could not engage in unilateral action to shift their group in a new direction because boards and general members often had competing ideas for the organization in terms of tactics, strategies, and goals. In addition, they had to contend with uncontrollable members who were at odds with the group's mission and focus. Perhaps most important, after working on these issues for years, they had yet to witness a "true revolution" in family law that they so strongly desired. Their particular approach to the most important of these issues, child support and child custody reform, to be covered in the next two chapters, partially explains this failure.

5

Money Changes Everything, or American Child Support Policy

Gathered on this cool fall day in an urban center on the West Coast are the two leaders of Dads Love Their Kids, Jasper and Veronica, and fourteen racially diverse members, of whom only one, besides Veronica, is a woman. The room in the YMCA where the group is meeting is obviously used to teach young children about important personal values. Signs hanging from the walls reinforce these values by proclaiming "Welcome!" "Respect," "Caring," and "Responsibility."

With Veronica primarily silent and Jasper running through the agenda, this fathers' group meeting carries an air of a gospel revival. Every time Jasper makes a statement, the group answers with exclamations such as "Amen," "Yes," and "Right on."

The meeting begins with Jasper asking members to identify themselves, tell how many children they have and the ages, and how often they see their children. After these introductions, Jasper describes his philosophy about the court system to a resounding series of clapping and other forms of verbal approbation from his audience.

JASPER: I really want to get cameras in court, but I cannot do this alone. What is my purpose? Tapes are cheaper than transcriptions. Cameras also get people to act properly in court. All of the crooked judges in the system need to be scared. Judges are like tyrants. They rule over the court and the transcriptionists listen to them. Anytime they do something wrong, the transcriptionist will write "inaudible" on the transcript to cover up for the judge.

(This philosophy about the court's abuse of power pervades the group meeting. At the end, Jasper cuts to the chase of his argument, especially as it relates to child support.)

JASPER: Judges are too powerful today. They are simply political hacks.
DADS LOVE THEIR KIDS MEMBER 1: Sometimes my ex uses child support money to buy things for herself.
JASPER: Your lawyer's job should be to get you to pay the least amount in child support.

From this snapshot of a fathers' rights group in action, it is clear that men want to pay less or no child support to women. But what would this type of reform, if enacted, do to the financial well-being of America's female-headed households? There is little debate that women in the United States have made strong socioeconomic gains since the 1970s. More specifically, between 1970 and 2002, women increased their presence in the labor market, moving from a participation rate of 43 percent to 60 percent.[1] They also are obtaining better jobs and holding onto more lucrative careers. In 1983, only 22 percent of all women were in professional or managerial occupations; by 2002, this number had grown to 34 percent. Commensurate with these gains has been their increase in educational attainment. Over the last three decades, the percentage of women between the ages of 25 and 64 with a four-year college degree tripled from 11 percent to 32 percent. At the opposite end of the educational attainment spectrum, the percentage of women in the labor force who were high school dropouts decreased from 34 percent to only 8 percent.

Yet despite these gains, other statistics demonstrate that women still have a long way to go in order to catch up with their male counterparts.

---

1. All statistics from these first two paragraphs are from U.S. Bureau of Labor Statistics 2004.

Perhaps most pointedly, dollar for dollar, women earn far less money than men. As of 2002, women brought home only 78 percent of what men earned. They tend to be crowded into part-time jobs, which ultimately has negative ramifications for their pensions, and little to no maternity leave protection, especially in comparison to women in other industrialized countries (Gornick and Meyers 2003). Occupational segregation is still rampant as well. Even though women are filling professional and managerial positions in greater numbers, within these broad categories, there is still hyper, sex-based segregation. For example, even though both professions can enable one to achieve a middle-class lifestyle, engineers tend to earn much more than early education teachers. Yet only 11 percent of all engineers are women, but 98 percent of all preschool and kindergarten teachers are women. Among those with lower skill levels, women suffer in comparison with men as well. Women age 25 and older are more than twice as likely as men to earn the federal minimum wage or below. And poverty still exacts a much higher price on women than on men. For those who logged at least twenty-seven weeks of work per year, 5.5 percent of women compared to 4.5 percent of men live below the poverty line.

Given these sobering statistics, a particular area of concern for women is what happens to them economically after a familial breakdown. Research in this area has moved in two directions. First, scholars have focused on estimating the financial impact of separation or divorce on women and their children. Second, researchers have aimed to document the benefits for these affected families of strong government intervention in the area of child support, which has emerged as one of the principle state-assisted methods by which to address economic instability among female-headed households.

Women, Economic Losses, and Family Breakdown

For over two decades, researchers have studied the financial well-being of families affected by separation and divorce. These studies vary in terms of sample selection, data sets utilized, and methodology employed, but perhaps are most significantly distinct in their measurements of pre- and post-breakdown measures of well-being. These measures include changes in poverty rates, family income, and income-to-needs ratios. Yet, although focusing on different measures and therefore producing a diverse range of interpretable impacts, these studies are most remarkable in their convergence on a single theme: when it comes to the effects of a family breakdown, women fare much worse than men.[2]

Several studies have compared the percentage of women and men living in poverty during marriage and post-marriage. This measure helps us understand the dynamics of what might happen in the worst case scenario in the event of a family breakdown: the risk of falling below the poverty line. Morgan (1989), in her analysis of a cohort of women from the National Longitudinal Surveys during the period 1967–1982, found that although only 10.2 percent of women were poor or near poor prior to divorce, this number rose to 25 percent of all women who did not remarry in the five years after the family broke down.[3] Duncan and Hoffman (1985) endorsed these findings by noting that in their study of couples from 1967 to 1981 drawn from the Panel Study of Income Dynamics, the portion of women living below the poverty line increased from 7 percent prior to separation to 13 percent only one year after separation. When comparing the experiences of women and men, the results of other studies of this type only grow more grim. For example, Bianchi, Subaiya, and Kahn (1999) analyzed data from the 1984–1990 panels (except 1989) of the Survey of Income and Program Participation and reported that only 25 percent of men who were in poverty during their marriage remained in that state after the family broke down, but that 75 percent of women remained in poverty.[4]

In addition to exploring the impact of divorce on poverty, the overwhelming majority of studies use family income prior to and following familial disruption as a measure of economic well-being. Employing this metric helps researchers capture all forms of financial decline, not

2. For two exceptions to this generalized finding, see Braver and O'Connell 1998 and Comanor 2004.

3. The National Longitudinal Surveys, sponsored by the Bureau of Labor Statistics at the United States Department of Labor, have collected data on employment and employment-related events (like job changes and periods of unemployment) for select groups of men and women since 1966.

4. The Survey of Income and Program Participation has sampled panels of thousands of adults since 1984 in order to examine the effectiveness of federal, state, and local public programs. It is conducted by the United States Census Bureau.

just those that occur in the worst case scenarios of poverty. In their overview of the literature, Holden and Smock (1991) found that out of a total of seven rigorous academic studies, three showed losses of 30 percent for women, and the remaining four generated drops in women's family income in the range of 40–50 percent. Interestingly, these declines do not affect all women in the same way. Black women suffer more than white women, and upper income women experience greater declines than middle and lower-income women (Duncan and Hoffman 1985; Smock 1993; Weiss 1984). The only way out of this economic dislocation for many of these women is to remarry, although even in these cases women tend to fare less well than those who remained continuously married (Duncan and Hoffman 1985; Nestel, Mercier, and Shaw 1983; Stirling 1989). By way of contrast, men experienced a much lower decline in family income—under 20% (Hoffman 1977). Some studies even reported an increase in family income for men of between 7 and 13 percent (Smock 1993, 1994). And in contrast to women, the majority of men increase their income over time (Duncan and Hoffman 1985; Phillips and Garfinkel 1993). Studies that adjust this income level for the number of people in the family only amplify these findings (Holden and Smock 1991; Smock 1993, 1994).

Finally, although studies that examine the poverty rate and straightforward income measures provide strong and consistent evidence that family breakdowns disproportionately impact women, they do not capture a family's ever-changing consumption patterns after a disruption. The income-to-needs measure solves this problem by not only encapsulating a family's income, but also its size and spending dynamics. The income-to-needs measure is simply a family's income as a proportion of the official federal poverty line for a family of that size; a family earning exactly the amount of income to reach the poverty line (100 percent of the poverty line) would have an income-to-needs ratio of 1.00. This measure became well-known in the mass media when one study inaccurately concluded that women's standard of living decreased by 73 percent after a divorce, but men's standard of living rose by 42 percent (Weitzman 1985). Nevertheless, despite the publicity surrounding this particular error, the majority of scholars using this alternative measure have shown that women still suffer dramatically while men improve their standard of living during the postdisruption period. For example, for women, the income-to-needs ratio dropped in the range from 6.7 to 30 percent (Duncan and Hoffman 1985; Hoffman 1977; Peterson 1996; Stirling 1989). Notably, black women and higher income women do worse than these averages. In contrast, men fare much better. Duncan and Hoffman (1985) found, for example, that men experienced a 13 percent increase in their income-to-needs ratio one year after a divorce, which then escalated to 24 percent two years after their divorce. In summarizing these findings, most scholars agree that although the majority of women end up "making it" in the postdisruption period, their standard of living declines while that of men advances upward.

How can we account for these dramatic differences in outcomes between men and women? First, as noted above, women are disadvantaged economically in comparison to men even prior to being married or as part of a nonmarital couple. They earn less than men—even with similar levels of education—and tend to be segregated in jobs that are historically underpaid, such as teaching and nursing. These differential starting points may be the result of personal preferences in terms of job selection. However, they also may be the product of a whole host of other, more complex factors, such as socialization, educational tracking, and discrimination. The end result is that most women are already "behind" their male partners when they first decide to be part of a couple.

Second, while they are married, they tend to work fewer hours than their husbands, primarily due to the responsibilities associated with child care (Blau, Ferber, and Winkler 2001; Smock 1994). The need to take care of children reduces their work experience levels, forces them to accept part-time jobs with little, if any, pension protection, and interrupts their employment trajectories. More specifically, these women delay pursuing additional education, acquiring more technical skills, and exposing themselves to emerging innovations in their particular occupations. In addition, even after controlling for these human capital differences and various job characteristics, research has demonstrated that women still face a "motherhood penalty"—a reduction in wages simply for having children. Estimates of this penalty—which might be caused by decreased productivity or outright employer discrimination against mothers—vary, but some studies have reported a penalty of 7 percent for the first child, and others have found a 5 percent penalty for the first child and 10 percent for the second child as compared with childless women (Budig and England 2001; Waldfogel 1997). These divergent paths for women can lead to wide, cumulative discrepancies in earning power, with women with two children earning approximately 80 percent of what women without children earn by age forty-five (Sigle-Rushton and Waldfogel 2007). Men, for the most part, continue to make their way upward on their occupational ladder, and may earn double what a forty-five-year-old woman with two children has earned up until that point in her life (Ibid.).

The third and final piece of this puzzle is to understand how women earn money in the postdisruption context and how these efforts—however well intentioned they might be—produce inadequate results. Simply put, women sustain themselves by cobbling together a whole range of income-producing activities (Duncan and Hoffman 1985; Smock 1994). One of the most significant modifications they make is to increase their participation in the labor market. They may return to work if they left completely to have children or increase their hours if they simply scaled back. However, after potentially years of under-investing in their own human capital, this move is often not enough to sustain themselves and their children. They then turn to other income sources, such as financial help from relatives. Parents, sisters, brothers, and cousins may be called in for aid. They may also apply for welfare benefits, housing assistance, and food stamps if their income falls below a certain level. Lastly, they round out their budgets by turning to alimony, which is only awarded in about 15 percent of divorce cases (Shehan et al. 2002), and most important, as we will see, child support.[5] In sum, women suffer enormous financial hardship in the post-breakup context—and, as a result, so do the children who remain predominantly in their care.

The Impact of Child Support Enforcement on the Well-Being of Single Parent Families

The economic difficulties facing women once their families break apart are very real and challenging. One of the foremost goals of the child support enforcement system is to help these predominantly mother-headed

5. As Crittenden (2001) has noted, even when alimony is awarded in contemporary family breakups, it is done so for only a limited amount of time. Therefore, most scholars have turned their attention to child support as a way to even out differences in standards of living between separating partners.

families overcome the worst periods of economic insecurity that result from losing male earning power in their homes. Yet the child support enforcement system is far from perfect in completely addressing these financial hardships. Table 5.1 illustrates these shortcomings in dramatic detail.

Considering single mothers from all socioeconomic backgrounds together, in 1978, 59.1 percent had a child support order in place and 23.6 percent received full payment. By 2001, these numbers had only marginally improved; 63 percent had an order in place, and 25 percent received full payment. For women above the poverty line, their precarious economic situation shockingly stayed the same over this time period. About 67.3 percent had an award in 1978, and only 65.4 percent had an award in 2001. The likelihood of these women collecting at least some of this award improved only marginally, from 41.1 percent to 44.3 percent. For women living below the poverty line, the situation improved more

TABLE 5.1.
Child Support Payments for All Women, Women above the Poverty Level, and Women below the Poverty Level, Selected Years 1978–2001

Category of women	1978	1981	1989	1993	1997	1999	2001
All women							
Total (in thousands)	7,094	8,387	9,955	11,505	11,872	11,499	11,291
Awarded (%)	59.1	59.2	57.7	59.8	59.6	62.2	63.0
Received payment (%)	34.6	34.6	37.4	39.1	40.4	39.8	41.1
Received full payment (%)	23.6	22.5	25.6	18.9	24.8	24.5	25.0
Women above poverty level							
Total (in thousands)	5,121	5,821	6,749	7,271	8,062	8,194	8,468
Awarded (%)	67.3	67.9	64.6	64.4	62.8	66.1	65.4
Received payment (%)	41.1	41.4	43.1	44.4	45.7	44.9	44.3
Women below poverty level							
Total (in thousands)	1,973	2,566	3,206	4,234	3,810	3,305	2,823
Awarded (%)	38.1	39.7	43.3	51.9	53.0	52.3	55.7
Received payment (%)	17.8	19.3	25.4	30.1	29.3	27.2	31.3
Aggregate payment (in billions of dollars)							
Child support due	17.1	18.4	22.5	28.8	32.0	34.3	34.9
Child support received	11.1	11.3	15.4	18.8	21.3	20.2	21.9
Aggregate child support deficit	6.0	7.1	7.1	10.0	10.7	14.1	13.0

Source: U.S. House of Representatives. House Committee on Ways and Means. *The 2004 Green Book.* Washington, DC: U.S. Government Printing Office.

significantly, with 38.1 percent having an award in 1978 and 55.7 percent obtaining one in 2001. The percentage of these poor women actually receiving at least partial payment increased as well, from 17.8 percent to 31.3 percent. Another way to understand the shortcomings of the child support system is that in 2001 the child support program was supposed to collect $24.7 billion in current support; it actually succeeded in collecting only $14.2 billion. According to the Office of Child Support Enforcement (2006), not much has changed in terms of effectiveness by this measure; in fiscal year 2005, $17.4 billion was collected in current support of $29 billion due. Overall, far too few women have an award in place, and far too few women are collecting on the awards that have been established. In sum, for a variety of reasons, fathers are simply not supporting their children at the level that the law requires.

Despite these problems, however, considerable evidence indicates that the child support system has produced benefits in the lives of the many women who are able to collect. First, consider the effects of child support on poverty and welfare dependency. Census data suggest an association between the receipt of child support and a mother's poverty status. In 2001, approximately 25 percent of all custodial mothers had incomes below the poverty line. In contrast, only 15 percent of all custodial mothers who received their full child support payments lived below the poverty line (Grall 2003). In addition to the program's relationship with lower poverty rates, academic research has demonstrated that stronger child support enforcement reduces actual welfare dependency in at least two ways (Garfinkel 2001; Huang, Kunz, and Garfinkel 2002; Mead 1999). First, it prevents women from applying for benefits. Simply put, tough child support enforcement provides single-parent families with the income they need to sustain their households over the long run. It smoothes out their earnings and enables them to pay their bills and avoid public assistance. Second, it promotes removal from the welfare rolls by channeling enough resources to single-parent families so that they no longer need help from the state. In fact, at the end of fiscal year 2004, the Federal Child Support Enforcement Program reported that it had closed 16.6 percent of all of its Temporary Assistance for Needy Families cases, or 331,447 TANF cases in total, due to a child support order that was put in place that year (Office of Child Support Enforcement 2006).

Second, even for families who are not poor—the more likely constituency impacted by the activism and claims of fathers' rights groups due to their members' predominant middle-class status—child support has the potential to make a massive difference in reducing the gap in earnings between both halves of the dissolved family. On this point, Bartfeld (2000) analyzed data from the Survey of Income and Program Participation over the years 1986–1991 in order to estimate the impact of a variety of child support scenarios on income-earning outcomes; these scenarios were no support, current support, and possible support under a set of state guidelines that are assumed to be perfectly enforced. Of those custodial mother households with no support, about 10 percent would live in relatively advantaged circumstances, with incomes three times the poverty threshold. When these families receive their current support, this statistic jumps to about 13 percent. If they were to receive exactly what the various state guidelines predict that they should receive, about 17–22 percent of these custodial-mother families would be in this highest income category. Interestingly, these modest increases in a mother's standard of living come at little expense to a noncustodial father's standard of living. When they do not pay any child support at all, about 54 percent of noncustodial fathers fall into this highest income category; at current support levels, about 45 percent of them still do. Even under strict compliance with various state guidelines, between 37–45 percent of all noncustodial fathers would fall into this highest income category. Thus, even with this effective enforcement, it is critical to note that better-off custodial-mother families would continue to be at a significant financial disadvantage relative to noncustodial fathers.

Finally, an important caveat to this discussion relates to the plight of lower income fathers and the question of whether or not they can truly afford to pay the child support that they are ordered to contribute (Huang, Mincy, and Garfinkel 2005). For those fathers living near the poverty line, research has documented that these men face many difficulties in their lives, including low levels of education and few stable employment opportunities (Sorenson and Zibman 2001; Waller and Plotnick 2001). In addition, the regressive nature of the child support system virtually guarantees that they will be paying a higher percentage of their income in support than their wealthier counterparts. Moreover, if their families ever received public assistance at any point in time, they might be charged, in addition to their child support obligations, with the Medicaid costs related to their children's birth as well as all TANF monies expended on their children. These rules can place them in significant arrears before they even begin to pay on their current orders.

But even those fathers earning incomes marginally to moderately above the poverty line might experience some strain in making their child support payments. From 1979 to 2005, real median weekly earnings in 2005 dollars for those men twenty-five years and older with less than a high school diploma fell from $629 to $455 (U.S. Department of Labor [DOL] 2006). Those who had only a high school diploma saw their earnings drop from $769 to $652, while those with some college or an associate's degree saw a decline in their earnings from $821 to $766 (DOL 2006). Only those with a bachelor's degree or more saw a rise in real earnings from $987 to $1167 over this approximately three-decade span (DOL 2006). During this same time period, men witnessed the transformation of the child support system from one that was virtually nonexistent, to one that was increasingly effective. The combination of a decline in real earnings with a stronger child support system could definitely produce a burden on some men.

Although these problems are very real and are beginning to be addressed by policymakers, the fathers' rights activists included in this study were, as noted above, relatively economically advantaged. Although income data were not collected from this sample, education data and other measures of socioeconomic status were considered. No participants claimed to fall into the very disadvantaged category, as defined by having a child currently receiving TANF benefits. The majority also did not seem to suffer the fate of declining wages in combination with a tougher child support system that afflicted those in the lower-middle class categories, since 60 percent of this sample held a bachelor's degree or more. Perhaps most important, regardless of the specific sample studied here, fathers' rights organizations do not claim to represent men from lower socioeconomic groups. Therefore, although it is possible that some of the men in this study may have had very real difficulties in meeting their obligations, for the majority, this was not their central complaint. The multipronged critique by fathers' rights groups of the child support system focuses on—in their view—the inappropriate actions of the state in its encroachment on their financial lives. Promoting equality between the sexes commensurate with their former partners' past economic and emotional contributions is simply not a concern, as we shall see.

The Response of Fathers' Rights Groups

Overall, then, the scholarly research suggests that women suffer severe economic hardship when their families dissolve. Government programs such as effective child support enforcement, although not perfect, can help ameliorate these negative outcomes by transferring money from fathers to mothers and their children. Yet this approach is not without controversy, especially within fathers' rights groups. For these organizations, the child support system embodies all that is wrong with government today. More specifically, in this study, fathers' rights members expressed their disdain of the child support system through the lens of three distinct critiques of the state: (1) the state as abusive and corrupt, (2) the state as unnecessarily interfering in "natural" family life, and (3) the state as overly "feminized."[6]

Distrust of State Action Because It Is Abusive and Corrupt

First, and at one extreme, some fathers' rights activists vocalized distrust of any state intervention in their lives following the dissolution of their families. In other words, they demonstrated a hardened view of the state and its capacity to address their needs. But their concerns went beyond the notion that the state is simply not responsive to them; rather, they viewed the state with disdain because they believed that those working in positions of power are abusive or corrupt. Fathers with this perspective also were least willing to engage with the architects of the child support system, whom they believed would only pursue incremental and thus insubstantial reform.

6. Most fathers in this chapter and in chapter 6 described their critique of the state as falling into one of these three categories. However, sometimes individual father's concerns fell into more than one category.

Vocalizing one extreme conceptualization of this abuse, fathers' rights group members oppose governmental intervention into their lives with respect to the child support system because of their belief that it forces them into "slavery." In other words, they maintain that the child support system is a form of systematic oppression that relegates them to a life of poverty and empowers their ex-partners to do relatively well financially. On this point, Nolan, a young father of a boy and a girl, experienced an extremely difficult divorce from his wife after he caught her having an affair. After the couple parted ways, she moved on several occasions; at one point, Nolan—who at the time was paying $500 per month in support—decided to follow her in order, in his words, to maintain a relationship with his children.

[Child support] reduces the other parent to slavery and starvation.... My ex-wife lives in a palace and I live in a trailer house. What made me decide to go to [the state where my children live now] is I had one can of pork and beans left, I ate them, and then I had no food left. I said, why am I staying here? When my kids were here with me in the summer, we went to the day-old bread store. I turn my air conditioner off during the day. [I am] living like a Nicaraguan and she is living in a plush palace, which is fine. That is wonderful and my children are living there during the school year against my will and their will. They lose half their family and I am languishing in this little trailer house. That is all I can do. It is slavery. I am in a slave cabin. NOLAN

Other activists echoed this same theme but indicated that slavery was not induced because of their status vis-à-vis their ex-partners but because the current system did not permit them to move ahead financially. Noelle, a sixty-two-year-old mother of seven children, became involved in the fathers' rights movement when one of her sons experienced a familial breakdown. Although he never married the mother of his two young children, Noelle's son had a long-term relationship with her. One day his girlfriend abruptly left the family. Much to his chagrin, the court only permitted him to have limited access to his children, even though he ultimately had to pay $1,000 per month in child support.

[The main reason that child support is unfair] is it makes a slave out of the father.... [Say] he pays a certain amount of money for two children in child support. Then it may be that he is living on $100 a month for himself. He can go out and get yet another job to help support himself. [Yet] because he is making more money, [his ex can] take him back to court and get a part of that. It doesn't matter, and he gets to claim none of this on his taxes.   NOELLE

Still other members maintained that they are slaves or "indentured servants" because the state gives them "no choice" over the support decision. For example, Devin had two sons, one with his wife and one with a girlfriend whom he unexpectedly impregnated when he was separated from his wife. As his two sons were toddlers and therefore relatively close in age, Devin found it difficult to accept that he could control the money that went to the one son with whom he lived but could not control the money that was being sent to support his son with whom he did not reside.

I figure I pay all the daycare for [my son who does not live with me] and she still walks away with $300 or $400 extra a month in her pocket. I'm thinking, wow, that's a great deal.... I wish I could make $300 or $400 a month off someone. The reason I look at [child support] as theft is I don't have a choice over whether I pay this or not. I have a choice if [the son who lives with me] goes to daycare or camp or if we are going somewhere and he says he wants something. Well, I say you're not getting that, you shouldn't have candy, or you shouldn't have that. That's a choice that I can make. I don't have a choice here [when it comes to paying child support]. I'm an indentured servant, which is another constitutional violation, because if I quit my job, they are going to tell me I still owe this money. If I don't pay it, they are going to lock me up.   DEVIN

For men like Devin, the child support system makes them feel as if they have "no way out." Devin specifically resented the burden that his unplanned offspring placed on him—and the way in which the government forced him to pay without his consent. Most important, he argued that the government was placing him in an untenable position, and he expressed his complete distrust of the system, which he maintained was impoverishing him using extralegal means.

Another central, overriding theme for fathers' rights activists who have complete distrust of the state is their belief that the child support system is not necessarily designed to help children but primarily exists for a corrupt state to make money. Recall from chapter 2 that over the last decade, the federal government has rewarded the states with incentive payments based on their performance in various areas of child support enforcement. Despite these incentive payments, since the beginning of the program the federal government has lost money, and since 2000 the states have lost money as well. In other words, both levels of government are expending more money on the program than they are taking in. Nevertheless, the simple existence of the incentive payment structure, which reduces these state losses, has enabled men such as Ricardo, who has five children, to question the integrity of the process as a whole.

> One of the...problems with child support is the incentives the federal government pays the [states] to collect child support has: (1) made the [states] more aggressive, and (2) sometimes the way the money is reported, they are actually committing what we consider [to be] taxpayer fraud.... A lot of the child support that [the agencies] collect would have been paid anyway; [but it is now] deducted straight from an individual's check and sent straight to the other parent. [By] the child support enforcement agencies getting involved in this, not only do they get a cut of it, but they also get taxpayer dollars for collecting that which would have been collected anyway. It is padded income for the child support enforcement agencies.   RICARDO

Prior to the creation of the child support enforcement program—for nonwelfare families only—monies flowed between parents privately (of course, this was only true in the small number of cases where compliance existed). To fathers like Ricardo, the state simply has found a way to make money by unnecessarily inserting itself into this financial transaction. Moreover, this system has significant, positive spillover effects for other players in the process, such as lawyers. Harold, another fathers' rights activist, described his view of the nefarious secondary profits that are generated by the child support system:

> [The system is unfair] because it creates, I call it a subconscious [idea] within the law community to look at [child support] more in the value of the money side of it, the economic side of it, rather than the justice side of it....[The] states...are actually making money or collecting money from the federal government as a result of collecting child support....Because it isn't one of those types of things where you can tangibly point to one thing and say this is causing it, but because you've got your [state] attorney benefiting from it; you've got your attorney benefiting from it; you've got everybody that is in the entire judicial system benefiting; and the Department of Children and Family Services, all those departments that work together are actually benefiting by the increased amount [collected]....As a result of that I think there is a subconscious bias then to...give the custody to the woman and make [the man] pay child support, the maximum amount of child support, because that will maximize the amount of money the state will receive. HAROLD

With these suspect motivations, Harold argued, the child support system loses credibility with fathers across the country. Rarely, however, if ever did these members acknowledge that such incentive payments might help the states in adopting new procedures to increase efficiency; moreover, it was unclear how they would replace these incentives with a new method of helping ensure administrative performance if they were so able.

Distrust of State Action as Interference in "Natural" Family Life

The second way some fathers' rights activists vocalized their distrust of state action in the area of child support was due to their belief in "rugged individualism." Some activists expressed an attitude toward basic economic principles that had deeper roots than the men's interactions with the child support system. In discussing their opinions about the fairness of the system, these members revealed a fundamentally distinctive, laissez-faire attitude toward the economy. They held that government intervention in redistributing wealth in any form is necessarily bad because it distorts individual initiative in the marketplace; therefore, child support enforcement policies—which function to transfer wealth from fathers to mothers—are damaging. Like their counterparts who distrust government action because they believe it is abusive and corrupting, activists holding this hands-off view in the area of child support expressed little desire to work within the system to pursue reform.

Because of these beliefs, some activists renounced any claim that they must minimize the financial impact of family dissolution on their ex-partners. Vince, describing the difficulties that he had trying to maintain contact with his nine-year-old daughter and five-year-old son, argued that every individual should be responsible for himself or herself. In this view, child support should not exist at all.

> Each one has to live on what [he or she] makes....I read a statement from this social worker [recently]. She said, "This child support business is a bunch of crap, because when you get foster children, all the state cares about is to have a roof over their heads and three meals a day, that's it." So if you are a person who is in a relationship and wants to get divorced, I think you should think about what you are doing before you get divorced. In [my state] it has created this arena where [a woman] could walk out, take the house, take the money. [The woman thinks], he can go live in an apartment and I'll have my house, my car, my kids, and his money. They've made it that way, which is wrong. Absolutely wrong! VINCE

Fundamental to Vince's philosophy was the use of the possessive "my" and "his" when he described what a typical woman thinks about the divorce process. "[The woman thinks], he can go live in an apartment and I'll have *my* house, *my* car, *my* kids, and *his* money." Even though she gets control over the main material goods and the children, Vince must abdicate *his* money to her as well. According to Vince, "his" earnings were not a product of shared enterprise accumulated during the relationship to which his children may now be due, but rather payment for individual productivity (his) to be protected at all costs. Franco, a twice-divorced father of three, agreed with Vince's assessment of post-family breakup economics.

> [My second wife], ten years ago, before we were married, earned approximately $36,000. I know all this stuff because I went through all these numbers. When we went through the divorce, she stayed at home and the court system allowed her to do that because she and I had an oral agreement that said of course she'd stay at home until our son is in kindergarten. I also had an oral agreement saying we'd stay married no matter what, too. Then she took a job part-time at his school initially as the assistant librarian, and now she is the lunch lady. The best I can guess to you is that she makes $12,000–$14,000 a year. She has the same level of education that I do. In fact, she graduated college in a shorter amount of time than I did. Granted, her education is twenty-something years old, [but] I offered to her that I would help her pay for school while we were going through the divorce....She said, "No, I have to be home for the kids." I said, "Yeah, but I do, too," and I earn six or seven times that amount of money. FRANCO

In Franco's view, his ex-wife was clearly making personal economic choices that resulted in her lower standard of living. Interestingly, he did not acknowledge the advantages of wage discrimination and occupational segregation that had benefited him over time, nor did he note how his uninterrupted work history as the children were born and being raised, which enabled him to make "six or seven" times as much money as her, had come into play once they broke up. To Franco, his ex-wife is equally situated and she must modify her current earnings-related decisions if she wants to do better financially.

Other fathers' rights activists rejected government intervention even when they knew that a family breakdown would result in a lower standard of living for their ex-partners and children. Elliot, father of four, summed up this belief system when he focused on his responsibility versus his ex-partner's responsibility in caring for his children.

> If the money [were] going to be used for the child, I don't have a problem with giving my children that money. But the fact of the matter

is, the ex-spouse uses that for her survival, not for the survival of the children....That's where I have a problem because the expectation is that [only mothers] have to keep a house for [the children]. Well, I have to keep a house for myself, why wouldn't they have the same expectations?...[The] other side is that she needs to be able to support herself....I know in my situation, [my ex] could not live on her income; without [my help] she couldn't have a house or anything like that, she couldn't survive. So is that my fault? I don't think so, but it is my responsibility to make sure my kids have a house and a roof over their head and food and clothing and stuff like that. At least that's half my responsibility; I don't know that it's my whole responsibility.   ELLIOT

In this case Elliot recognized that without the purchasing power of his income, his ex-partner would not be able keep her house. But his acknowledgment of her predicament went much further. In fact, he clearly admitted that without his income, "she couldn't survive." His awareness of this fact, however, did not change his attitude toward the child support system overall; mothers should be financially independent to the point where they are forced to live on whatever they earn.

In a more extreme vein, fathers' rights activists argued that they should be given the freedom and latitude to make their own decisions about how to spend money on their children, even when their families break down. In their view, as parents, fathers have a strong sense of how to care for their children; no state needs to remind them of this responsibility. Mel, a father of three grown children and one teenager, encapsulated this view succinctly as he described the current child support system as producing nothing but "travesties."

The only...reason I have a problem with the child support guidelines is interference with my right as a parent [to spend money on my children as I see fit]. [There is] the presumption...that I'm an irresponsible person and therefore the state has to control, regulate, and determine what [it] thinks is fair [with respect to support]. It takes that opportunity from me as a parent and I think the government has overstepped its boundaries in many, many areas. I understand why, I understand the irresponsible people. But when you have very caring, loving parents, the government should take a hands-off approach to it....[As] an example,...I had gone [to the courthouse] a couple of years ago just to listen in on some of the things [the court] was telling other people that were trying to go through a divorce. There was a couple coming in—a husband and wife getting a divorce and they were still friends. They were amicable with each other, they wanted to be sharing in their child's future, [and] they didn't want child support because they were going to have equal time. The court would not let them make a decision....[The court wanted] to calculate the child support and everything else. [They] went through the whole process; they left crying. Here [are] two people that really wanted to do it, work it out, agree on everything, but when they tried to use the system to get the legal paperwork, [the court] said, "No, you can't, you have to do what we say." They left crying. I've never seen such a travesty in my life. MEL

With this example, Mel highlighted his belief that in the majority of cases, parents are able to work out their differences and provide for their children without acrimony. Therefore, state action to guarantee this outcome is unnecessary.

Another activist named Ted echoed this view that fathers should be given the benefit of the doubt in terms of supporting their children. Men should be held at their word to do their best by their children; with this promise, no child support need flow in any direction.

You know, first of all, in this country, in the United States of America, a parent [will] go in front of an elected official (which is what these judges are) and say, "I want to be an equal part of my child's life. I stand up before this forum and say, I will take care of everything I need to take care of and I demand to be an equal part of my child's life." Who is one of our elected officials to look at us and say, "No, you can't do that?" With that as a basis, for anybody to be forced to pay money when [he] will go in front of a judge and say, "I will take care of my half of everything," is wrong. For somebody who wants to turn [his] back on a child, wants nothing to do with the child, okay; force those people to pay. For somebody that goes in there and says, look, I want to be an equal part of my child's life, [he] should not be

forced to pay money. You have to pay money to guarantee your freedom and the opportunity to see your own child. That is not what this
country is about. TED

These optimistic views about parental behavior, however, stand in stark
contrast to the well-established history that shows a significant percentage of men do not do the "right thing" by their children. In fact, this
lack of responsibility for their children's welfare, resulting in wide-scale
poverty, was exactly what prompted the government to finally create
the child support enforcement program in 1975. Nevertheless, fathers
holding these views remained adamant about them. They consistently
rejected the idea that the government should engage in the business of
transferring finances between adults once a family dissolves and were
very hesitant to suggest policy reforms of any kind to modify what they
viewed as a wholly unnecessary system.

Distrust of State Action Because the State Has Been "Feminized"

The third way some fathers' rights members expressed dissatisfaction
with the government in the area of child support enforcement is through
their view that the state has been "feminized." As of the year 2000,
approximately two-thirds of all divorce filers were women (Brinig and
Allen 2000), making them the immediate "culprits" in a relationship
breakup according to fathers' rights activists. Yet despite this fact, fathers' rights members consistently complained that the government is
on the woman's side when a family dissolves. As a result, in their view
the policies that have been developed around child support enforcement
automatically favor women over men. Despite this perception, however, fathers who reported these attitudes were the most amenable to
suggesting ways that the system could be modified to promote their
interests in what they viewed as a more favorable fashion.

   One of the most common charges against the system as overly "feminized" was the notion that the child support money that they were paying out was inappropriately enriching their former partners rather than
taking care of their children—with the complicity, of course, of lawmakers. For example, Carey, father of one child, articulated his resentment over the fact that "his" support dollars were being used not to

provide necessities for his child, but rather to fulfill the extravagant desires of his ex-partner.

> Too often the money is not put towards the actual raising of the child; it goes for extras for the parent that is receiving them. I talked to a guy last night whose ex used the money to get a new nose....I know of a father here in [this] area whose ex took him to court to increase her child support and then went out and got herself a new boob job. That is not money being spent on the child. CAREY

Gerald, another fathers' rights activist, also complained that child support is simply disguised alimony that is meant to benefit women.

> Chances are [the average man will] have to end up paying...alimony disguised in the child support formula to his ex-wife, and we think that's ridiculous. If we truly want equality between the genders today,...we have to treat men and women equally in terms of parental rights and responsibilities. We get many cases where [a] woman quit[s] [her] job after a divorce, finds a new boyfriend, collects child support from the old husband, and the ex-husband doesn't get to see enough of his kids to have a decent relationship....He is just struggling to get by [through] paying child support....The mother gets everything her way and has this leisurely, favorable lifestyle, because we all know the male pursues the female....[Women] have a real big advantage over men there and it's not fair when it comes down to family law decisions. GERALD

In his interview, Gerald maintained that women follow a normal pattern after they seek a divorce. Because they have a gender-based "advantage" in the pursuit of a mate, women can tap both their ex-husbands and new boyfriends in order to achieve a "leisurely" new lifestyle. Like many others in fathers' rights groups, Gerald held this view despite the preponderance of scholarly evidence that suggests that child support helps the majority of women simply make ends meet.

Related to this idea that the government requires "too much" child support to women was the concern voiced by group members that there is no oversight over the use of their child support payments. In particular, fathers argued that they are required to support their children by law but that there is no way to guarantee that the money that they send is actually being spent on their children. Some fathers like Jay maintained that without this accountability, their children lacked basic necessities.

Well, child support to me, the way it is right now, is a way of transferring wealth from one parent to another under [the] auspices of child support. In my own particular case, I am paying the money every month, but I see that money is not spent on my children. I see them, [and] they have no clothing. They don't have [any] proper clothing. They don't have [any] shoes. They come to daddy. Anything they need, mommy sends them to daddy to go buy it for them. So, in other words, mommy takes the money and puts it in the bank or does whatever she wants to do with it, and expenses for the kids come back to daddy. Now if they put together a system that this money is spent on the children, I think most parents who are paying the child support wouldn't have too much of a problem. In my case, my main problem is my money is not spent on my children, but is spent on other things. Jay

Other fathers, like Lawrence, echoed the idea that without a strong accountability system in place, mothers simply use child support awards to buy luxury goods.

There is very little accountability because the money could go for buying a brand new car for the custodial parent or, in my personal experience, it went to buy a timeshare condo in Florida....We went through, after we got a divorce, we went through a short period of an attempt at reconciliation and she confided in me that she was using the money that I was giving her for child support to pay for a time-share in Florida. Lawrence

Fathers' rights activists also perceived a lack of equal justice with respect to the issue of accountability. If they are late with their payments, they can face jail time. However, according to activists like Clifford, father of two, the recipients of the money (women) are not held to the same standard of responsibility.

> There is no accountability on the side of the person who has custody. You know, if I don't pay my child support, they can garnish my wages, they can take away my driver's license, and they can throw me in jail. However, there is absolutely nothing provided in the law to give the child support payer recourse as to what the custodial parent does with it. I found that very upsetting. CLIFFORD

Several fathers suggested a simple technological solution to this accountability issue—the introduction of some type of debit card that would only permit purchases of approved items. In the view of many fathers, child support is actually "their" money and not to be spent in what they suggest are arbitrary ways.

> There is no accountability. Basically, she comes in with beautiful hair and nails, new clothes, [and] new cars. It's pretty amazing. So, I can go to jail for not paying her. And she can take my money to the liquor store or beauty store and feed her face and body. It doesn't matter. No accountability.... I think that there [should be a] debit card situation where you can actually use a card and only buy things that were pre-approved for use by the children themselves. I'm learning about it. It sounds like a wonderful idea. It's a check and balance. NATHAN

Interestingly, although a few fathers like Nathan offered specific examples of their child support dollars being spent on extravagant items for their ex-partners, for the most part, fathers' rights activists just assumed through observation of their ex-partners' behavior that this was true. There was strong resentment against all former partners who appeared to be "making it" above the mere subsistence level. Indeed, this attitude was indicative of a much broader sense of anger against women who demonstrate economic resiliency with the help of government intervention on their behalf.

Beyond this accountability issue, fathers' rights activists also maintained that the state was overly "feminized" in the ways in which it calculated their ex-partners' awards. At every stage in the process, these fathers pointed to evidence that the rules of the game favored women's interests over their own. Paramount among these concerns was simply the amount fathers were required to pay. Recall from chapter 2 that child support guidelines are designed to preserve a child's standard of living based on parental income; they are not based on what a child needs merely to survive. Fathers' rights activists tend to object to this principle at its core. They want only a child's needs to be used in determining child support awards and are not concerned about more equitable standards of living between the two households. For some fathers, such as Jonathan, father of two, injustices arise because a family breakup brings out the worst instincts in couples as they argue over scarce resources.

> Well, the main reason [child support is unfair] is it creates a contest. Well, I don't know about the statistics, but in many of the cases, the amounts that are being disbursed are far, far in excess of what is necessary to support the child. As such, there is a game to be played to commandeer those resources. Facts become distorted, [and] motivations become obscure in the process of trying to commandeer those resources....The state has seen fit to set very unrealistic guidelines of what constitutes a reasonable figure. [The game is] played on people who are in an emotionally bad place and needing perhaps to seek out revenge or a desire to put other people down or something.
> JONATHAN

For Jonathan, more often than not in the game he described, women turn out to be the winners and fathers the losers. Diego echoed this concern by arguing that raising children is not as expensive as the actual awards might indicate. Here he described the disparity between what the government ordered him to pay to support his only child and what he believed it really cost to raise that child.

> For some people, I [have] heard [that they] pay upwards of a thousand dollars per month for child support. That's as if that child makes $1,000 a month at the age of two. I have never spent $1,000 a month on my child. On rare occasions, I spent $300 a month on my child.
> DIEGO

In many cases, awards were so high that fathers in the study claimed that they could not support themselves. Wayne made this point as he detailed his budget after taking care of his three teenage daughters.

> Just in my case, I know, my ex-wife persuaded the court she couldn't work because if the children got sick [and had to stay home] from school, she needed to be home. . . . So besides paying child support, I also pay 84 percent of all nonreimbursed medical expenses for my daughters, [and] educational expenses. Basically I'm left with $74 a week to live on, and to me that's unfair. The options that I'm left with . . . is I either get a second job and give up visitation, or I struggle along so I can see my girls. . . . It just seems like it's all just fixed.   WAYNE

In some situations, parents earned close to the same amount of money when they were living together. However, when they broke up, the courts ordered child support to be paid, usually from the father to the mother. This arrangement made it difficult for the paying parent to survive, according to fathers' rights activists. Harry encapsulated the feelings of these fathers when he explained his financial circumstances after his separation.

> [While my ex-wife had] temporary custody, I had to pay child support. I was only making $23,000 a year and my ex-wife was making $18,000 a year, so there wasn't a real big difference. The magistrate in our case ordered me to pay a little over $700 a month, and that left me with two [semimonthly] paychecks of only $315, but yet she defaulted quite a bit of her time with the kids. I had them, like, 60 percent of the time, which meant she had all of this extra money coming into her house when she did not have the kids. I was trying to survive buying food. I lost my apartment and I had to move back in with my parents. It was very tough and I think sometimes [judges] need to sit back and say, how much does it really cost to raise a child? For instance, . . . does it really cost them $3,000 a month to raise a child? I am not saying men shouldn't have to pay or this or that. They need to really look at how much does it really cost to raise a child and how much time that child spends with each parent.   HARRY

A key corollary of Harry's argument was fathers' stated belief that no sound, economic basis is used for the award guidelines established by the states. Timothy became a member of a fathers' rights group when one of his five children—a son—faced a crisis in his own parenting life. When Timothy's son separated from his wife, they had two children, a boy and a girl. At first the wife received temporary custody and the husband was ordered to pay child support. He eventually received sole custody of the children when the wife simply left the state. Although Timothy's son was happy to have custody of his children, the child support obligation that he was ordered to pay while they were living with their mother was, in his view, extremely burdensome. To activists like Timothy, who was exasperated by the financial pressures facing his son, child support guidelines simply cannot be defended on their own merits; in the activists' minds, these guidelines work to fundamentally disadvantage men and benefit women. As Timothy stated,

> I even attended child support commission meetings in this state. [The commission sets the guidelines.] There is nobody on the panel that is an economist, nobody on that panel. So they take the amount of money that the father makes, the amount of money that the mother makes, add the two together and they come up with the magic figure of how much money the father is going to have to pay....I know one [case] now where the father is paying 87 percent of his income for child support; now how is that person supposed to live? See, I've got friends who have had to go back to live with their parents, live in a trailer, live in their car.   TIMOTHY

Although Timothy's own son did not have to resort to such drastic measures in order to survive, other fathers in his experience clearly suffered from the effects of what they perceived as the onerous burden of these obligations.

Another primary source of concern over the calculation of awards related to the perception that the government refused to consider the needs of fathers struggling to keep two homes running rather than one. Lukas, a father of three with only a modest income, made the case that families frequently must make hard budgetary decisions when they are all living together, including the establishment of priorities regarding rent, food, clothes, and so on. Yet in Lukas's mind, this type of normal household budgeting is no longer deemed relevant when the family faces a judge in the courthouse.

> When you go into that courtroom, you are treated as though you are still living with your spouse and...your standard of living is not considered. They are not realizing that the family is now divided. The father has to provide not only for his family now, but he also has to provide for himself as far as a house, transportation, food, clothing, and utilities. Now that family pot, let's say, is divided, but the courts say, "No, you have to keep up the standard of living for your children. You have to continue to provide for their utilities, their food, their clothing, and a lot of times you are not able to do that. You were not able to do that much when you were together as far as buying your kids clothes. You know what I mean? Families have to struggle and get by and they sacrifice. But now all of a sudden that sacrificing and not getting the tennis shoes and the clothes is thrown out the window and now they are saying you've got to pay. So we feel that the court system is taking advantage of fathers that way and making them pay as if they were still with the family, yet they have to be able to provide a home for themselves. In a lot of cases, it is hard and some guys find themselves homeless or having to move in with relatives or friends or whatever just to get by. Then the courts punish you by threatening you with jail time or taking your license or whatever they can do to get you to pay. LUKAS

Compounding the difficulty of this situation, many fathers believed that their former partners were not doing enough to make the transition to two households smoother. Felix articulated this point when he described the hostile relationship between him and his former partner regarding expenses for their two children.

> [The] majority of custodial parents are mothers, so the majority of the people doing this wrong are mothers. What happens is mothers will take your money, but they sure won't share the clothes [that] they buy with [your money], they sure won't share the toys they buy with [your money]. So when you have a two income household and now you are

broken up and you have a one income household, [things change]. Now part of your one income goes to fulfilling another household's [needs]....From my standpoint, I have one income, and part of that income is to go to make this other household whole, but what about my household? I have to make it whole. I have to go buy beds. I have to go buy toys. I have to go buy food, et cetera. So you go from a two-income household to less than one income....You have to buy a full household [of supplies] because the mother is not [going to help you]. I beg you to show me one mother who would share fully the clothes and the toys she bought with the child support money. [My] kids came here for six and one-half weeks, and there was nothing but the clothes on their backs....Now, ...I completely expected that because I've been through this for years. Everyone that I talk to—they go through the same thing. It isn't anything new; we are all used to it and it is wrong.   FELIX

In these circumstances, Felix carefully described his view that the courts retain a responsibility to make sure that both halves of the former partnership remain economically viable units. However, in Felix's perspective, the government consistently abandons fathers while ensuring that mothers retain economic independence; the courts simply will not compel women to carry their share of the financial burden. Yet, interestingly, neither Lukas nor Felix made any mention of financial difficulties faced by their ex-partners in the postdissolution context.

Fathers' rights activists also expressed the idea that the government was failing men by not considering the cause of the breakup in the awarding of support. Although it has never been a fundamental part of public policy, men with this view held out the hope that this new type of linkage would be introduced. The link would function like the concept of "fault-finding" in the case of a divorce settlement, whereby bad behavior in a marriage is ultimately linked to a range of negative outcomes—such as reduced property settlements for the "offending" party—when the union dissolves. Patrick, father of a nine-year-old daughter, described his preferred mechanism for awarding child support in the following terms:

[There] is no consideration, based on a case by case basis, as to whether the noncustodial parent left the kids with a custodial parent or whether the custodial parent kicked the noncustodial parent out. To me, [these are] two different situations and should be held differently.... [It] comes down to [this]: if you want to take something away from me, I shouldn't be expected to provide support for it. No service, no payment. PATRICK

In this case, Patrick clearly defined his position by stating: "No service, no payment." What exact "service" his wife was supposed to provide to him while he was married is unclear, but nevertheless, now that she had taken this "service" away, Patrick no longer felt obligated to take care of his child. But governmental officials, according to Patrick, refuse to consider the issue of fault when they calculate awards. This practice once again revealed to fathers' rights activists the state's favoritism toward women as the overwhelming recipients of the male largesse.

In terms of other nuts-and-bolts procedures that appear to favor women, some fathers' rights activists found fault with the government's use of imputed income as a way of determining child support obligations. Judges may impute income under a variety of different circumstances. For example, in situations where a person's true earnings may be ambiguous or undocumented, as in the case of a recently incarcerated father, judges may impute income at the minimum or median state wage. In other cases, judges may impute extra income to a father who simply has access to overtime at work—even though it may not be used—a presumption on which they then make a child support award. The idea behind imputing income is to ensure that mothers receive a steady stream of payments from these potential extra hours of labor. However, fathers' rights advocates have argued that the availability of overtime is unpredictable, and the assumption that it is dependable results in overly generous orders that they then have to struggle to fulfill. Philippe, who has three daughters to support of his own, described the dilemma that he maintained many of his male employees faced.

I had 160 people working for me, and I would see young people get married, have kids, and then they would have a divorce. We were working seven days a week and they were getting a lot of overtime. [Judges would] base this child support on overtime, which you're not supposed to do....They would come to me for their salary to pre-sent to the court and I would always say that this is not a steady income....The overtime could end at any time, and I saw that happen to them. PHILIPPE

Even though Philippe would document that the overtime was not permanent for his employees, he found that the judges would ignore this fact.

Similarly, Laura had married a man who had a daughter from a pre-vious marriage. She joined her local fathers' rights group because her husband wanted to spend more time with his daughter and could not find a way to easily negotiate that with his ex-wife. In the meantime, she discovered what she thought were unfair practices related to imput-ing income. Here, Laura explained what happened to her family when her husband switched from working the second shift at his job to the less-lucrative first shift.

What we found shocking [with] going to court [was that] my husband had 45 percent [of the time] with his child [and] he still paid full child support....[In addition, the court] decided he should have been pay-ing more; he made $25,000 at the time. They decided he should be making $35,000. Remember I said he wanted to go to first shift? If he stayed on second, they said he would be making $35,000. So [the court said] he should be making $35,000, and that's what they based his child support on. They also said he should have been doing that for two years, so they made it retroactive. So even though he never missed a payment, he is now in arrears. So he is paying based on a salary of $10,000 more than he makes and paying on an arrearage even though he never missed a payment. We were impoverished. That little bit of income wiped us out. When my stepdaughter was with us, sometimes we didn't have food. LAURA

Although these concerns are valid, neither Philippe nor Laura indi-cated knowledge of the financial circumstances of the children's mother. Given the extensive body of research demonstrating that the majority of mothers fare far worse than fathers in the case of a family breakup, it is possible that without these adjustments ordered by the court, these children could have been living in poverty or in a less severe but still disadvantaged environment when they resided with their mother. Nevertheless, these activists consistently branded the imputing of income as a policy that systematically disadvantaged fathers while inappropriately raising the standard of living of mothers and their children.

Fathers' rights activists also complained about the treatment of their income in the tax code. In most states, child support obligations are based on gross income rather than net income. Fathers' rights activists maintain that this is unfair because they never experience what it is like to earn a "gross income." After all of the deductions that their employers and the government take, they see much less in take-home pay. Women gain once again because policymakers favor them when they create these rules. Ray, a divorced father of two young children, expressed his indignation with the system on this point.

> You know what they consider child support? They base it off of gross income...not giving any allowance to your basic tax burden. I mean, if you have an income in the $100,000 area, by the time you pay sales tax, property tax, and income tax in [this state] you are looking at, basically, I believe the figure is around 51 percent of your income in taxes. I believe the child support burden for two children by the tables would be in the [range of] 25 to 27 percent of gross income, ...I've seen stories where people making $160,000 are left with $20,000 a year to try and live on. I don't know anybody who wants to do that.   RAY

In addition to problems with the determination of child support based on gross rather than net income, other fathers found fault with the system as it relates to the tax deductions that they are permitted to take. Simply put, custodial parents may claim children as dependents on their income taxes, but noncustodial parents may not. A fathers' rights activist named Maury expanded on this injustice.

> [The] noncustodial parent has to pay a rather significant portion of [his] income and often [it is] so much so that he is left in a state of semipoverty. I actually have a very good deal, so I am not complaining, but in a lot of cases that's how it ends up. In [addition to that], they don't get the tax deduction, they don't get any of the tax breaks,

and they often don't even get access to their child. All they get is the responsibility of sending money.   MAURY

In this case, Maury indicated that he had "a very good deal" with respect to child support, paying less than $200 per month for his only son. Although he could not claim the income tax dependent deduction, he continued to benefit from an order that made his monthly obligation relatively low. Again, without knowing his ex-partner's financial circumstances, we cannot assess whether this obligation is "a very good deal" for his son as well. Regardless, fathers' rights activists simply oppose the current tax code because, they argue, it favors custodial parents, who are, more likely than not, women rather than men.

Another frustration voiced by fathers' rights group members is that child support obligations do not take into direct account the quantity of time a child may spend with his or her noncustodial parent. Fathers' rights activists repeatedly complained that the child support money simply "does not follow the child"; instead, the state ensures that the money follows the mother. Ivan, father of two teenagers, expounded on his view of the problem.

Just like I explained to you, I have my kids more than their mother has them....I have to clothe them, feed them, but still give money to their mother. I will lose my house if I can't get this straightened out....The money needs to go where the kids are....They need to take into account where the child is [when they think about] where the money needs to be. Don't get me wrong—guys who are out running around and horrible fathers who want a divorce—it's not the mother's or the child's fault, and he should be responsible for them. But when that's not the situation, the child support needs to be adjusted.   IVAN

Although Ivan acknowledged that some men are irresponsible, he also argued that the current system of money flowing from father to mother does not reflect the reality of where his children spend their time.

However, consistent with Ivan's preferences, one of the newest trends in child support law is for judges to make proportionate reductions in child support awards based on the amount of time a child spends with the noncustodial parent (Crowley 2003). In states where this type of formulaic adjustment is used, the noncustodial parent must reach a certain threshold of overnights for the child support obligation to be reduced. Yet despite this movement away from the "winner-take-all" system of child support, in which the custodial parent—usually the mother—receives all of the money because of her custodial parent status, fathers' rights activists like Samuel still rejected this new practice as arbitrary and constructed by policymakers to favor women.

> I believe that in my case it is just about a 60/40 custody split [60 percent for mom, and 40 percent for me]. The thing is, I pay child support whether I have the child or not. I don't think [fathers] get enough of the credit and I'll tell you why. I am paying mom $180 a week. That is a lot of money for a three-year-old child. Now if I didn't have my child any nights of the year, I'd still pay $180. I have my child, like, I'll say 143 nights a year, [and] I still pay $180. I am saying that the 143 nights a year [that] she lives with me, I've got to have a home. I've got to drive the car and spend [money on] gas. I've got to feed the child. I've got to buy toys. I've got to buy clothes. I've got to entertain her. I have exactly the same expenses during my 40 percent of the time that the mother has in her 60 percent of the time.... The other thing is I think I should get a proportionate deduction based on the time I have her, but there is a threshold for that, and it is 40 percent. I have 39.17 percent, so I missed it by 83–100ths of a percent.... This is why deadbeat dads, that lousy term, is created. The system asks a man to support his ex-family to such a degree that he can't support himself and another family. [He also has] a support order and alimony order, a mortgage payment and [is trying] to live and [is trying] to work two jobs. You know what he does? He beats it out of town. He's to the point where he can't make it.... Give a person the credit for the time and understand [that he has] expenses, too.... Proportionate credit for the time spent with the child [is all we want]. SAMUEL

Carlos echoed the concerns of Samuel. Although his three children either had already or were close to "aging out" of the child support system, Carlos continued his fight on behalf of child support reform because of his inherent objections to the ways in which the government refuses to acknowledge how fathers must expend substantial resources on their children both when they have them at their residence and when they do not.

> The calculations...do not make any allowance for ordinary parenting time with the children. So a parent who is paying guideline child support and has his children according to the local parenting time rules...in the county I'm in, it's every other weekend, one evening a week for three hours, and half of the holidays, but when you count up half the holidays and summer and everything, that's about 27 percent of the time. So that parent is actually paying twice, even if [he is] not incurring any of the direct expenses for clothing, and school, and so forth. [He is] paying twice for housing and all of that, and that, I think, you know, the unfairness bothers me. CARLOS

In some cases, fathers argued that the child support awards were so unreasonable that the impetus behind the law had to be policymakers' low opinion of men as providers. And because society is so vested in protecting women over men, all fathers ended up suffering because of several "bad apples."

Finally, fathers' rights activists took the government to task for its perceived harsh enforcement of child support laws. These activists maintained that although law enforcement officials are quick to punish those who get behind in their child support payments—which are most likely to be men—they are loathe to enforce access agreements—which are controlled and repeatedly violated by women. Louis, a group member who went through a particularly hostile divorce, claimed that his ex-partner did everything in her power to restrict access to his three children, even to the point of filing a false domestic violence claim. This accusation had the result of reducing his ability to see his children, even after the courts cleared him of these charges.

> Being a child support-paying parent doesn't give you the right to see your children. The courts don't enforce the laws on the books when visitation is interfered with, [even though] the other party is supposed to be sanctioned. Not only don't the courts enforce the existing laws, they don't enforce their own court orders. When somebody is found in

contempt, they will find them in contempt again, but they don't punish [her] on it. They don't do anything. Child support doesn't mean
you get to see your children.   Louis

For Louis, in order for the system to have any credibility, the government
must do much more to make sure children continue to spend time with
both parents. Toward this end, paying child support on time and providing access to children must be treated as equally important duties.

But Louis went even further in these remarks. He implied, as many
fathers' rights members do, that there should be a close link between
child support and access. In other words, paying child support should
entitle a person to access to his children. Both the federal government
as well as the states, however, do not condition access on the timely
payment of support, or vice versa. To Louis as well as other activists,
this is further evidence that the state is excessively "feminized"—in
other words, captured by women's interests at the expense of equally
important male needs.

Frustrated Payers

Child support policy represents a never-ending source of consternation
for fathers' rights activists. Their primary criticism revolves around the
actions of an overly intrusive state that, in their view, forces them to
make ill-conceived transfer payments to their ex-partners. Their level of
hostility toward the state can be arrayed along a continuum of extreme
antipathy to strong opposition. Near the side of extreme antipathy are
those who maintain that all state actions in the area of child support
are abusive and corrupting or, alternatively, completely unnecessary.
Activists with these views have very little patience for incremental reform in this policy area; they would like to see the child support system
completely abolished. Somewhat more open to the prospects for change
are those who strongly oppose the current system as excessively feminized, that is, overly allied with women's interests. Regardless of where
they are on this spectrum, however, all activists argue that because the
system is so stacked against them, noncustodial fathers suffer inordi-
nate consequences. The most disadvantaged are relegated to living on

the economic margins, and the still less fortunate are jailed for their inability—not unwillingness—to pay their ordered amounts.

How can we evaluate their views? Since this study did not collect divorce documents, police reports, bank information, or interview data from other members of these fathers' families, it is impossible to assess the factual basis of their statements. What about the inner motivations of these fathers as they described their particular views? These too are difficult to discern, but two possible extreme positions can be outlined that are not necessarily mutually exclusive. On the one hand, some fathers' statements related to the child support system appear to come from an honest position of pain and injustice, informed by their own particular experience with the losses they faced when their families dissolved. No social program is perfect, and individual cases of hardship are bound to occur in a system that relies on award guidelines that are uniformly applied across thousands of families every year. Their voices in this study were loud, clear, and despondent, as only can be expected given their circumstances.

On the other hand, a number of these fathers' statements regarding the child support system are blatantly antifeminist and antagonistic toward women as a group. This mindset was particularly apparent when fathers described child support policy as emerging from a state that is excessively "feminized." In these interviews, fathers expressed frustration with the presumed notion that women had successfully captured the state for their own interests. For example, in demanding an accountability system to monitor how child support is actually used and in decrying what they viewed as their ex-partners' suspicious use of "their" money for luxury goods, these fathers revealed an inappropriate desire for control over a woman's right to make autonomous and independent decisions about her economic life without male interference.

Regardless of their motivations, their antistate attitudes stand in stark contrast to the overwhelming academic research that points to the *necessity* of state action in enforcing child support as fundamental to the economic security of female-headed families. Study after study has indicated that women continue to earn less than men and make significant career sacrifices while married or romantically involved in order to care for their children. When these unions dissolve, women rely on child support to at least partially compensate themselves for labor market discrimination and other types of occupational sacrifices—including those that enabled their partners to advance up career ladders unencumbered by child care responsibilities—that they made while the family unit was still together. Indeed, they often need this money in order to raise themselves and their children above the poverty line. To this charge, however, fathers' rights groups have a ready answer. Policymakers should make joint legal and physical custody the presumptive law in all fifty states. If this were to occur, according to fathers' rights activists, then no money whatsoever would need to change hands between parents. Fathers' grievances against the current custody system, as well as an analysis of their particular policy reform suggestions, are the focal topics of the next chapter.

6

The Custody Wars

The local fathers' rights group, Papas for Participation, tries to cre-
ate a warm, inviting atmosphere when it meets every month. A small
Golden Retriever puppy dashes among the ten round tables that are
set up in the expansive room donated by the Lutheran Church in a
suburban northeastern town. As his owner tries to gain control over
the puppy, other members gradually trickle into the room. Including
the male leader and his female vice president, twenty-one people are in
attendance on this breezy day. All attendees are white, and there are a
total of six women, two of whom appear to be grandmothers. One man
boasts his commitment to the cause by wearing a "World's Greatest
Dad" tee shirt.

Five minutes behind schedule, the meeting begins with Lawrence,
the president, and Cathleen, the vice president, introducing themselves
to the group. They each provide the names and ages of their children
and ask the members to do the same. After pausing a moment, most of
the members reach in their wallets and pocketbooks. They begin circu-
lating pictures of their children to all of the other members. With each
member taking his or her turn, they describe their family situations to
the rest of the group. Some members state that they do not need to be
coming anymore as their children are grown, but they are committed

to the cause of forcing their state to pass new, father-friendly laws. One father cries out that he does not believe he will ever see his children again due to false allegations of abuse.

Once the introductions are over, Lawrence first reviews the activities planned for the summer. Papas for Participation is aiming to attend a baseball game as a group social event, rent a booth at the state fair to publicize its issues, and sponsor a candlelight vigil at a local park in support of shared parenting. Then two female members speak. One recently completed training in family mediation, and she describes to the group the importance of this option for settling disputes as opposed to the adversarial court process. The second woman describes her efforts to establish a neutral site for both the transfer of children between parents and, when needed, supervised visitation.

After these initial presentations, Lawrence gets the group's attention by asking them all to fight for their most important goal: encouraging the state to pursue joint custody legislation.

> LAWRENCE: I hope that all of you are voting, because we must get joint
> custody legislation passed through this legislature. I want to read
> to you a list of several individuals who are running for office in the
> state. Some of them are divorced with kids. We must invite them
> to our meetings, because more and more of our representatives are
> in the same boat as us. I have an important rule of politics to share
> with you. Help candidates out with the election and they will help
> us with our issue of joint custody!

Beyond overhauling the child support system, fathers' rights activists consider child custody reform to be the most important issue facing legislators and judges at all levels of government today. Unlike material assets accumulated during the course of a relationship or a marriage, the law has had much more difficulty "dividing" up children once a relationship has broken down. When considering the dilemma as to where children should spend their time after a family dissolves, one potential starting point would be to answer the question: Who handled the majority of child care when the family was together?

Scholars have approached the study of how much effort each parent expends in caring for his or her children in a variety of different ways. Up through the 1980s, these analyses explored how much time each parent allocated to general household labor, which included child care. This early research accounted for time each parent spent in broad categories of work, like preparing meals, washing clothes, and cleaning the house. However, because these studies did not specifically focus on child care per se, they were in constant danger of either over or underestimating attention paid to child-centered activities (Ishii-Kuntz and Coltrane 1992). More recent research has relied on time diaries, which ask participants to recall, sum up, and report the total amount of time that they engage in a variety of household tasks (Sayer, Bianchi, and Robinson 2004). Of course, these studies rely on participants actually recording accurately how they spend their time, but overall, these diaries are more likely to be a reliable means of collecting data because researchers can code themes and activities that are solely related to child care.

Overall, we would expect that since the mid-twentieth century, fathers would be engaging in more active child care than they had in the past for three central reasons. First, as discussed in the previous chapter, women have dramatically increased their participation in the labor market. This is true of both married and single mothers; and we might predict that with this trend, some of the tasks previously undertaken by women would be assumed by their male partners in the name of fairness and more efficient time management (Cohen and Bianchi 1999). Second, with the spread of contraception and the growing acceptance of the notion of parenthood as a voluntary choice, those having a child might be expected to dedicate a significant amount of time to their offspring. In other words, now more than ever, men would "self-select" into fatherhood, and ultimately these men would be the ones who would demonstrate a strong desire to participate actively in child care (Sayer, Bianchi, and Robinson 2004). Third, strong social forces have encouraged men to become more involved in child-related activities (Burgess 1997; Coltrane 1989). In other words, there has been a fundamental shift in the "culture of fatherhood" whereby men assume more active roles in raising their children than in the past. Newspapers, magazines, television shows, and movies all have begun promoting more vigorously than ever before the merits and virtues of fathers taking a vital interest in their children's well-being.

Despite these potential positive influences, however, the scholarly literature almost uniformly concludes that women continue to do a majority of the child care in comparison with men (Ahmeduzzaman and Roopnarine 1992; Aldous, Mulligan, and Bjarnason 1998; Hofferth and Sandberg 2001). When the studies first began, promising signals indicated that a behavioral change might be underway, despite a slow start. In fact, the "slow start" was actually a "nonstart," because during the decade between 1965 and 1975, men did not substantially alter their child care activities at all (Coverman and Sheley 1986). But during the 1980s and 1990s, fathers began to share some child-rearing tasks with their wives. Yet, because the initial care gap was so wide, this marginal improvement did not make much of a difference; today, women still do considerably more work in the care of their children than men. In one of the most recent analyses on this topic, in fact, Bianchi, Robinson, and Milkie (2006) found that although there is greater gender equality between married partners in terms of total paid and unpaid work than ever before, in the year 2000 women still did twice the child care work, spending 12.9 hours on these activities per week versus 6.5 hours per week for the male.

Of course, gender is not the only variable that matters in understanding how these arrangements get mapped out; many other factors influence the amount of time and energy each parent dedicates to child-oriented activities. Pleck (1997) has described the five categories of parental influences that shape who exactly takes care of the children: sociodemographic factors, motivation, skills and confidence, social supports, and other institutional dynamics. Sociodemographic factors include inherent parental traits and attainments, such as age and education (Cooney et al. 1993; Zick and Bryant 1996). Motivational factors include an individual's own upbringing, personality, and ideology regarding egalitarian gender roles, and skills and confidence relate to perceived competencies regarding child care (Baruch and Barnett 1981; McHale and Huston 1984; Radin 1981). Social supports refer to how each partner views the other partner's capabilities and networking resources in the area of child care, and institutional factors highlight how each parent's employment commitments impact his or her participation in child-oriented activities (Aldous, Mulligan, and Bjarnason 1998; Nock and Kingston 1988). In sum, all of these influences may play a role in either increasing or decreasing the amount of time a parent spends doing the work of child care. However, pointing out that other dynamics may be important does not negate the central finding of interest here: fathers still do much less than mothers on the child-rearing front.

Fathers' rights activists maintain that they have a strong rebuttal to these conclusions. When parents are living together, they each specialize in providing certain services to the household (Nock 1998). Although women may do more of the child care—and may prefer to do so to preserve their authority over the domestic sphere—men engage in equally important activities as breadwinners. In other words, in a united family unit, fathers model strong social behaviors like a vigorous work ethic and individual responsibility for their children. They also bring a steady income into the household, which research has shown to be important in inoculating children against a whole host of risky behaviors such as teenage pregnancy, juvenile delinquency, and substance abuse. Once a family breaks up, fathers should not be penalized for having played the primary wage-earning role when everyone lived together. Instead, children should spend roughly 50 percent of their time with each parent, whose former earning-versus-care specialization histories should no longer apply in their new households. These fathers are also likely to remarry within four years, with their new spouses providing coverage for any gaps in care that may arise (Coleman, Ganong, and Fine 2000). In considering these arguments, it is important to examine the scholarly research that explores the direct impact of various custody arrangements on familial well-being in the postdissolution context.

Joint Versus Sole Custody: Is There a Clear Winner?

In the case of child support enforcement, a strong consensus has evolved in the research community about the importance of financial transfers from fathers to mothers. Child support clearly makes a difference in moving female-headed households out of poverty or preventing them from falling into poverty in the first place. Moreover, these payments can help keep families off of the welfare rolls or can extract them from the throes of welfare dependency if they are already there. For more advantaged families, child support also functions to maintain the child's standard of living in both homes after a dissolution takes place. In addition, the academic research shows that these benefits for custodial mothers can occur without significantly harming the economic well-being of most fathers, especially the more advantaged fathers in fathers' rights groups. As chapter 5 illustrated, however, fathers' rights activists distrust state activity in this area, regardless of the benefits for women and children. Some members were suspicious of any type of state intervention in their lives because they perceived the government to be abusive and corrupting, while others were more critical of state action because they charged that it constituted unnecessary meddling in their "natural family lives." A final group of activists objected because the technical rules of the child support game, in their minds, are overly biased towards women.

The case of child custody policy—and this chapter uses the short-hand term "joint custody" to mean joint physical rather than joint legal custody, unless otherwise specified—is somewhat more complicated (Kelly 1993a). Scholars agree that in cases with a primary custodial parent (usually the mother) and a noncustodial parent (usually the father), contact between children and their noncustodial father decreases over time; and this "dropping out" effect may be more rampant among low-income families (Furstenberg and Nord 1985; Seltzer 1991). In an ideal world, no child would have to experience such a tragic separation from a parent. This has led researchers to take a hard look at joint custody arrangements as a way to prevent any type of alienation from occurring. However, as demonstrated below, there simply is not an overwhelming case for joint custody either (Johnston 1995). Instead, the research results—generated mostly by sociologists and psychologists—have been much more mixed and even contradictory. Scholars have documented these uneven findings when examining how different custody arrangements impact parent-child relationships, parental happiness, and childhood development overall.

When considering the influence of custody decisions on children's lives, scholars have first focused on how these arrangements impact the parent-child bond over time. The starting point for these analyses is the question of time allocation. Even children in joint custody situations do not necessarily spend 50 percent of their time with each parent. Because judges often accommodate individual family's circumstances, joint custody can mean a child splitting each week with each parent, alternating weeks, or settling into some other type of arrangement. In general, however, children in joint custody arrangements spend more time with the lesser-seen parent and transition more frequently between houses than children in sole custody situations (Amato and Gilbreth 1999; Ferreiro 1990; Kline et al. 1989; Lee 2002). This result is robust over time; that is, children who initially spend more time with a lesser-seen parent with joint custody will continue to see that parent more consistently over the years than children in sole custody circumstances. Children in sole custody relationships simply do not have these consistent opportunities for interaction that can provide the basis for the parent-child bond to flourish (Bowman and Ahrons 1985).

What about the impact of these arrangements on the quality of the child's relationship with each parent? Here the results are very mixed. Donnelly and Finkelhor (1992) explored how different custody arrangements influence the level of affection and support communicated between parents and children. They found no relationship between joint custody and higher absolute levels of these measures of well-being. On the other hand, some scholars have focused on co-residential arrangements and have argued that these are beneficial to fathers because alliances build between parent and child more readily (Shapiro and Lambert 1999). However, these types of studies might simply be picking up the effects of improved access and contact rather than the benefits of the joint custody arrangement itself. Moreover, these positive effects are likely to be reversed in cases of high parental conflict (Kline, Johnston, and Tschann 1991; Maccoby et al. 1993).

Second, scholars have examined the role of different custody arrangements on parental happiness. The process of a family breaking up can be devastating for both parents. Mothers and fathers have to adjust to living on their own, including making financial and emotional decisions on issues to which they might be unaccustomed. Managing their children's well-being in this turbulent context can also be very demanding. The attitudes, needs, and behaviors of their children can serve to either support parents during this period of transition or, alternatively, create more stress. To what extent, then, does where their children live contribute to their parents' personal well-being? Which custodial arrangement, in other words, makes parents happiest?

The answer depends on how one measures "happiness." One way to do so is by examining stress levels. Joint custody's requirement for constant consultation and meetings over children's schedules might produce additional anxiety among parents who are already demoralized by the dissolution process. However, the opposite may also be true; joint custody may actually decrease parental stress in the following sense: Children consume parents' time and energy, and during the transitional period of family dissolution, these pressures are likely to increase in magnitude. Parents with weak social networks may have difficulty managing these problems if they become the primary caretakers for the first time in their children's lives; this might be an especially important consideration for fathers, who may have fewer close friends than do mothers on which to rely during this critical time. Under this scenario, joint custody might facilitate lower levels of stress because parents with this arrangement might be more inclined to share child-rearing responsibilities between them. Over the long run, this practice could result in decreased emotional burnout for each parent. There is some scholarly research to suggest that this, in fact, is what transpires: reduced stress levels do occur for certain families with joint custody agreements (Arditti and Madden-Derdich 1997; Maccoby and Mnookin 1992).

Another way of exploring parental happiness is to examine satisfaction levels with various custody arrangements, which tend to divide along gender lines. Fathers, for the most part, prefer joint custody arrangements, perhaps because they sense that this type of agreement will provide them with greater access to their children. Interestingly, however, researchers have found that "too much" time for these fathers can be a negative; Shapiro and Lambert (1999) found that men who lived with their children were less happy than continuously married men and nonresident fathers. For fathers, then, there appears to be a "happy medium" of involvement. Mothers, on the other hand, consistently express a strong preference for sole custody (Arditti and Madden-Derdich 1997; Shrier et al. 1991). This preference may be due to the high likelihood that they were primary caretakers when the family was intact and have a strong desire to continue in this role.

Third, in addition to their focus on the impact of various custodial arrangements on parental adjustment, scholars have also explored whether these residential agreements influence children's adjustment.

Many factors can shape a child's well-being after a family dissolves, including the internal, temperamental characteristics of the child him or herself and contextual/environmental conditions. For example, traits unique to each child, such as his or her age and gender, may help predict how well he or she will adjust to the family's dissolution. In addition, the absence or presence of intense parental conflict clearly matters in influencing a child's behavior. Of course, parents who are abusive, neglectful, or mentally ill dramatically reduce the likelihood that their children will flourish. In sum, all of these factors may be equally or more important than custody arrangements in determining the status of a child's well-being. It is therefore important—to the extent that it is possible—to isolate the impact of custody arrangements by themselves on a child's prospects for healthy development (Johnston, Kline, and Tschann 1989).

Unfortunately, the research that explores the influence of various custody arrangements on child well-being indicates no consensus as to "best practice." On one hand, scholars have found a variety of positive outcomes in childhood development associated with increased access in the form of joint custody (Bender 1994). In one of the most significant meta-analytical studies conducted on this topic, Bauserman (2002) reported, for example, that children who spend roughly equal time with both parents have fewer emotional and behavioral problems than children who spend the majority of time with only their custodial parent. These children also have higher levels of self-esteem, improved family relations, and a healthier attitude toward their parents' separation. Importantly, these children do not report feeling as if they are being torn between their parents as a result of their living arrangements, which is a fear commonly voiced by joint custody opponents. In fact, children in joint custody arrangements were no different in terms of their adjustment across a wide range of measures than children from intact families. Indeed, retrospectively, adult children of divorce also frequently express a preference for equal time between parents (Fabricius and Hull 2000).

Other scholars, however, have noted the negative consequences associated with increased access to both parents, especially if access is granted under conditions of duress. Johnston, Kline, and Tschann (1989), for example, compared children under a variety of court-mandated and voluntary custody arrangements with respect to children's behavioral and emotional development. They found that those children who were most troubled had the highest levels of access to both parents, more transitions between households, and parents who were more verbally and physically aggressive with one another. Researchers have speculated that not all children react equally to the stresses of the family dissolution process. Some are able to compartmentalize their parent's conflict from their own developmental growth. Other children do not cope as well, and they quickly become overwhelmed by adult problems, which can create so much stress in their lives that they manifest emotional and behavioral pathologies. Certain children also might value more *quality* parenting time with each parent rather than splitting their *physical* time with each one exactly equally (Smart 2004b; Smart, Neale, and Wade 2001). Overall, scholars focusing on the child adjustment effects of joint custody point to the importance of determining the contextual factors that are unique to each family before embarking on such a living arrangement. In other words, no hard and fast rule regarding the most appropriate custodial determination is warranted without considering each family's interpersonal history.

The Response of Fathers' Rights Groups

Overall, then, the scholarly research on matters pertaining to custody has produced several important findings. Concerning actual child care responsibilities when parents are together, women do the overwhelming majority of the work. If past practice is to be used as an indicator of future behavior, then this evidence would support the principle that women should be the primary custodial parents when families dissolve. Moreover, the research that has explored the impact of different custody arrangements on familial well-being in the postdissolution context has produced mixed results. No consensus exists on the correlation between custody arrangements and parent-child relationships, parental happiness, or childhood adjustment. Some studies favor sole custody agreements, but others indicate that joint custody agreements are more desirable. In sum, no strong, compelling reason exists to promote joint custody at the expense of other arrangements from the perspective of the academic research that has emerged on this topic.

Despite the findings from this scholarship, however, fathers' rights groups are firm in their support of joint custody laws in the fifty states, which have inched only tentatively in this direction over the past several decades. This slow movement has become an unsettling source of strain and frustration for the men involved in these groups. As in the case of child support policy, their opposition to current child custody law is channeled and expressed in ways that reveal their intense distrust of the state; nowhere in their arguments do they discuss promoting equality in child care based on past family contributions. And again, similar to the case of child support, the membership articulated their disdain for child custody policy through three specific critiques of the state: (1) the state as abusive and corrupt, (2) the state as unnecessarily interfering in "natural" family life, and (3) the state as overly "feminized."

Distrust of State Action Because It Is Abusive and Corrupt

At the extreme end of this antipathy, many fathers' rights members charged that current custody policy is vacuous because the state itself engages in activities that are both abusive and corrupt. Fathers who voiced these types of concerns viewed the state as an unwieldy piece of political machinery whose representatives, once granted the power to intervene in family breakups, systematically ruin people's lives without looking back. Because of their strong antistate belief system, these fathers were the least likely to predict that reform would be possible in this issue area.

For these fathers, their most formidable enemies in the custody battle are the judges who arbitrarily reign over the family court system. Fathers' rights members maintained that these judges have no qualifications to make decisions about what is in the best interest of children whom they do not know, but they still act in extremely dictatorial ways that disadvantage men. Jonathan expressed his consternation when he described how judges use and abuse their extraordinary discretion in the courtroom.

It's highly politicized what's going on. There is what's called the "best interest of the child" [standard]. And what it is, in my view, is a Rorschach test. It says more about the person who is interpreting it than it does about the subject. And so a judge or a person in the system will look at the facts and make his own conclusions based on very arbitrary criteria. There are no thresholds in the law. If the judge wants to decide that my giving my kids piano lessons is abusive because they complain about the practicing, which did occur, he is able to make that conclusion. Without fact, without access to the children for a rebuttal, he is able to do all of these things because his power is absolute in that he has broad discretionary power to ascertain facts. And when you give a person that ability to ascertain facts, it's a very dangerous situation because the facts are then used to the ends that the party is trying to accomplish rather than . . . you know, any other [purpose]. It's absolute power corrupting absolutely. And that's the basis for the unfairness in the law.   JONATHAN

Like Jonathan, Carey had a similar complaint about this absolute power, even though on the surface he did not have a strong reason even to be involved with his local fathers' rights group. Carey reported sharing joint custody of his thirteen-year-old son with his ex-wife. Both parents lived in the same town; Carey had his son one week, and his ex-wife had the son at her residence the following week. It had been extremely difficult to achieve this arrangement, however, as his ex-wife had put him through two custody battles at the time of his interview and expressed a desire for more fights in the future. Carey argued that these types of challenges by his wife were only possible due to the abusive power that judges hold, which, in his view, is similar to that imposed on countries by reprehensible, communist political systems.

The only people who can really determine what is best for a child are those child's parents. If you take somebody who is totally outside of that family circle and have him deciding what is right for that child, I think that was called communism. Somebody who comes in from the outside has no idea. A judge would have no idea what my son's actual needs were. . . . I think it was put best by someone when he said to me, "[The] best interest of the child is whatever that judge wants it to be." If that judge decides that it is in the best interest of the child for [him] to play in the middle of the freeway during rush hour, [then that is considered in the best interest of the child].   CAREY

Another fathers' rights member named Brandon agreed with Carey's assessment and pointed to the ways in which this unpredictable, excessive authority had ruined his own chances for custody of his only son.

> As far as my own case, the judge's exact words to me the first time [I appeared in the courtroom] were, "I don't care what the circumstances are, you are going to lose." Those words are burned in the back of my brain and I want to know where on the LSATs, where in law school, where on the bar exam is the answer to any question—"I don't care what the circumstances are, you are going to lose." That is corrupt. BRANDON

With this extreme power, these fathers maintained, judges learn that they do not need to respect the petitioners who come into their courtroom; rather, they can simply ignore fathers' wishes with impunity. Marvin, a father who was in the process of fighting for sole custody of his daughter, also represented many other fathers in custody battles in his occupation as a family law attorney. In one particular case, he described a situation in which a father of two daughters, ages ten and twelve, had an order of protection issued against him by his former partner. This order of protection also mandated that he stay away from his children, even though there was no evidence of violence or threats against them. Marvin wanted the judge to overturn this decision and returned to court to represent his client in these proceedings. In a dejected voice, Marvin described his interaction with the judge as follows:

> So I brought a motion...to say to the judge, look, give [my client] a temporary order of visitation until we go back to court. Take the kids off the order of protection. The first time [I went to court], he wouldn't do it. He said, "I don't see what the big emergency is."...I said, "The guy hasn't seen his kids in a month and he is not going to see them for another month." And he rejected the motion, so I [filed again]. We came back two weeks later and he did change the order because he really had to, but already a month and a half had gone by. He just had no respect for, he didn't care to look or think about anything for the kids or the father. He's a typical judge. Is that the worst [situation imaginable]? MARVIN

As the attorney representing this father, Marvin believed that the judge in this case simply had no regard for the father-child relationship. The judge's power was all-consuming, making him blind to the day-to-day needs of children who, Marvin maintained, should see their parents on a regular basis.

In addition to their concerns about the excessive power of judges, activists also voiced disgust at the ways in which the courts and the institutions "feeding off" of the courts seem to profit from families breaking up. As described in chapter 2, the courts may require parents to hire mental health evaluators in order to determine the best possible living situation for their children. In addition, the courts may order that a guardian ad litem or an attorney represent the children's interests in court. Of course, these professionals can cost parents thousands of dollars in fees. Joanna, a divorced mother of four, had difficulty seeing her children on a regular basis. She complained in harrowing terms about the financial stress that this corrupt process had inflicted on her:

> I think…attorneys, by nature, are adversarial and greedy. The American society is greedy. The more money attorneys can bill through conflict, the more heartache they create and the more, really, everyone suffers.…I've totally depleted my retirement [funds]. It has just been hemorrhaging because of attorney fees. I love my children dearly and I ache every day because they are not part of my life and so do they. They want to see their mom but the guardian ad litem says, "No, that is not a good idea." Well, why? "Because it is not a good idea."…I think also the courts have too many people who profit from custody situations. The guardian ad litem in my case [charges clients] $50,000. That's more than I make in a year. She sent her bill and I said I disagree with this, this, and this. She wrote back and said, "I justified all these expenses and it took me time to do that, so I am going to charge you even more." JOANNA

In this case, Joanna explained that the courts had placed her in an untenable situation. The judicial system required her to retain a guardian ad litem at her own expense, and then the guardian ad litem recommended that the children not spend time with her. She, in other words, had paid to receive a decision that ultimately separated her from her children. To Joanna and other like-minded activists, the courts as a whole foster unnecessary conflict between parents from which all professionals linked to the system then financially benefit.

Fathers' rights activists also asserted that this corruption emerges because professionals and other interest groups profit from partnering with women who make unsubstantiated allegations of misconduct during the custody decision process. Primary among these unholy alliances is that which has emerged between what fathers' rights members call the "domestic violence industry" and women seeking sole custody. Members of the domestic violence industry include lawyers, shelter workers, and other mental health advocates. In lodging their complaints, fathers' rights members acknowledged that women might have had inadequate protections from abusers in the past, but that today the law has gone overboard in terms of providing them with remedies to address their allegations, especially through the passage of the initial Violence Against Women Act (VAWA) in 1994. This legislation brought social service, criminal justice, and nonprofit agencies together to work toward ending domestic violence. It also introduced the federal prosecution of interstate domestic violence incidents and sexual assault crimes and guaranteed the interstate enforcement of protection orders. With these mechanisms now in place, once an abuse allegation is made, these activists complained, fathers can do little to protect themselves from the resulting quagmire of investigations from law enforcement and social service agencies. Timothy explained how this plight affects fathers:

> In our state, if you allege that I abused you, then you can go into town and get an EPO [emergency protective order] against me.... That's one part, then on top of that...when it comes to asking for custody, then the judge says, "Well, he's been accused of abuse. So therefore he has no standing to ask for custody." How can that be? I've got a preacher who has been charged with that, and for him to see his children, he has to go before a court-appointed overseer that watches [the visit].... He's got to pay $30 an hour for somebody to stand there and watch him, and he can't even touch the kids. So, there is no fairness. TIMOTHY

From experiences such as those described by Timothy, fathers' rights activists have learned that members of the domestic violence industry who claim to protect women from abuse do so at the expense of honest, innocent dads. In this way, however, the harm caused by domestic violence as an ongoing problem predominantly to women and children is minimized.

Distrust of State Action as Interference in "Natural" Family Life

Fathers' rights group members also distrust state action in the area of custody because they view it as unnecessary interference in the "natural state" of family affairs. Family life, in other words, is private and should not be micromanaged by the government. This argument manifested itself in different ways as these members described their encounters with the child custody system. On a more abstract level, some fathers' rights activists asserted that custody decisions are simply unconstitutional. Emmy, who joined her local fathers' rights group because of her new husband's difficulties in seeing his children, articulated the constitutional issue in the following way:

> The U.S. Constitution allows every parent the right to parent [his or her] child. The judges, legislators, and feminist groups have decided that they should go against the Constitution and there are now trials about who's fit and unfit [as a parent]. Nobody has the right to take your father away from you. Nobody, no judge, nobody. I am very passionate about this. Wouldn't you be? EMMY

Roland carried this argument a step further by maintaining that the Constitution gave him the right to parent his child in the best way that he sees fit.

> The bottom line is [that] I believe it's a constitutional right for one to...pursue life, liberty, [and] happiness. Part of this is the ability to control one's own children in loving them and being able to nurture them and being able to care for them....Unless there is an objective reason to the contrary, both parents should be equally involved with the children. The children did not divorce the parents. Because the

parents couldn't work out the marriage, [that] doesn't mean the kids don't need them any less. That's really the answer—[our] constitutional rights are getting trampled.   ROLAND

To Emmy and Roland, the government's ability to become involved in their personal lives to the extent that it does during custody deliberations is simply unacceptable. Their families are private units that only they themselves should have the authority to govern.

Other fathers' rights activists vocalized similar condemnation of the state's involvement in their "natural" family life. In contrast to those who positioned these claims within a constitutional framework, however, these fathers made arguments based on what they perceived as the necessary contributions each parent makes to the child's well-being. In this view, as Malik described, children need two parents in order to become complete, emotionally stable adults, and the government should not play a role in eliminating either one of these positive influences.

In an intact family when you have mom and dad in the family, there is always this tension between the parents; the two together make better decisions than one alone.... The tension between those two creates a better situation for the child. If you have one parent, you have one perception for the child. [The children] get short-changed. [The children] lose the relationship with the other parent, and it is harmful. And visitation—going to see dad on Saturday—is not enough; you can't just have lunch with [the children]. You need enough time with them and to be involved in all facets of their lives. If the child comes over on Saturday and the child does something wrong, dad isn't going to discipline the child and say, "Go to your room," because that's the only time he sees him. It's not a natural relationship and the children are damaged because of that.   MALIK

Another activist named Kyan echoed this sentiment by outlining his views regarding the biologically determined contributions of each parent based on gender. From his perspective, mothers and fathers have unique approaches that they bring to child-rearing, and these approaches cannot be duplicated by the other parent. No state, therefore, should have the power to interfere with or remove the influence of either parent.

> Custody laws [are such that] right away you are going to have one parent that is pushed away, and children need to know both parents. Mom and dad both have qualities [that are critical to the upbringing of a child]. A dad has qualities that only a dad can offer and the same goes for the mother. One can't make up for the other.   KYAN

Blayne put it more bluntly when he described what he views as the vital contributions of both parents to a child's emotional and developmental growth. Like other activists in these groups, Blayne argued that since it took both partners to make the child, both partners should raise the child.

> I think that it takes two people to make a baby and at least two people to raise a baby, child, and teenager. I think the older [the children] get, the more people you need to help out. [Seeing children] Wednesday and every other weekend is not being a parent, it's being a visitor, and that's why they call it "visitation."   BLAYNE

To these fathers, the "natural" system of parenting is being systematically violated by the government. This "natural" system involves a mother, a father, and a child. When the family unit dissolves, the parent-child links should not also dissolve, even if, as many mothers claim, fathers did little parenting when the family was together. Consequently, they see child custody policy that does not automatically promote joint parenting as working against their family's best interests by actively undermining their vital paternal role.

Distrust of State Action Because the State Has Been "Feminized"

In addition to those who distrust state action because it is corrupt and abusive, as well those who view this type of intervention as in violation of "natural" family life, some activists are skeptical of the state's involvement in custody matters because, in their view, the government has become overly "feminized." As in the case of child support, this means that group members believe that the state, for a variety of reasons, has become overly identified with women's interests at the expense of men's interests. Unlike with child support, however, fathers whose views fell into this category were not necessarily more optimistic that custody policy would change, nor did they tend to be more inclined to propose particular reforms.

In one sense, members maintained that the state is excessively feminized because the rules of the custody game are explicitly designed to favor women and have no relation to children's needs. Even worse are the outcomes. By not guaranteeing 50/50 custody from the beginning, courts insure that one parent—typically the mother—will unfairly have more influence over the other parent—typically the father. In this case, Tomas explained how these rules do a disservice to children everywhere.

> I think [current custody laws give] more power to the person who holds the children. I'll have to beg and plead to see my kids for a few hours here or there, and she'll say, "Well, it is not your weekend." There have been a couple of times when I didn't have to work on a Friday and I wanted to spend the day with my boys so they didn't have to be in daycare while she is at work. . . . She said I couldn't have them. I shouldn't have to wait until my weekend to see my kids. Tomas

Tomas pointed out that vengeful custodial parents, still hurting from the dissolution process, lash out against the noncustodial parent by withholding access to their children. Blinded by their own anger, custodial parents will frequently choose to place their children in alternative, group care settings, such as daycare, rather than permit them to be with their fathers. Britney became involved in her local fathers' rights group as a result of her husband's difficulty in spending time with his two sons, ages five and seven. Britney reported that her husband never had problems seeing his children until he married her; from that point onward, his ex-wife made their lives very stressful by repeatedly withholding access—simply because, in Britney's view, the judicial system allows such manipulation. Like Tomas, Britney echoed this theme in her comments on what she perceived as the gender-biased process of custody determinations.

There are a lot of good fathers out there who can do just as good a job [raising their kids as mothers], which is why I think that [a] joint physical care law would be a good thing because [both parents] could both be equal, [with] equal time and equal decisions. The kids have enough love to go around. There is no excuse for [this type of attitude]: I am mad at you from ten years ago, so I am going to keep the kids from you. I think the custody laws...give the mother way too much control to use the kids as pawns.   BRITNEY

Ray, who had two daughters, ages eight and thirteen, when his wife had an affair and left him for a man who made a substantial amount of money, echoed Britney's views. In addition to adultery, Ray alleged that his ex-wife repeatedly left the girls at home so that she could "party" with her friends. When Ray sought custody of his children—even with numerous psychologists recommending that the children live with him—the courts refused. With this victory in hand, his ex-wife used every opportunity to assert her power in the relationship vis-à-vis the children. Ray described the pain that this type of excessive control caused him on his birthday each year.

People have a tendency to treat children as a possession....My ex-wife plans vacations on my birthday and on the days I am supposed to have my children....Of course, as a parent, I am not going to stop them from going, but I just don't agree with that....As long as both parents are adequate in parenting, I don't think that one should have that much authority over the other. It gives them a tool, it gives them leverage [to use] if they are angry. They use the children, you know what I am saying? And that is not fair to the children.   RAY

In the extreme, according to fathers' rights activists, this system creates a dynamic whereby one parent must actually prove that the mother is "unfit" in order to achieve a 50/50 custody arrangement. Lester explained how this type of distorted process wreaked havoc in his own life.

You know, my son lives with me half the time and I had to prove or had to show evidence that his mother was in many ways unfit or was parenting him in a negative fashion. I don't think you should have to do that just to get equal access to your child. In my particular case, I felt that was true and I had asked my ex when we separated that I wanted my son to live with me half the time. She absolutely, flat-out refused. She did not want me to have anything more than one overnight every other weekend and one after-school visit during the week. That was not acceptable to me. So the way the system works right now is that for me to get equal parenting time with my child, I had to sue for full custody. That's how the system works, that's undeniably the truth, that's the way it works. There is no suing for joint physical custody. You have to sue for full custody and then you know, carve out how much time you could get or have a judge rule half or whatever, 70/30, 60/40 whatever.... When I interviewed lawyers, and I interviewed quite a few before settling upon one to represent me, they all told me unless the mother—and I didn't want full custody, but they told me it was going to be very hard to get joint—and that even to get full custody, I'd have to prove that the mother was an alcoholic, drug addict, or physically abusing the child. You know, I don't think you should have to prove those things to get equal access to your child.   LESTER

Even though Lester has a "good" situation in terms of his son living with him 50 percent of the time, he felt that the process he had to go through to achieve this arrangement was based on false premises. In other words, he had to sue for full custody, even though he wanted only joint custody; simply put, he had to overshoot his goal in order to be taken seriously by the courts. In addition, the lawyers that he interviewed to represent him all stated that if he wanted a substantial amount of time with his child, he would have to prove that his ex-partner was an unfit parent. Like many other similarly minded fathers, he found this "rule of the game" to be unconscionable and even detrimental to himself, his ex-partner, and most important, to his child.

Some fathers interpreted the driving force behind mothers' restrictions of custody for fathers to be control over their children and their ex-partners' lives, but for other fathers, the mothers' motivation was clearly money. Clint described this less-than-noble motivation:

[In my state, there is only] sole custody, and that creates problems. That creates a war. It creates an attitude that you have to get custody of the children because the [system] ties money to the children. You get the children, you get the money. Everything is linked together and that pits one parent against the other parent; the children are in the middle, and they suffer as a result of it.   Clint

In either case—control or money—fathers noted that evil intent of the mothers was not necessarily what prompted this type of sparring, although it could be. Rather, more often than not, the biased rules of the game, as interpreted by attorneys and other members of the judicial system, transform mothers into parents who are solely focused on acquiring as many "prizes" from the separation process as possible. Felix reflected on the difficulties of his own particular case in making this argument.

When I was going through the divorce, it was yeah, joint custody, we'll split the kids, blah-blah-blah. Then when she [hired] an attorney, [she said], no joint custody and [she'll] have them the majority of the time. If I increase the time I have with my kids substantially, I could go back to court and lower my child support payment. In theory, my child support payment will go down this summer because the kids are with me for six and one-half weeks. That is right there why mothers want their kids all the time, because it gets them money.   Felix

Felix did later point out that mothers, like fathers, are driven by the strong emotion of love to be with their children, in addition to desiring control of the family and financial security. But if this is true, Felix wondered why these games should have to be played at all, but for the fact that the state is excessively captured by women's interests?

Another common justification public decision-makers use in siding with women on custody matters, according to fathers' rights group members, is that they erroneously perceive mothers to be better nurturers than fathers. Vic reported that the court awarded him standard visitation with his son after his divorce, which meant that he saw his son every other weekend and on alternating holidays. Although his ex-wife never violated this agreement, Vic still complained that it was not enough time for him to parent effectively. Vic argued that the courts were unaware of the fact that although women might have an "innate" advantage at parenting when their children are small, men have an advantage in parenting as children age.

When you have a baby, a newborn baby and you've got a room full of men and women, when you bring that baby into that room, the women go right over there, they have to look at it and interact with the baby and the men won't. As the child grows up a little more, the attraction isn't there with the women. But the men have an attraction to try and teach that child, especially when [the child has] an ability to learn. So I think when a couple goes through a divorce, the reward is given to the mother because the mother makes the best parent for the child in the beginning and I think that's okay. But later on in life, and this is in my own situation with my fourteen-year-old son, as [children] develop into teenagers and they develop...their own sense of self, that's when the fathers kick in and [because fathers are kept out of their children's lives] we are having trouble in society.   Vic

Other fathers' rights members maintained that the mother and father are equivalent parents throughout the child's life and that women never have an advantage in terms of parenting skills, even when the child is a baby. Nonetheless, the state continues to award custody primarily to mothers. At the time of his interview, Nathan had a twelve-year-old daughter and a nine-year-old son. At first the court ordered that he only see them every other weekend plus two evenings on his "off" week. Nathan reported that his ex-wife repeatedly violated the visitation order and made false allegations that he verbally threatened her. After going back to court in his estimation between twenty and forty times, Nathan was able to secure his children 42 percent of the year. Yet despite these shenanigans that women commonly practice, according to Nathan, judges still continue to place children predominantly with their mothers.

I think we're still living in the dark ages. We still feel [that] if you have mammary glands, you're a good mother. I disagree with that. Obviously there are really bad women who are mothers and really good fathers out there. It's the luck of the draw and case by case. But I think the courts are still thinking [that] if you are born with mammaries and if you sit down to use the rest room, you're a good parent. And that's all there is to it. I think there needs to be some eye-opening that...good parenting comes from the person, not the gender.   NATHAN

Ashton, father of a nine-year-old girl, had to fight for his current custody arrangement, which now enables his daughter to reside with him 40 percent of the time. But for Ashton this decision was still unfair because it did not guarantee him true equity—50/50 sharing of his daughter's time—with his ex-wife. He therefore seconded Nathan's view when he depicted how most local judges view the male sex when making custody determinations.

> Again...some judges are very biased and very prejudiced. Instead of using good judicial discretion, [they just assume custody will go to the woman]. As a matter of fact, there is a judge down here who said point blank, "I never give custody to a man because I've never seen a calf following a bull." Well, you know, personally, my daughter is not a cow. That is an insult to me.   ASHTON

To these men, the state has inappropriately allied itself with women's interests because of inaccurate beliefs regarding the child-rearing capabilities of each sex. To address these prejudices directly, they conclude, policymakers need to treat both mothers and fathers as equally able parents.

For other fathers' rights members, their central reason for distrusting the state as overly "feminized" comes from their perception that they are devalued as breadwinners. To Elliot, most fathers work very hard to support their families, and this is a role that should not be penalized if their families ultimately dissolve.

> The other assumption is...if dad works and mom didn't work [while the family was together], well, obviously mom is the better person [to have custody] because she has been there [for the children]. That may have been a family decision at the time, but that shouldn't make the father a worse father because he went to a job forty to fifty hours a week. And it doesn't make him a worse father for actually supporting his family. But you are penalized for having a good job and working

forty to fifty hours a week. You are penalized for that if the other one doesn't work. Well, [current custody law says that you] can continue to work and [the law will] just make you pay more money. That will be your half of the support and she'll just stay at home with the kids. That is unfair; the laws are very unfair.   ELLIOT

Other activists echoed the views of Elliot. Recall from chapter 5 that Laura had joined her local fathers' rights group to support her new husband in his quest to have more access to his young daughter from a previous marriage. From her perspective, judges do not consider the traditional jobs of fathers in intact families to be important when custody decisions need to be made.

I also know that a lot of things they look at for custody [relate to] who makes the most meals [and] who is doing the laundry. [They look at] the things that are more traditionally the mom's job. They don't look at who is getting up at 6:30 in the morning every day to go to work and get a paycheck. That is a need. Who is going outside to show the kid [how] to catch a ball? Who is mowing the grass? Who is changing the oil? We need to look at the whole picture, not one side. All [of those things] are important. The bottom line is truly if parents are doing the traditional roles in the home, once they split up mom will be mowing the grass and dad will be cooking. So...[let's] look at everything [when awarding custody], not just one side.   LAURA

Elliot and Laura reflected the views of many men who maintain that the state has inappropriately allied itself with women's interests when families dissolve. In the traditional division of household labor, men have performed more significant breadwinning activities, while women have controlled the domestic arena. In awarding physical custody primarily to women, according to fathers' rights activists, the state has signaled that the work women do is more important than the work men do in maintaining the household. Fathers' rights members argue that this ranking of responsibilities is inappropriate because task assignment while the family was one unit might no longer be relevant when the family dissolves and because men's work under this faulty reasoning is devalued.

Finally and interestingly, some men blamed their own gender for the feminization of the state in the area of child custody. These activists claimed that in the past if their adult relationships did not work out, men made mistakes by abandoning their children; as a result, now judges view all men with the same suspicion of irresponsibility. Glenn, a fathers' rights activist who sees his son only rarely because of a restrictive visitation agreement with his ex-wife and the fact that they live in two different states, described this thought process and how it continues to permeate judicial thinking.

> You know, oftentimes when you hear about people walking away from children, more often than not…it's the man.…You know, judges are not unaffected by that mindset, that thought pattern. [They think]…if anybody's ever going to walk away from the child, it's going to be the father, not the mother. GLENN

In his discussion, Glenn empathized with the judges who have come to hold these generalized views at the same time that he hoped for change. Another activist named Conner expressed the same perspective as Glenn but was slightly less patient in his desire for reform.

> I do think [that] I understand a little bit of the favoritism, because certainly in the past, in some situations women have been victims and still in many instances [today—in domestic situations]—continue to be the victims. The unfairness comes in [because] now all men are painted with this brush of potential abuser [and] probable philanderer; [judges have this idea that] he did something wrong to cause their relationship to break down. Therefore the system, in somewhat of a major fashion, does everything that it can to protect the woman's rights. In doing so, it probably tramples a little bit on the man's rights and probably on the children's rights, too. CONNER

Glenn and Conner distinguished themselves as only a handful of fathers who took some responsibility for the current state of custody law and the de facto preferences for mothers. In doing so, however, they were not by any means signaling their acceptance of the status quo. Instead, they encouraged others like themselves to continue pressuring all policymakers in positions of power to promote more equitable custody laws.

Custody in Contention

On the hot-button issue of custody decisions in America today, fathers' rights activists perceive nothing but injustice. They claim that they were actively involved in their children's lives when their family units were whole. The fathers brought children to school, made them dinner, played with them, disciplined them when necessary, and witnessed their growth with pride as any normal parent would. Once the core family unit dissolved, however, these fathers no longer had the centering experience of fatherhood in their lives. As in the case of child support, in many ways they blamed the state for this outcome. Through the government's abusive, corrupt, unnecessary, and female-biased actions, activists maintain that children continue to be placed physically with their mothers at the expense of their fathers. To these fathers, this practice represents a slap in the face to all men who desperately want to remain connected to their children through every year of their young lives.

As in the case of child support enforcement, however, we must also ask the question: How can we evaluate their views? Here again, since this study did not collect corroborating documents from fathers in the study or those related to them, it is impossible know whether the statements that they made about their particular custody circumstances have a basis in fact. What about the inner motivations of these fathers as they described their specific views? There are, again, at least two extreme possibilities that are not necessarily mutually exclusive. On one hand, some of these fathers' statements related to the child custody system contain undeniable hurt and anger, which are understandable emotions in light of the strong love and devotion that they expressed for their children. Separation from their beloved offspring is almost too much for them to bear, and their words reflect their strong sincerity. Indeed, a family breakup is a devastating event, and the losses that are inevitable in the process, especially losses involving regular, daily access to one's children, are undoubtedly extremely tumultuous and painful transitions to manage.

On the other hand, similar to those pronouncements that they made with respect to child support policy, some of these fathers' statements regarding child custody decision-making in America are blatantly anti-feminist and, at times, unnecessarily harsh in their assessment of women as a group. For example, when fathers indicated their view that the state is excessively feminized, they tended to paint mothers with the broad-brush stroke of being intrinsically motivated, at least in part, by greed. In this view, mothers did not seek out custody because they had done the majority of the child care while the family was intact, or because the children might benefit from the continuity of care, but rather because they desired the money in child support that they would gain if they had sole possession of their children. In addition, fathers devalued the difficult work mothers do in parenting newborns, toddlers, and older children and privileged their experience in the working world as entitling them to custody of their children when their families dissolved.

Unfortunately, regardless of their motivations, as in the case of child support reform, fathers' claims regarding their participation in children's lives as well as the benefits of joint custody are simply not borne out consistently by the scholarly research. Even though gender roles have been changing over time, women continue to do the majority of child care work when families are together. Judges may simply be recognizing this contribution after a separation by awarding custody to the children's primary caretakers: mothers. Moreover, it is not clear that joint custody would necessarily be in the best interest of families recovering from the dissolution process. In fact, there is no overwhelming consensus that parent-child relationships improve under joint custody arrangements, nor do scholars agree that such physical sharing of children enhances parental happiness or improves a child's level of adjustment across a whole range of behavioral and emotional measures. All of these questions are still being vigorously debated by researchers of both genders and across multiple disciplines. In the meantime, however, fathers' rights groups battle the state, an institution that at least gives mothers some recognition of their child care work by placing children overwhelmingly with them.

In terms of political activism in the areas of child support and child custody, therefore, fathers' rights groups seek reforms that have very little merit. Under the most benign interpretation, these men simply have not exposed themselves to or assimilated any of the scholarly work that challenges their worldview—a worldview that is overtly hostile to the state and all of its allies, whether they be attorneys, judges, mental health professionals, or women's groups. Alternatively, like all other interest groups in American politics, they simply choose to highlight the research that supports their preferred policy positions and downplay research that is at odds with their views. The bottom line is that the political agenda of fathers' rights groups today is potentially damaging to the health of American families. But this does not mean that the entire organizational movement should be dismissed; fathers' rights groups have value, and it is embodied in the interpersonal relationship goals of these groups, which are the subject of the next two chapters.

7

Frayed Ties

Fathers' Relationships with Mothers

The leader of Fathers for Kids, Sarah, is a middle-age, white woman who married a man with considerable experience battling the family court system. The meeting is at Sarah's home, located in a small town in the South, and members gradually trickle in one by one. Everyone traverses through the garage littered with campaign signs to congregate in her dining room: Sarah not only leads Fathers for Kids but is quite active in local Democratic politics as well. The house smells strongly of cigarette smoke, as Sarah puffs away by the kitchen sink. Finally, when eight members (including one other woman and one black member) are present, Sarah begins the meeting by asking members to comment on current issues that they are struggling with in their lives.

> FATHERS FOR KIDS MEMBER 1: I am really frustrated. I have had two custody evaluations done. The first one was done right away. But we didn't get to court in time so the evaluation became too old for us to use. So, we had to begin again with another custody evaluation. But the latest news is that my ex-wife went ahead and registered my daughter for summer camp. I am sure that she did this to keep me away from my daughter.

FATHERS FOR KIDS MEMBER 2: Well, my ex blocked me from obtaining my child's school records. My ex also keeps registering my kid for camp without my permission.

(A general discussion ensues about which ex is worst. Finally, Fathers for Kids member 2 redirects the discussion by declaring that he should change his own personal web address to www.shootthebitch.com. After some laughter, Fathers for Kids member 1 brings the group's attention to another one of his personal problems with his ex-partner.)

FATHERS FOR KIDS MEMBER 1: That's not all. My ex also filed an order of protection against me. The judge then made this crazy suggestion that I should try to talk to her.

(Name calling breaks out. One man suggests that the judge in the case is a "bonehead." Another man, referring to Fathers for Kids member 1's ex-wife, calls out, "The bitch!")

FATHERS FOR KIDS MEMBER 3: I thought my ex was "the bitch."

(Laughter ensues. But soon thereafter the meeting takes on a decidedly different tone when Fathers for Kids member 2 elaborates on several problems that he is experiencing with his fifteen-year-old son.)

FATHERS FOR KIDS MEMBER 2: Recently I noticed that my son had a lot of money in his pocket. I found out that his mother was giving him all of this money without making him do any chores. This made me so mad! I never do that, and that makes me a better parent. I know that my son knows that inside, too. I said to him, "Who teaches you fiscal responsibility?"

FATHERS FOR KIDS MEMBER 1: You are so wrong to do that! You are asking your son to choose between his mom and you. You are trying to alienate your child from his mother, when you should be trying to work with her in your son's best interest.

(Everyone in the room agrees with this last statement, and Fathers for Kids member #2 falls silent).

The political goals of fathers' rights groups are, in many ways, the public face that these organizations present to decision-makers and the media. To the extent that Americans are beginning to recognize the influence of these groups at all, they are familiar with this public face. There is, however, a much more hidden face of fathers' rights groups in the United States today; this is the hidden face of their activities in the "personal" arena.[1] Recall that in chapter 3, changing public policy was one of only three reasons individuals offered for joining their local fathers' rights group; personal case management and support were the other two reasons individuals tended to join. But what exactly do these groups offer in terms of "personal case management"? And what exactly do they provide their members in terms of "support"?

Unbeknownst to most observers who know only the political face, fathers' rights' groups offer their members a wide-ranging set of services designed to help them improve their private lives now that they are living apart from their former partners. The breadth and depth of these services vary from group to group, but most organizations included in this study spent a significant percentage of their group meeting time addressing members' individual family issues. These needs might include finding out which legal forms to fill out under what circumstances in order to modify a custody arrangement, learning how to effectively speak with a former partner over a child's poor academic performance, or facilitating a discussion about how to explain to a young daughter that she now has two homes: mom's house and dad's house.

From these groups' political goals, it is difficult to imagine that fathers' rights groups would provide a beneficial environment for men to address their legal challenges and work out their new family relationships. As we saw in chapters 5 and 6, a noticeable divide exists between the solutions that fathers' rights groups want society to adopt regarding child support and child custody policy and what the academic research shows is in the best interest of the majority of families after a dissolution. More specifically, fathers' rights groups want to push forward with their reforms even though the scholarly research demonstrates

1. Note that many of these types of services are also offered to low income men specifically by pro-marriage and economic empowerment organizations (see Anderson, Kohler, and Letiecq 2002).

the benefits of child support for women and children and has yet to come to a consensus regarding all of the ramifications of joint custody. Most significant for the discussion here, the interview data suggest that many of these fathers—while not denying their individual pain regarding their personal circumstances—hold strong antifeminist and overly harsh views of women as a group in the area of family law. It is not an enormous leap to believe that any services these groups offer on the "personal level" would be thoroughly colored by these views. Even individual fathers who do not share these perceptions initially might be influenced to think differently and negatively as they become part of the group and its particularized organizational dynamics.

However, the next two chapters—focused on fathers' relationships with their ex-partners and then on their interactions with their children—demonstrate that this is not the case in the majority of circumstances. Whereas there is a disjuncture between the political goals of fathers' rights groups and the academic research as to what is best for American families, there is much more convergence between the personal goals of these groups and what the scholarship suggests is the most productive way for fathers to mediate these critical relationship connections. This is not to say that fathers' rights groups always create an atmosphere where family relations are given the highest priority; as we saw at the beginning of this chapter, fathers freely called their ex-partners "bitches" as they discussed their family lives. But note too that the membership also reprimanded one particular father who was putting his son in the position of having to criticize his mother. These contrasting group dynamics show that although human behavior is complex, and sometimes less than laudatory, the organizational culture of fathers' rights groups can promote positive relationships among family members if they remain committed to this goal. Overall, then, in this particular realm of fathers' rights activities, there are reasons to be cautiously optimistic about their work.

Parents Getting Along after a Split: What Hurts? What Helps?

With the high probability that many families will dissolve after children are born, researchers have spent a significant amount of time thinking about the roles that mothers and fathers should assume vis-à-vis each other when they no longer live under the same roof. Scholars have recognized, in other words, that not all family dissolutions need end badly and that parents have the capacity to engage in moral and care-based decision-making regarding how they choose to relate to one another (Smart 2004a; Smart and Neale 1997; Smart and Neale 1999). This means that broadly speaking, adults need to focus on successfully coparenting, which refers to the actions of any two adults who are actively engaging in child-rearing practices (Adamsons and Pasley 2006; McHale et al. 2000). More specifically, coparenting involves attitudes and behaviors that are distinct from the romantic, intimate, and sexual relationships shared by adults in one-on-one, "couple" relationships. It is, in a sense, a skill that has little to do with what emotions the two parents may feel toward one another, but reinforces the recently emerging social view that ideally both parents must be given the opportunity to offer their children ongoing love and support (van Krieken 2005). Although some parents do drop out of their children's lives after their adult relationship ends, many continue to want to play some type of role in caring for their minor children; the question is exactly how to go about interacting with the other parent. In answering this question, it is important to note that the majority of research on effective coparenting has focused on previously married parents rather than nonmarital parents. The central insights gained from studying this one group of parents, however, can likely be extended to other groups of parents as well.

Perhaps not unexpectedly, one of most important predictors of a positive adult relationship after a breakup is the nature of the relationship prior to the breakup. In other words, those partners whose union ended mutually or on good terms are most able to establish a positive coparenting relationship with one another in the postdivorce period (Maccoby, Depner, and Mnookin 1990). Of course, in many cases parents do not split under such amicable circumstances (Ahrons and Rodgers 1987). Instead, the strong emotions of anger, fear, betrayal, and sadness can rule their lives for substantial periods of time after the breakup, creating possibilities for arguments and hostility at every interaction. Long, drawn-out, and bitter divorce battles can add further fuel to these fires as financial and other property settlements are painstakingly worked out (Braver et al. 1993; Emery et al. 2001). Moreover, the logistics of organizing childcare transitions, as well as information inadvertently provided by the children themselves about the "other" parent's new life, can heighten the probability that these pent-up emotions will explode. Remarriage by one or both former partners may also generate more animosity, as "new" family members compete against "old" family members for the time and attention of the involved children (Buehler and Ryan 1995; Hetherington 2003). Researchers have, however, identified two key factors that mitigate against the possibility of a rapid deterioration in adult relations: satisfaction with current parenting plans and the ability to focus on compromise as a way to resolve differences.

The issue of satisfaction with current parenting plans revolves around how mothers and fathers perceive the sharing of child-related expenses and time. If both parents sense that these arrangements are fair, then they are much more likely to get along with each other and work together on behalf of their children's needs. For example, if mothers are satisfied with their child support payments, there is a greater chance that they will be able to enjoy a better relationship with the fathers of their children. The economic security that the money brings functions to alleviate some of the significant stress under which most single mothers find themselves (Madden-Derdich and Arditti 1999). This stability, in turn, leads them to more productively work with their former partners in protecting their children's best interests. Likewise, in some cases joint custody arrangements might produce more happiness for parents because under the right circumstances, each comes to perceive the other as a truly equal partner in raising the children together. Indeed, the research has demonstrated that fathers' satisfaction in the area of physical care responsibilities might be particularly important to solid, long-term relations with mothers (Arditti and Kelly 1994).

The second key factor that helps determine the strength of parents' postdissolution relationships is their ability to communicate well with each other. In general, the level of interparental hostility declines over time after the initial separation, which ultimately can provide a positive environment in which to pursue better relations (King and Heard 1999). But in the interim—especially right after a split—parents need to know how to speak to one another and how to listen to each other effectively. With these goals in mind, researchers have pointed to at least two distinct ways in which parents can meaningfully negotiate differences (Afifi and Hamrick 2006; Camara and Resnick 1989). The first relates to the nature of parental interactions in general. Parents who interact in highly structured ways on "safe" topics do best by minimizing the conditions under which emotional, uncontrolled exchanges might emerge. These parents develop tightly defined boundaries with one another in managing the privacy of their new lives, while at the same time maintaining an appropriate level of cohesion with their former partner in order to raise their children together with love and devotion. Second, if differences do arise, "give and take" is much more likely to occur when feelings are expressed in a neutral way that does not involve verbal attacks on the other parent. Researchers note that it is important to present all concerns to the other parent in a nonthreatening, nonaccusatory manner (Ahrons 1994; Masheter 1997). This gives the recipient of the query the opportunity to thoughtfully consider the issue at hand rather than react through the lens of charged emotion. In these ways, researchers conclude, parents can maximize the possibilities for positive conflict resolution and work toward building as loving an environment as possible for their children.

Divorce Education Programs as the Solution?

In sum, then, satisfaction with current parenting duties—with respect to both the finances involved in caregiving and the quality of care over time—as well as solid communication skills—promote positive, interparental relationships. The challenge then becomes, how do parents achieve these prerequisites to harmonious, future interactions? This is a critical question because parents who are no longer together and do not get along well in matters related to their children present policymakers with a variety of difficulties. They are more likely to return to court to re-litigate issues of contention, thereby clogging the judicial system with complaints that are intrinsically resistant to resolution. They might engage in harassment by making petty accusations against one another through local law enforcement, wastefully appropriating scarce public resources. Perhaps most important, they are likely to harm their children as a direct result of their animosity, especially if their sons and daughters are put in the middle of their arguments. If these children develop antisocial behaviors as a result of this tension, taxpayers may end up paying all of the costs associated with juvenile rehabilitation, teen pregnancy, substance abuse treatment, and educational failure.

In recent years, the courts have become active partners with nonprofit organizations and family court professionals in trying to fight these potentially negative outcomes by engaging parents directly in an examination of their own attitudes and behaviors about the separation process (Blaisure and Geasler 2006). The result has been the creation of government-sponsored and sanctioned divorce education programs, which have spread rapidly throughout the country since the early 1970s—a volatile period that some observers argue was especially fertile for creating the rise of the "therapeutic state" (Reece 2003; Salem, Schepard, and Schlissel 1996). By the late 1990s, approximately 50 percent of all counties in the United States had such programs in place (Geasler and Blaisure 1999). Except in the case of extremely high-conflict couples, attendance in these programs, which typically take place over the course of several hours on a single day, is mostly voluntary and classes are mixed by gender.

In many different ways, these programs are built on individual counseling strategies that used to be available only to those who could privately afford them. For years, mental health practitioners have met with parents one-on-one to help them define proper new roles in dealing with each other during this difficult time (Arditti and Kelly 1994; Baum 2004; Camara and Resnick 1989; Madden-Derdich and Arditti 1999). These sessions also served to equip parents with the knowledge that they needed to manage their own emotions for the well-being of their children. Divorce education programs have simply seized upon many of these same principles to deliver this information to a wider audience of parents in a classroom-oriented setting. Counties across the United States use prepackaged curricula or develop their own content to meet their specific communities' needs (Geasler and Blaisure 1998). Programs typically present parents with information in the form of a videotape, lecture, or discussion. In a survey conducted in the mid-1990s, Braver et al. (1996) found that most programs covered material related to both relationships with ex-partners (legal and interpersonal) and relationships with children (interpersonal) (see table 7.1).

TABLE 7.1.
Content of Court-Affiliated Divorce Education Programs

Adult content: legal	Adult content: interpersonal	Child content: interpersonal
Additional community resources available for divorcing parents	Benefits of parental cooperation versus costs of parental conflict	Typical postdivorce reactions of children
Custody options (joint, sole)	Responsibilities of custodials (permitting, encouraging visiting)	Brainwashing
Dispute resolution options (mediation, litigation)	Conflict management skills	Different reactions and needs of children of different ages
Issues concerning domestic violence	Parenting skills	
Financial responsibilities of noncustodial parents (child support)	Emotional responsibilities of noncustodials	
Legal rights of parents	Typical postdivorce reactions of parents	
How to properly file the legal paperwork	Benefits and costs of developing a formal coparenting plan	
How to calculate child support under the guidelines		

Source: Adapted from Braver et al. 1996. "The Content of Divorce Education Programs: Results of a Survey." *Family and Conciliation Courts Review* 34 (1): 41–59. Tables 3–5.

Do these programs make a difference in the lives of the people they serve? Evaluation research is still in its infancy, but some preliminary conclusions can still be drawn. A handful of studies have found that parents report high levels of satisfaction after attending such a program, even among those who were mandated to participate (Shifflett and Cummings 1999; Stone, Clark, and McHenry 2000; Stone, McHenry, and Clark 1999; Zimmerman, Brown, and Portes 2004). These parents indicated that they were more aware of the divorce adjustment process and were more willing to seek out compromise solutions with their ex-partners rather than focusing all of their energies on "winning" an argument. Another set of studies has focused on the actual effectiveness of these programs in reducing re-litigation rates among parents (Geasler and Blaisure 1998). Although the evidence is still relatively scant, some researchers have reported that parents in high-conflict relationships who participate have lower rates of re-litigation than similar high-conflict parents in a nonparticipating control group (Kramer and Kowel 1998). Scholars have also noted that parents must not simply passively receive the information presented in these programs; instead, they must show evidence of mastering new communication skills in order to reduce their chances of re-litigation (Arbuthnot and Gordon 1996; Arbuthnot, Kramer, and Gordon 1997; McClure 2002).

Fathers' Rights Groups Respond

Although evidence is emerging that divorce education programs provide parents with some assistance in adjusting to the family dissolution process, fathers' rights groups argue that they do not do enough for men as *fathers* in these situations. First, the programs are not uniform or mandatory, so fathers may or may not receive services by accident of geography. Second, and most important, the goal of these programs is to help *parents,* not fathers specifically. As indicated in table 7.1, the mixed-gender classes cover topics that are broadly defined to respond to *all* parents facing the challenges of dissolution. Mothers in particular may benefit from learning about domestic violence and child support laws, but fathers may see these issues from a completely different perspective than that presented in these seminars. For example, fathers may be concerned about the problem of false allegations of violence and how to seek a downward modification in child support. In the area of interparental relations specifically, programs again must be general enough to cover the concerns of both mother and father, thereby favoring breadth over depth. Fathers' rights groups, therefore, see massive, troubling holes in these government-sponsored services and have responded in their own way by providing assistance to their members in helping them get along with their ex-partners. As in the cases of child support and child custody, where fathers' rights groups demonstrate a marked rejection of state intervention in their lives, their focus on self-help here thus represents another instance of these groups' inclination to "turn away" from the state in meeting their needs. Unlike with issues of child support or custody, however, "turning away" from the state is not damaging because these groups provide solid substitutes for government-sponsored services.

In brief, fathers' rights groups try to promote *satisfaction with parental responsibilities* and strong *communication skills,* the two factors the scholarly research has consistently identified as necessary for improving father-mother relationships over time. They do this in four ways: (1) providing legal information (satisfaction with parental responsibilities), (2) promoting constructive discussion techniques through anger management (communication skills), (3) encouraging nonconfrontational "phraseology," (communication skills), and (4) propagating special "group rules" in directing individual behavior (communication skills).

Providing Legal Information

In a variety of ways, fathers' rights groups provide legal information to their members that is designed to improve their satisfaction with their current parenting arrangements and ultimately their relationships with their ex-partners. This information can be divided into two categories: (1) defending themselves against past, current, or potential wrongdoing and (2) promoting positive, legal harmony. In the first category, many members of fathers' rights groups maintain that they do not have the legal information they need in order to assert their parental rights to be with their children. More often than not, fathers sense that they do not have any rights at all with respect to parenting, especially if they occupy the noncustodial parental role. Ex-partners sense this insecurity, fathers' rights members assert, and engage in a whole host of obstructive, manipulative, and even illegal behavior regarding their children. For example, recall from chapter 5 that Noelle, a sixty-two-year-old married mother of seven children, described that one of her sons had a terrible relationship with his ex-partner. That state of affairs encouraged her to join her local father's rights organization, which she found to be an excellent source of support for those going through the family dissolution process. Over time, as she learned more and more about the law, Noelle herself became one of the primary providers of legal information for those fathers walking through the organization's door for the first time.

> As a group, one of the main things we try to do is teach them how to go to court. We teach them what their rights are first of all, because most people don't think they've got any rights. We try to tell them

to be civil with each other. Do the best you can; don't be the one to throw the first punch. If you could just be civil....It is the number one thing. NOELLE

Noelle's group, like many other fathers' rights organizations throughout the country, utilizes many different methods of communicating this legal information to parents in need of assistance. The Internet is the most common tool groups use to link members to relevant resources, not only by posting educational materials, but also by sponsoring chat rooms and Listservs. Groups also generate their own printed publications in order to direct fathers to the legal forms that might be most relevant to their particular familial situation.

As Noelle described above, a significant number of fathers feel that they do not have any rights at all. A critical role, therefore, that fathers' rights groups play is to provide their members with specific and concrete legal information regarding one of their most important rights: to see their children. Issac, a highly educated father of two adult children at the time of his interview, found that his relationship with them when they were younger was quite positive in the period immediately following his separation. The boys would regularly come over to his home after school to spend time with him. He easily talked with them, offered his advice and guidance on daily events, and sought to be a loving and stable presence in their lives. In fact, Issac deliberately moved closer to them in order to promote this contact. However, when he started dating the woman who would eventually be his next wife, this type of easy access ended. His ex-wife rebelled against him and withheld the children from him repeatedly. According to Issac, time and time again he would go to his ex-wife's home to pick up his children, and they simply would not answer the door. Even though she was found in contempt of court on numerous occasions, she never complied with the court order to permit access. Nonetheless, Issac struggled desperately to stay involved with his children, and this battle taught him the importance of being assertive in protecting his paternal claims.

[We provide referrals to lawyers based on their] aggressiveness and fees....Well, some people [may] need somebody who is going to be real aggressive because they are going against somebody who is just

absolutely unwilling to talk. You don't want somebody that's going to
go in there and just chit-chat.   IssAc

In a similar way, Bruce's relationships with his two daughters, although
still quite positive, nonetheless suffered because he had less access to
them simply because they lived apart. Bruce believed that his group
helped other fathers learn about their legal rights without having to
spend thousands of dollars in legal fees.

> If we can teach an individual or empower an individual that there are
> laws available to help a noncustodial parent get access to [his] kid, it
> gives [him] some emotional courage. Most of the people that come to
> us come to us with their tails dragging between their legs. They are
> distraught. They are ready to give up. They are out of money, [and]
> they don't know what direction to turn. We give them the path to
> take so they can get access to their kids or enforce the access they
> do have by court order or get them a court order. That gives them an
> emotional boost. It also makes it easier for the individual to get the
> stuff into court because [otherwise] the financial costs are horrendous.
> The average legal fees in this state run about $10,000 to $15,000, but we
> can cut that down to $1,500 to $2,000 or less. We've had guys come
> to us with no court orders and end up with custody for less than $600
> or $700. We've created an environment that can take them through
> the entire process quickly, for very little money, and give them some
> emotional empowerment.   Bruce

Bruce thus argued that his group provides fathers with an incredibly
important service. When their ex-partners are not complying with the
law or are threatening not to comply, fathers' rights groups give their
members the wherewithal to continue applying pressure for legal access
to their children.

Beyond the issue of using the law to make sure that they spend time
with their children, many fathers fear that their ex-partners might make
up accusations against them—involving adult/child physical or sexual
abuse—that would be unquestionably accepted by local law enforcement and the judicial system. Recall from chapter 5 that Timothy was
a widowed father of five who, while in his seventies, took an active lead

in his local fathers' rights group because one of his sons faced many difficulties dealing with his ex-wife. In addition to his son experiencing a tremendous hardship in paying his child support obligations, Timothy's son also had to contend with his ex-wife's erratic behavior. At one point over a New Year's holiday weekend, she was supposed to pick the children up at a certain time but she never showed up. She actually disappeared from their lives for five years. Because of his own son's suffering, Timothy became involved in fathers' rights, and even though it was not an issue for his son, heard fathers tell story after story proclaiming how they were the victims of false allegations of abuse. Timothy described how he learned and subsequently trained other fathers to protect themselves against these false accusations.

> Well, now we try to more or less to let [all members] know that they have to keep notes; when they go to pick up the children, they should have somebody there as a witness. We've had cases where the father would go pick up the children and the ex-wife would say, come on in while I get their coats. Because it's cold outside, he goes on the inside and gets the children and leaves. She scratches herself or cuts herself, then she goes to the police station and gets a warrant for terroristic threatening. See, so we try to warn them to be careful [and to know] what they are doing....We also try to let them know if you can have a relationship with [your ex], it would be much better for the kids.
> TIMOTHY

Timothy argued that all fathers need to be prepared against charges that could be made against them: charges without merit or substance.

Likewise Jose, a divorced father of two teenagers, was in an extremely high-conflict parenting situation. His ex-partner had called the state's department of family services and protection on him several times and made, according to him, false charges of abuse. The group helped him through this difficult period by encouraging him to take measures to protect himself against what he viewed as destructive and unsubstantiated claims.

> [The group] educates you to think differently. It's a shame that you have to be like this, but you should always be on your guard; make

sure, for the most part, that you carry a tape recorder. [No matter] what, never lose your cool and always answer in a very nice, pleasant way. [The group] teaches you to rethink the way you would normally react to a situation and, to be quite honest with you, I am not the same person I was before joining this group in 1997....I am a very outgoing person and I am a very emotional person; I am not afraid to talk to anybody. I always wear my emotions on my sleeve....I have learned to keep a lot of my emotions bottled up almost like in a co-coon and [it is] a different way of thinking. You have to because any-thing, especially for a male person, if you overreact or if something is perceived to be an overreaction, it can come back to haunt you. You have to keep your emotions bottled up inside. Not that that is a healthy way of doing things, but legally it is to your benefit not to show a reaction of any kind that could be perceived in a negative way....The knowledge and the education I got made me a different person. In some ways that's good, and in some ways that's bad....Why is [it] if a male shows an emotion such as anger, he is dangerous? Why? Why are we not allowed to be angry? Why am I not allowed to take my hand and slap it on the desk and say, oh shit, but if I do that, that could be [evidence] that I am violent....So if I get angry at you, I can't be angry at you. Jose

Interestingly, Jose clearly reported having mixed feelings about what the group has taught him in terms of protecting himself. On one hand, he knew that the techniques of controlling his emotions are important in terms of shielding himself against the actions of his ex-partner. On the other hand, he resented his inability to be fully "himself" and to show his anger when he needed to express this emotion. This is a di-lemma that the group seemed unable to solve. However, like Timothy, Jose agreed that by documenting his actions and monitoring his tem-per, the likelihood of a dispute over perceived false allegations would diminish—an outcome that would be worth the internal sacrifice.

Not all legal information is provided in the context of defending fathers from the potentially hostile actions of their ex-partners. Fa-thers' rights group members also indicate that the legal information they receive serves an important, positive role in promoting greater understanding between partners in their shared enterprise as parents.

As discussed in chapter 4, some groups do this by only accepting new members who are currently paying child support. This philosophy is designed to "weed out" those members not committed to a mutually respectful and lawful relationship with their ex-partners. Although not all groups agree with this strategy, the organizations that do are ultimately aiming for reciprocity in law-abiding behavior between parents, with fathers paying child support on time and mothers encouraging access.

In addition to encouraging compliance with laws regarding child support, at the most informal level these groups also help fathers maximize their success in securing vital paperwork from their ex-partners that will help them parent more effectively. Tito, for example, had difficulty getting necessary documents from his ex-wife related to his sixteen-year-old daughter. He recalled how he had asked his ex-partner for a copy of his daughter's birth certificate so that he could help her get a learner's permit to drive. His ex-wife not only refused his request quite adamantly but denied the paperwork to the daughter herself, which resulted in her enormous distress. In his interview, Tito expressed a desire to avoid this type of bitter adult interaction in the future. Overall, he argued that the group was very helpful in encouraging its members to communicate effectively with their ex-partners over matters that would otherwise go to court, an outcome that would be financially damaging to all involved parties.

> We try to encourage what is called conflict resolution [on legal matters of paperwork], so part of our education is to teach our members how to facilitate that. There are some real good readings we encourage our members to [look at].... We also encourage our members to communicate with letters, short and to the point; [we ask men to write] two or three sentence letters.   TITO

On a more formal level, groups also promote the adoption of parenting plans, or detailed descriptions of how each parent will share child-rearing responsibilities with the other. Lisa, an active member of her local fathers' rights group, was an outspoken advocate of parenting plans. At the time of her interview, Lisa asserted that her relationship with her ex-husband had changed over time and at that moment was very positive. However, she still felt that the divorce negatively impacted her son and daughter and therefore dedicates much of her free time to working at her local fathers' rights organization. While there, she helps parents develop parenting plans so that future conflicts can be avoided.

> So we sit down with both parents, and they both have to be willing to do this. There can be some hatred in that and usually it gets heated,…but we discuss how you can cooperatively work out an agreement. Like a mediator, but we don't mediate. We are not mediating. We are facilitating and we let them work it out. We give them samples of parenting plans, but we let them totally work out all their agreements—even down to the property settlement. Once they have it all written up, we type them up. We put them into the computer as we are talking with them.…We have had a 100 percent success rate, which is unusual. The parenting plan that they have worked out, they work out their own glitches. It usually takes about five to eight sessions to do this.…What they do then is go before the judge for their preliminary hearing with this parenting plan, the judge reads over it, has both parents there or they don't even have to be there if they have an affidavit that they've agreed. He usually signs off on it and it eliminates a lot of problems. LISA

To Lisa, the primary advantage of a parenting plan is that it helps parents confront their differences over their child-rearing philosophies, work them out prior to appearing before a judge, and then move forward with their lives without expensive litigation.

Also at the more formal level, these groups try to encourage mediation among their members and their former partners so that as many families as possible can work out their disagreements without having to return to court. Aaron, who maintained that he was trying to have a cordial relationship with his ex-partner, asserted that mediation referrals represent one of the most important services fathers' rights groups currently offer their members for a variety of reasons.

> For example, last night I went to a meeting—I ran the meeting because the other person wasn't available. I had a mediator come in there—a mediator attorney who is one of the top notch people in the area.…The presentation was on the use of consent orders and

mediation.... Now mediation is something I highly believe in and recommend. It's in contrast, and I use the word contrast specifically, to
adversarial law or litigation that I think is very destructive to people
who are divorced or separating. So on the organizational services side
of it, we have legal self-help meetings so someone can avail himself
of information and if we have a good qualified speaker, hopefully the
quality of that information is going to be very good.   AARON

Like many fathers' rights activists, Aaron believed that mediation could
help almost all couples, even those in extremely tense relationships like
that of Jaime. Jaime, a father of a now-grown adult daughter, developed
stomach ulcers over his problems with his ex-partner. His daughter had
severe medical issues when she was young, and the anxiety produced
by this condition was difficult for his wife to manage at the time.
The couple tried to ease the pent-up pressure within the household
by taking jobs with non-overlapping shifts. Unfortunately, because
they were no longer seeing each other on a regular basis, cracks developed in the marriage and his wife had numerous affairs. He ultimately
gained primary custody of his daughter, and his ex-wife visited her
only sporadically. Despite his own personal difficulties, through his
occupation as a counselor and as an active member of a local fathers'
rights group, Jaime remained committed to the goals and practices of
mediation.

One of the first mediation sessions I [helped with] was with two parents
who were almost violently opposed to each other and fighting for custody of the child. I went to the lawyers' offices, [and because the] parents couldn't be in the same room, I did interviews in separate rooms.
Talking with the dad, he was firmly claiming he had 45 percent of the
time and responsibility for raising the children. I used a relationship
questionnaire and a weekly time chart. Both indicated he had about
45 percent of time with the children. I interviewed mom using the
same tools. I found she was claiming 60 percent.... So we were talking
about a difference of percentage points. I suggested to the lawyers that
they offer dad a settlement such that he would have 42.5 percent [of
the time] with the kids and mom would have 57.5 percent. That comes
out to about six overnights for dad out of every 14.... Not only did they

agree to it, but they walked out of the office together, laughing, talking, and chatting how they would handle the next birthday.   JAMIE

The case that Jaime described, of course, is extremely optimistic. Realistically speaking, many fathers' rights group members may not be able to utilize mediation services, especially if their ex-partners are opposed. However, the overall philosophy of these groups is to discourage litigation whenever possible and to encourage even recalcitrant parents to consider mediation to promote an agreement that is in the best interest of their children. The end goal, of course, is that all of this legal information will promote satisfaction among both mothers and fathers, thereby producing greater familial harmony overall.

Promoting Constructive Discussion Techniques through Anger Management

Beyond assistance in the legal arena, fathers' rights groups also aim to build the communication skills of their members—another area documented by substantial academic research as essential to promoting positive interparental interactions. One of the most significant ways these groups foster productive communication is by advocating calm dialogue between parents. Of course, during the dissolution process it is extremely difficult to foster a sense of equanimity between separating partners. Emotions are raw, feelings are hurt, and tempers are likely to flare. Yet fathers' rights activists maintain that achieving a state where constructive dialogue is, in fact, the norm is possible if both parents work toward this goal. Lukas, an active fathers' rights group member at the time of the interview even though two of his three daughters had aged out of the child support and custody systems, argued that organizations like his provide an excellent service in this regard.

[One of the leaders in our group] heads up [the counseling] portion of [the meeting] and what she tries to do is [to get] the parents [to] talk....It is important that people are able to sit down, be civil with each other, and not be at each other's throats. As I said, we are not a women-hating group and I would love to see more [civil communication]....A lot of times, that is the problem. People haven't just sat down, talked things over, and are not able to get things resolved. I believe that, I believe it is possible and I believe it is something we need. We need to be able to talk with our ex-spouses civilly and be able to visit with the kids on a holiday and not have all this anger.   Lukas

Members with strong negative feelings toward their ex-partners often reported that they had transformative experiences by participating in a group's monthly discussions. Vic, for example, had enormous anger over his belief that current public policy does not give fathers enough time to have a strong impact on their children's lives. Eventually, however, he came to the conclusion—with the help of the group—that he needed to put his anger aside for the sake of his teenage son.

Another thing we do,...we say, "Keep the emotions out of it. You're going through a very difficult time and the first thing you want to do is react. Men react. So try to keep it at a professional level and work for the best interest of the child. The thing to do is to put up a stop sign [up where you can see it] and put your offspring's picture on that stop sign. Who are you hurting [by being angry]? Are you doing it for your own pleasure or to feel better? Or is it a thing for your family?"   Vic

In this case, Vic described his sense that men in general do not handle the important work of keeping parental relationships civil in the post breakup process. Instead they "react." Fundamental to the work of fathers' rights groups, then, is education with the goal of turning these potentially damaging inclinations around.

Fathers' rights groups use a variety of "teaching" tools to signal to their membership the importance of reducing levels of anger when dealing with their ex-partners. For some, the key is simply removing the association between anger and strength that men may have assimilated from the wider society. In its place, fathers need to learn more effective methods of coping and the beneficial emotional association between respect and strength. Allen echoed this theme in his comments about his local fathers' rights group. After his wife got pregnant, he noticed that her attitude toward him completely changed. Quite abruptly, she expressed a strong desire to leave the marriage without attempting counseling or other means of reconciliation. After they split up, she admitted to him that she only had married him so that she could have a baby. Needless to say, Allen reported being devastated. Nevertheless, while he was still getting over the hurt of this disclosure, he soon realized the need to protect his son from his mounting sad and angry feelings. He proactively worked through his loss, and once he did, he noticed that his son's school performance started improving in response to his changing attitude. His son also seemed happier and healthier in other aspects of his life. As a result of these positive changes, Allen made it his mission to spread the word to other members of the group about parents' need to reduce their level of animosity toward each other.

> Mainly, when [the group] first got started, I did a lot of [talking about anger management] in the meetings.... The message I tried to send to them is that you are not helpless, but you do have to be the better parent by avoiding the conflict. Stay away from it; it is bad news for your kids. I still throw out little reminders to members on the mailing list, plus I coach the parents for free and that is mainly it.   ALLEN

For Allen, the key point in promoting recovery from a devastating situation was telling fathers that they are not helpless in their situations. Instead, Allen advanced the idea that fathers would gain strength by showering focused respect on their ex-partners.

Another anger management strategy encouraged by fathers' rights activists is for members to redirect their hostile feelings they might be experiencing toward their ex-partners and instead rechannel that energy toward changing public policy. Jack, father of an adult daughter and a five-year-old daughter from two separate marriages, described his relationship with his second ex-wife as something that would be nonexistent except for the fact that his child needs her parents to get along. In his view, his ex-partner wanted to leave the marriage, and ultimately, although it made him very sad and frustrated, he had come to terms with her decision. In his personal case, Jack stated that it would have been really easy for him to live in his anger; instead, however, he decided to convert his hostility into a positive force for political change.

> Mostly, there is a lot of group solidarity. [We say to each other] gosh, I know how it feels, I've been there, [but] you've got to get beyond this.

You don't need to accept the legal injustice here, but you certainly do need to accept that your former spouse isn't your enemy and you and she need to get along for the sake of the kid. If you have a sense that injustice has been done here, you need to understand that it really isn't your ex-spouse that's done it, it is the state.... Let's go after the state, let's put this energy to good use. JACK

Jack articulated the importance of a powerful resource that he believed should be harnessed by all fathers' rights groups: strong emotions. Family dissolution will inevitably produce intense feelings, but those feelings need not be directed at ex-partners. Instead, the energy behind the anger should be funneled toward informational campaigns in the public arena in order to promote positive legislative change.

In encouraging fathers to modify their behavior, still other members focus on the long-term consequences on their children of displaying their anger against their former partner. Jake, who described his relationship with his ex-partner as tense, argued that not revealing anger toward the other parent can be beneficial over the long run. In many ways, Jake had a multitude of reasons to have antipathy against his ex-partner. He fathered a nonmarital child, and it was not until his daughter reached her first birthday that he found out that he was her father. In the beginning of her life, his daughter lived with her mother and her half-brother (the boy was the result of another relationship). Through careful monitoring of his daughter's behavior, as well through a tip from a friend, he learned that his former partner was engaging in sexual acts in front of both children. He also discovered that not only had his daughter's half-brother been physically abused by a caretaker within the mother's house, the half-brother also had sexually assaulted his daughter. After these incidents, he was able to convince the court that he, rather than the child's mother, was the best parent to raise his daughter. Despite these multiple tragedies, however, Jake remained committed to never "bad-mouthing" his ex-partner in front of his daughter.

One of the most common things I've heard over and over again, not just from our group but from other groups I've interacted with, is that the parent that badmouths the other parent initially will have the edge over having a better relationship with that child; however, over time, when that child learns the truth, the [bad-mouthing parent] will actually alienate [him or herself] from the child. That is a very common theme. I've heard where a guy will say, "My children are seventeen and eighteen now and we went through hell back when we first got divorced. Mom was always badmouthing me and it hurt my relationship with the children, but now the children don't want anything to do with the mom." JAKE

Although Jake's situation is extreme, which makes his ability to control his emotions extraordinary, notably, other respondents reported similar examples of bad behavior on the part of their ex-partners, along with a corresponding commitment to treat them well, especially if the children were at an impressionable age. Gilbert, for example, had a tense relationship with his ex-partner because he had successfully placed an order of protection against her new boyfriend to stay away from his two young sons, ages three and six. In his testimony, Gilbert had argued to the court that the boyfriend was involved in criminal behavior, and he did not want those kinds of activities around his children. Even though he knew that this action would place a strain on his relationship with ex-partner, he tried never to argue about any issue with her in front of his children. He described his philosophy in the following way:

I try to encourage [all group members] to learn how to coparent. Whatever they do, they cannot argue with the opposing spouse in front of their kids. Make an effort when you have a conversation with the ex; make an effort to wait until after bedtime maybe, when the kids are in bed, [so] they don't hear what is going on. Whenever you've got to talk to your ex-spouse, you know there are going to be disagreements. It is just natural. One is going to disagree with the other in most situations. The best thing to do if your ex-wife calls you and the kids are up—unless it is an emergency—tell that person you will call back at a better time, especially when it is going to be pertaining to child support or whatever the circumstances are where it could generate an argument. Unless it is an emergency and needs to be talked over, try to come to an agreement to where hey, on certain days if you need to talk to me, make it at this time. Most kids are in bed at 8:00 or 9:00

on school nights; [say] "Call me at 10:00 and we'll discuss any matters concerning the children." GILBERT

Even in the face of potential hostility generated by his order of protection, Gilbert recognized that the long-term best interest of his young boys was never to witness their father treating their mother in a disrespectful manner.

Positive, unemotional communication may be a laudatory goal, but fathers may have difficulty reducing their anger unless they are constantly reminded of the importance of doing so by the group. This type of group "correction" actually takes place within the context of fathers' rights group meetings. Blayne, the father of a three-year-old girl, illustrated this method of "correction" by the group when he made the distinction between being a good *mother* and being a good *custodial parent*. For Blayne, his ex-partner was a great mother in that she made sure that his daughter received all of her necessities for a healthy life, including a loving home. However, she was a horrible custodial parent because she consistently froze him out of his daughter's life by not providing details regarding her activities. For example, Blayne complained that his ex-partner never told him about his daughter's doctor's appointments or basketball games. At first, he found himself getting very angry. Fortunately for him, the group was quick to point out when he was wrong and how he should take action to remedy his mistakes.

[The group gave me] advice, basically: "Calm down," is what they told me; "You're not the first person that it's happened to. If you get mad and start a fight, she's going to know that's how to get to you and she's going to do it again later, so just calm down and act like it doesn't bother you." I guess [the group gave me] advice [as to] when to react and when not to overreact....I sent her a card one time when I think I said something or yelled at her or cursed at her or something. [Well,] you go to the next meeting, [and I say,] "You know what she did last time?" And the cofounder [of the group]—I was telling her the story— and she says, "I actually think you were wrong to do that. I think you should send her a card and apologize to her," and so I did. When you are wrong, you're wrong. I am not afraid to admit that. BLAYNE

Felix, father of both a son and a daughter, was in many ways in a similar situation to that of Blayne. He had a lot of anger toward his ex-wife and was faced with a parenting dilemma whereby if he acted in a certain way regarding his son's future plans, he could get even with her, but such an action would hurt his son. However, the group counseled him to take action in another direction.

> You've got a group of people and if you recount the situation that you are in, they'll say, "Hey, here is a way to handle this. It's happened to me and it helped me...." Again, I am pretty pissed off because I am a visitor in my kids' lives. I am going to miss so many events in their lives. My kids are here for six and one-half weeks. My son is going to play football for the first time in pads this summer. Now my son is telling me, "Dad, I've got to practice. It starts at the end of July, and I want to go to practice." That would mean he would leave two weeks early from being with me. Now part of me wants to say [that] I am keeping my kids as long as I physically can because I want to be with them as much as I can. That's part of me and I also know that would piss off the mom. So when I was at that [group] meeting, I told...them about the football practice and I said part of me wants to keep him here. I am already screwed out of raising my kids and if I could keep [them] two weeks I would like to be able to do it. One guy said, "What is best for your son is to go play football. That is what you need to do." Even though I knew that, hearing that from somebody else helped me. I didn't even think about it. Just hearing that from him, I was like, you are right, and that is what I am doing. I am not saying I am a big hero for letting him go back; that's the way [it should be].   FELIX

Interestingly, note that Felix pointed out that he did not want to be congratulated for doing the right thing. Instead, he wanted to illustrate the key role of the group in focusing positive peer pressure on him to make the best decisions for his children without demonstrating anger toward their mother.

Perhaps just as important, several respondents indicated that they had internalized these group norms of anger reduction and actively monitored themselves against potential future violations of this standard.

Ben, a father of a fifteen-year-old and a nineteen-year-old, explained that he had nothing but disgust for his ex-wife. He described how she took no interest in her children's lives, never attending their sporting or scholastic events, and instead focused exclusively on her own life. However, despite these feelings, he made a conscious effort not to argue with his ex-spouse, especially in front of the children. This does not mean that he has been able to meet this goal all of the time; he recalled the regret he experienced when he fell short of his high standards for his own personal behavior.

> I can remember one time [when I really fought] with my ex....I actually, quite frankly, I didn't want to fight, but I had her husband out in the parking lot yelling at me with the kids in the car. [I really got angry and yelled]. [After that], I actually just broke down and cried, and I promised my kids that [they would] never see that again. I told them I was ashamed as a parent. I think [the group would say], because we are all friends, to try to look at [every situation] and be sensitive towards your kids.... If you are going to talk about things, the children shouldn't be present. You don't bad-mouth your ex in front of the kids. I don't care how bizarre mom is, that is still their mom. You've got to bite your tongue and say mom is a nice person.   BEN

Like Ben, Alvin was fairly settled in his relationship concerning his ex-partner at the time of his interview. His three children were grown, and he even had grandchildren. Yet he still could vividly recall the problems that he had with his ex-partner, and his temper was readily visible when any type of conflict between them emerged. Going to several group meetings, however, made a fundamental difference in his life, a difference that he compared to a religious conversion.

> I am pretty impulsive, so I can trace immediately back to hearing [the president of a fathers' rights group speak], because at the time I heard him I was embroiled in the hostilities; I was angry, depressed, frustrated—all of the things that follow hostile, continuing litigation. But what [the group leader] said made sense... that there needs to be systemic changes [in the family court system] and also that all

of this should stem from a more child-centered approach. [He said] that it's really the children that are hurt and even though you're hurt and you're in this muck, it is worse for your children and we need to change it for our children....It was like going to Billy Graham thirty years ago and [thinking], "I am going to walk down [the aisle], because I'd buy into this." Alvin

Both Ben and Alvin indicated that they had "bought into" the new philosophy that they learned from their groups. Regardless of how angry they might be, they had to calm themselves and proactively deal with the range of emotions that they were experiencing in order to produce the best coparenting relationships possible.

Encouraging Nonconfrontational Phraseology

The third critical task of these groups is to help fathers learn to speak in nonconfrontational ways about and with their ex-partners. On the most basic level, this entails changing the *way* men have learned to address their ex-partners. Not unexpectedly, many fathers experiencing family dissolution do not use kind words when they describe their ex-partners. Although the attraction to this type of language might be understandable, fathers' rights groups try to develop among group members a new "phraseology" of respect. Rachel, who has had a tumultuous relationship with her ex-partner at times and now is extremely active in leading her local fathers' rights group, described the ways in which she helps members use a new language to describe their interactions with their former partners.

We have incidents [where our members use bad language to describe their partners] and I tell them, "How great do your kids feel, how does your kid feel" knowing that you cussed out his or her other half?...I'm telling you that's going to haunt you like a nightmare, because you know what your kid's going to remember? My mom or dad said this to my mom or my dad....What I teach them to say when they say the broad, the bitch, the who, the what, or whatever, the asshole or whatever, you'll learn to say my children's mom, or my children's dad; that is very, very [important]....I'm straight to the point with that....So I'm telling you to get some control over it and get started telling yourself and everyone else that all the negativity ends now. RACHEL

In addition to encouraging members to avoid profanity when describing their ex-partners, these groups also aim to teach members to use cooperative language that will promote the parenting relationship as a fully functional, dual responsibility. Pablo, father of four, learned this important lesson from those emphasizing proper phraseology in his group. Even though his relationship with his ex-partner was strained, he remained committed to the practice of positive verbal framing to help control his emotions.

> We actually practice phraseology and stuff, as well as encourage people, whatever their spiritual discipline is, to make sure that they have those steam vents. Because if they don't blow it off with sports or with something else, they are going to take it out on the person they tend to blame. That is a big, big part of it.... Listen to the difference between ex-wife and coparent. It acts as a totally different mindset. This is a coparent for the rest of your life and you better learn to not just cope with it, but make it somehow work and flourish. "Ex-wife" conjures up all of those memories and it conjures up child support and spousal support and all of that kind of junk. So we work on just little things like that, which seem semantic at first, but they actually elicit a totally different state of mind. PABLO

For Pablo, the important point is that words can change attitudes. When a father learns to call his ex-partner his coparent rather than his ex-wife, he becomes empowered to see the world completely differently. He gradually becomes transformed into a person who envisions himself as a coequal adult with his ex-partner in his children's lives rather than a rival for their attention with their mother.

Some groups move beyond simply using more suitable terminology when fathers are describing their ex-partners by promoting a completely new way of using words to understand mutual pain. Ryan, a father of one child with a background in social work, leads his local fathers' rights group in this effort by explaining that most parents, even though they might be going through the dissolution process, have strong feelings for each other that include the concept of care. After all, even though the relationship did not work out, ex-partners usually have a substantial history of love or at least attraction that ended up producing the children whose well-being is now a source of struggle. The problem, as Ryan explained, is that the grieving taking place over the relationship ends up consuming these parents and puts them at odds with one another as they try to manage their children's lives.

> One of the perspectives that I've learned [is that] when people are very angry with one another, there is a lot of caring going on. [It may be] maladaptive, but there is a connection. In essence, because there is a connection, if you acknowledge there is a connection, that can be very empowering. So the next step is not to take the other person's anger as personal, but take it in terms of their pain, their emotional and psychic pain. What they are doing is trying to transfer their pain onto you by attacking you, so the key then is to not to compound the pain by responding to the attack and getting into the games of the victim, persecutor, [and] rescuer roles. [You need to learn] to side step the drama triangle and maintain your own self-esteem and acknowledge that the other person is in a great deal of pain [as well]. . . . Then you can find out from them what it is that they are scared of, what they feel their need is, and then instead of you doing something about it, you ask them what they feel they can do about their pain and their situation.   RYAN

Although not common across all fathers' rights groups, Ryan's dedication to promoting positive interactions between parents was striking. He remained committed to the idea that parents simply need training in using the right words to react to one another so that their old habits do not dominate their verbal exchanges and result in increased hostility. Ryan focused on teaching this new way of communicating with every father that he met in the group context and professed to obtain positive results from those inclined to make a difference in their own lives.

Propagating Special Group "Rules"

The fourth strategy used to encourage parents to get along is the development and propagation of group rules for directing members' behavior in productive ways, thereby improving communication between parents over the long run. These rules are not formally written out, nor do members need to take an oath that they will regularly abide by them. Rather, they tend to be unspoken norms to which the leaders and experienced members adhere and which they encourage all new members to learn and attempt to integrate into their daily lives. These rules govern many aspects of fathers' interactions, including how they should interact with their children and the type of role models they should become in their children's lives. However, many of these rules also pertain to treatment of their ex-partners in a variety of contexts, including in court and at home.

Franco, the activist mentioned in chapter 5, had a total of three children—two by his first marriage and one son from his second. Although he had a relatively amicable divorce from his first wife, his divorce from his second wife was disastrous, especially since the judge allotted him very little time with his son. Moreover, he explained that his second ex-wife was extremely inflexible in making any slight modifications to his scheduled time with his child. Relations between the ex-couple became so bad that both knowingly began tape-recording each other when they spoke on the phone. Perhaps because of these challenges, Franco became actively involved in his local fathers' rights group. Over time, he learned that most individuals coming to meetings were similarly upset over child access issues and likely to treat their ex-partners in disrespectful ways. Ultimately Franco came to the realization that he wanted to change his own life and help others change theirs. He therefore saw a need that he believed he could fill among his counterparts and developed a set of group rules for all members to understand and integrate into their daily lives.

We had six new people in June [in the group] and... everybody is angry and frustrated. I talk about my rules. One thing that somebody told me when I was going through [a dissolution is that] when you are going through it, your head is messed up and you don't think clearly at a time when you really need to. The problem is you can't focus on a lot of things at one time. You can read these books, the self-help books and all that, but you have to have some very basic things you remember that will pop in your head when you are going through the anger and the strife or whatever.

I'll give you four of them really fast:

1. Being right doesn't matter. You walk into court and you know that this is the right stuff for your kid. It doesn't matter if she is shooting up drugs in front of the judge; unless that judge recognizes that is what she is doing, it doesn't matter.
2. Logic doesn't exist. What is logical, which is children are entitled to be parented by both their parents unless one is an abuser, [is not recognized].
3. It is not what your ex says or does, but how you react to it. This is the biggest one.

These three rules literally are survival tools for these people.

4. Be reasonable. Don't go yelling and screaming because of rule #1, rule #2, and rule #3.

...[We] challenge new people [when they have these bad attitudes] and they look at us like we are crazy. I will look at a guy right in the eye who is just absolutely angered and frustrated, doesn't understand, and can't see his kid. I'll look him right in the eye and I'll say, "Are you this little girl's father?" He'll say, "Yeah." I'll tell him, "Start acting like it. Stop being this wimp who is whining and complaining about all this stuff. Would you take a bullet for your son or your daughter? Well, then, start doing it."   FRANCO

Franco explained that his unofficial job as "rule propagator" was never easy, especially with respect to rule #3. There were constant violations of the rules, even at the group meetings themselves. But Franco indicated that he never gave up, and would pull the violators over to one side in order to patiently explain the rules to them once again. To him, the most important guideline to keep in mind is that children have an enormous capacity to understand discord, and parents must do everything in their power to treat each other civilly in order to de-escalate this potentially dangerous conflict.

When the Group Does Not Help Parents Get Along

In many ways, fathers' rights groups engage in numerous activities that help promote positive relations among parents whose union is in the process of breaking down or has dissolved completely. Yet some respondents reported that they received little or no help in this area of their lives. These respondents tended to attribute this lack of success to two distinct causes: other, competing organizational goals or the nature of individual personalities.

First, some respondents asserted that their fathers' rights organization could have very little impact in the area of interpersonal relationships because the leadership had chosen a different central mission for the group. For example, Nigel contended that his relationship with his ex-partner was still very hostile. Indicative of this anger, during his interview, Nigel bitterly proclaimed that since his ex-partner was close to turning forty, she did not have many prospects for finding a new boyfriend. Nigel's lingering animosity, he believed, was endemic in his group for good reason, as fathers are consistently being denied access to their own children. Therefore, he argued that his group's leaders rightly had other, more important priorities at that point in time than helping parents "speak nicely" to one another.

> I wish [encouraging parents to get along] could be relevant [to our group's leaders]. That's a very good point that I don't think we considered too much. Right now we are just trying to consider how we [can] equalize [the law] and get everything in balance for our children, to do what is best for them. We have a section [of our group] where it is primarily mothers, grandmothers and second wives....Some...women in our group, too, are paying child support and don't have custody. [Encouraging parents to get along is] a point [that] we haven't considered, though. NIGEL

For other fathers, the main barrier to promoting effective communication between ex-partners is not so much a different set of group priorities independently conceived by the leadership, but rather the other issues most members pressure the group to focus on instead. Ricardo, father of eleven and fourteen-year-old girls (along with three adult children from previous relationships), had a very strained relationship with his ex-partner. He maintained that not only did she refuse to speak with him, she also demanded that he stay off her property on numerous occasions. Ricardo also reported that her new husband had physically attacked him twice. As these circumstances illustrate, Ricardo had survival on his mind much more than improving his relationship with his ex-partner. He believed that most other group members shared his view, and that these survival issues should rightly be the predominant focus of the group.

> I think the majority of fathers who are in this situation are looking for help since they've got the ex-wife against them and they've got the system against them. So they are trying to find some way to survive out of this whole thing and not totally lose their kids....I think the most important thing on their mind is spending more time with their children and not getting hosed with child support.   RICARDO

Still other fathers emphasized the importance of the group mentality in preventing the organization from tackling the issue of interpersonal relations. Keith, for example, remarked that there was nothing he could do to improve his "horrid" relationship with his ex-partner. But even if there were, his fathers' rights organization was not necessarily the best place for him to do so. Overall, the group conceived of itself as an organization of victimized men whose first priority had to be self-defense.

> In general we don't really have that much time to work with these issues, with this aspect of our personal lives, because in general we are men who feel we are victims. We are under a lot of duress and we have an immediate need, meaning that when we go to the group meetings we have to...get advice for legal matters that we might be encountering and, of course, political activism and all that. The reason why we don't address [relationship issues] is because we see ourselves as really victimized men and it has gone beyond the point where we can actually negotiate or communicate with our spouses. [This is true] because almost across the board our spouses have already victimized us in the courtroom and aggressively pursued things against us, like false accusations [of domestic violence and abuse], etc. Because of this, we focus mostly on defending ourselves and also actively/legally seeking to be with our children.   KEITH

Although Keith indicated that the group "mentality" of conceiving themselves as victims prevented his organization from doing more in the area of interpersonal relations, Tristan, who had been through the divorce process three times himself, painted a much darker portrait to explain why his own group did not get involved in this area: misogyny. In other words, Tristan argued that his group was not helpful in improving relationships with ex-partners because the group itself had a singular focus that was often hostile to women.

> I think [giving members relationship advice is] one thing the group could improve upon. Sometimes [group members] "bad mouth" the women who are keeping the children from them....A group member, and even [our group leader], can be kind of negative about women. [He is this way] because he went through his own ordeal, he was actually incarcerated on a number of occasions as an attorney trying to see his own kids, and he had to go through hell to get his own kids....Now that he's got them he's got a passion to help other people understand what it takes to get them. So, I think he's a bit bitter.   TRISTAN

Although Tristan understood where the anger of many of the group's members and its leader came from regarding their views of women, he did not endorse the vocalization of these sentiments himself. Nonetheless, he believed that the misogynistic culture of the group itself led it to avoid tackling the important yet neglected topic of interpersonal relations.

A second and far more common reason given for a group not helping with interpersonal relations had to due with the nature and decisions of the individual personalities involved. For example, some members had other support systems in place on which they could rely for these needs. One father named Diego declared that he chose not to seek advice from the group on the issue of interactions with his ex-partner because he did not see the organization having that role in his life. Diego, who does not have a relationship with his ex-partner at all, argued that for him, the group was not necessarily the best place to go for assistance regarding his personal life.

> I really don't go through that group for that type of [relationship advice]....I go to my church....They provide counseling. They are willing to see me through the whole situation of divorce and stuff. They

help smooth the water and stuff by contacting her maybe, sending her information, helping me spiritually and emotionally so I am not breaking down over it....[They also help me] to forgive and not hold myself responsible for her actions.   DIEGO

Diego was one of a handful of respondents in this study who was extremely religious. He had a clearly defined view of the role of the group in his life, which was to provide legal information and public policy advocacy. In contrast, he turned to his spiritual advisors for advice regarding relationships.

Although Diego decided not to seek out the group for help in relating to his ex-partner because of his view of the role of the group in his life, others did not utilize the group in this fashion due to their extreme antipathy for their ex-partners that, in their view, could never be overcome. Samuel, who indicated that his relationship with his ex-wife was only business-like in nature, argued that the group could not do anything to assist him become more cooperative with his ex-partner. Samuel and his wife split up around the time his daughter was born. At first, Samuel declared, his ex-wife would only let him see the baby for thirty-minute intervals within the confines of her house. Although he gradually received more time with his daughter, his ex-wife consistently tried to prevent contact by simply not being home when he was due to pick his daughter up and then later by alleging abuse (she claimed that he pushed her). Even though the court system eventually exonerated him, he and his ex-wife continued to clash, most recently over her efforts to bar him from the church that they all attended. Samuel concluded that the group could do nothing for him to help him communicate more effectively because his ex-partner refused to meet him at least half way.

I resent it (respectfully) when somebody says, "You two can't get along?" No, [I] can't get along because she won't let me. The reason she won't let me is because she has primary control of everything and the courts have empowered her to the point where she doesn't have to or want to. The reason she won't facilitate communications with me is because communications lead to compromise and she doesn't want to give up a second....What I am saying is [if a] person at the other end of the line doesn't want to talk to me—I can be the smartest communicator, I could be Shakespeare—I can't get her to talk. I could be the most eloquent Englishman in the world, but yet if the other party bogs down on purpose..., everything defaults to the mom.... I said to the mother, "Let's meet once a month for coffee, me and you without the baby and we'll bring ourselves up to speed on all pertinent issues. Let's just make a habit of it to keep in touch; away from everybody." [She said no]. I said, "Let's go to eat together." [She said no]. I said, "Can I talk to you on the phone?" [She said no]....As [far] as this child is concerned, in my heart I have done everything I can to be in her life [by being] a supportive father, a reasonable person, a financially supporting father, an emotionally supporting father....So, I mean, like the option a father is given is [to] just step back for the sake of the child [and not] fight with the mother. Well, what's worse? Staying out of the child's life so that no arguments occur, or having an argument and being part of the child's life? That's the [dilemma] the father is faced with.   SAMUEL

For Samuel, the critical issue was his ex-partner's reluctance to communicate effectively. For others like Jay, the distrust went much deeper because of the perception that mothers frequently make false sexual and physical abuse allegations against fathers. Jay also had an incredibly hostile relationship with his ex-partner such that the court required him to travel to a police precinct in order to pick up his young daughter for visitation. In this way, local law enforcement could ensure that neither parent unnecessarily provoked the other during their brief encounters. Jay indicated that most fathers are so busy trying to defend themselves against these baseless allegations that they have no time to worry about developing effective interpersonal skills with their former partners.

You've been bombarded with so many accusations; you are spending so much time trying to defend yourself. All you need really is information on how to defend yourself. Every day you turn around, you are slapped with a different accusation. That is typical for everyone who I see. How do I get out of this mess? There are a lot of issues; you are talking about accusations that can get you into trouble with the law, accusations that can destroy your career. You can't be talking about how to improve your relationship.   JAY

Jay did not think this was a positive state of affairs. In fact, he hoped that his own circumstances would change so that his child could adapt more easily to the family dissolution process. He also witnessed the devastating impact that the hostile relations with his ex-partner had on his daughter, who regularly drew self-portraits with missing limbs. Jay interpreted his daughter's drawings as evidence of her perceived handicapped status in the world, handicapped by parents who could not get along. At that time, however, with tensions running high, Jay concluded that the group could do nothing for him in this area.

Ex-Partners for Life

For some fathers' rights members, characteristics of the group itself, such as other priorities or negative approaches to women in general, prevented the organization from tackling the important issue of improving interparental relations. Other members looked to churches in their lives for this type of assistance. Still others maintained that the hostile natures of their former partners prevented them from rebuilding their adult relationships over time. However, the majority of fathers in this study realized that, for better or worse, they had to come to terms with the fact that in some way they were going to be bound to their ex-partners for life because they had produced children together. Despite parents' animosity, babies still had to be fed, toddlers still had to be transported to the doctor, young children still required direction in school, and adolescents still needed assistance in resisting the overwhelming peer pressure to engage in substance abuse, premature sexual activity, and other types of undesirable behavior. Ideally, parents would reinforce one another on all of these issues, no matter what stage of life the child is in, no matter how far apart they live, and no matter how painful the cause of the adult breakup.

Fathers' rights groups, consistent with their antistate attitude that dominates their overall philosophy to family policy, reject as not suitable to their needs the court-affiliated divorce education programs in place to help parents relate to one another. Although their antistate attitudes in the areas of child support and child custody policy can be harmful to families, their beliefs in the area of interpersonal communication have led them to provide valuable alternative services. In lieu of court-affiliated divorce education programs, for example, they have designed their own methods of sharing legal information with fathers attempting to navigate their way through the judicial system. By providing tips on how to manage their own cases, these groups aim to inculcate within their membership the principle that protecting their rights is indispensable to increasing their satisfaction with their child support and child custody arrangements, a critical factor clearly identified by the academic literature in helping improve parental relations over time. Perhaps more important, these groups attempt to implement the lessons of academic research that suggest that strong communication skills also reduce inter-adult conflict. By encouraging fathers to reduce their expressions of anger, learn new, unemotional ways of speaking, and adhere to the groups' rules about interacting with ex-partners in ways that are positive for their children, fathers' rights groups can make an enormous difference in the overall health of families that have dissolved.

These positive services, however, as this chapter has shown and others have documented (Flood 2006), are not automatically generated by all fathers' rights groups and available to all members. Each individual group has to make a decision to promote a pro-partnership agenda with mothers through which women are treated with respect and dignity. Groups that solely express hostility toward women and a victimhood mentality will not help fathers establish a functioning relationship with their ex-partners. Moreover, individuals who perceive their ex-partners as unable to work with them or who are blinded by unresolved hatred will never be able to construct healthy linkages with the mothers of their children. Only if these groups can minimize unhealthy inter-actions such that all members can find stability in their adult partnerships can fathers then turn to the most important relationships in their lives—those that they maintain with their children.

8

The Ties That Bind

Fathers' Relationships with Their Children

Ten people—eight men and two women—are gathered in a small class-room at a Christian college in the Northeast. Two of the eight men in this group, called Kids Need Dads, are black; the rest of the participants are white. The room is clearly used to teach religion to small children on the weekends. Paper chains with children's names decorate the room, and a list of Bible chapters is meticulously written on the front black-board in block letters. Children's drawings artfully depict a timeline that details major scenes from the Bible. As if to announce the presence of adults in the room, the Kids Need Dads' leader, Alvin, asks the ten attendees if they would like to help themselves to a cup of coffee.

The reason for the meeting is to train interested parties who want to become monitors at a new child access center that will operate at the col-lege. Child access centers are designed to facilitate peaceful exchanges of children when parents are having difficulty doing this on their own. Alvin, the group's leader, quickly begins expressing his view of the types of skills he would like to see in all of his child access center monitors.

> ALVIN: Current child access training is filling a void. We are actually
> pioneers in providing this service; there is no government program
> designed to do what we are doing. Since we are in a church, let's
> begin our meeting with a prayer.

(Members pray in silence.)

ALVIN: You should all know that we are not affiliated with a fathers' rights group. We are a children's rights group. There are millions of noncustodial mothers impacted by the types of problems that we are going to discuss today. Our focus is on the children. We educate people on issues related to children's rights.

(Alvin pauses, looks down, and then meets the eyes of the attendees once again.)

ALVIN: You know, kids have not received their appropriate civil rights. We want to be revolutionary, you know, just like black Americans sitting at those white-only restaurant counters in the 1960s.

There are over thirty of these centers in operation right now. Mostly all of these centers are located in churches. Motivated and trained people can all do their part in this crisis. We can help facilitate thousands of transfers. Hopefully, judges are more sensitive to these issues now.

If you would like to be a monitor, the number one thing is that you must remain neutral between both parents. You must always put the child's best interest first. You must help provide a safe, secure, and neutral place where children can be exchanged.

We also have a workable program to prevent violence from erupting in the first place. You simply need to follow these rules:

1. Start a program in a church (people are more respectful in church).
2. Treat people with respect.
3. There should be behavioral guidelines and parents must sign these guideline agreements. Monitors can send anyone home who threatens violence.
4. Let parents who are inclined to speak to one another do so, except if there are:
   A) Domestic violence protective orders in place
   B) If a parent requests separation
5. Parents get one warning to behave themselves if they are angry. If they get angry a second time, simply call 9–1–1.

Let me make another point. Most incidents of violence that we have recorded occur in the parking lot. We can prevent these incidents from occurring. The parent who is picking the child up should be allowed to leave first. The other parent should be held back, between 5–8 minutes, and then allowed to leave. Never allow people to sit in their cars in the parking lot.

I would also like to comment on several good monitor characteristics. Monitors in general should mind their own business and not give advice. We usually like to see teams of monitors, generally a man and a woman, working together. This type of teaming up tends to make both parents comfortable; neither parent thinks the center is biased against him or her....Ideally, this is the best way for the kids, too. They need to see the sexes getting along.

One of the least controversial programs run by some fathers' rights groups in the United States are child access centers, also known as transfer sites or safe havens. As we have seen, during the 1970s and 1980s as a result of the dual problems of rising divorce rates and non-marital childbearing, an increasing number of American children were growing up without a strong paternal figure in their lives. A small but influential set of fathers' rights groups began to suggest that the lack of father involvement was not due to paternal neglect but rather to the fact that fathers faced barriers to seeing their children on a regular basis.[1] These obstacles included orders of protection that many fathers contended did not have any basis in fact and a basic lack of cooperation from mothers in facilitating contact. The federal government began to respond to these claims in the late 1980s. The Family Support Act of 1988 initiated the process by authorizing a wide range of exploratory projects in order to improve fathers' access to their children. From this original legislation, Congress eventually provided $3 million to support seven access demonstration projects located in six states: Indiana,

1. The idea that children need fathers in their lives, and that there was once a period in American history where fathers played a more significant role in their children's development, is a core principle of the fathers' rights movement. However, numerous scholars have contested these claims, maintaining that the importance activists now ascribe to fathers is socially constructed and not necessarily supported by academic research (see Griswold 1998; Stacey 1998).

Florida, Idaho, Iowa, Massachusetts, and Arizona (Ellis and Levy 2003). Building on those experiences, the Personal Responsibility and Work Opportunity Reconciliation Act of 1996 specifically designated money for every state to begin or partner with existing family service or non-profit agencies to find solutions to the problem of lack of paternal contact. Several states have continued to respond to this call for action by financing a variety of child access centers.

Child access centers place the safety of the family in moving a child from one household to another at the core of their missions (Elrod 2001). Families can be referred by numerous sources, including judges, lawyers, and counselors. Families can also "self-refer" to access centers in order to reduce the opportunity for conflict and promote a more harmonious atmosphere for their children during transitions. Although some of these centers also provide "supervised access" for those parents accused of being or found to be abusive or neglectful (in which case the parent and child cannot leave the premises), the majority of these programs only cater to those parents for whom interactions around their children during pick-ups and drop-offs need to be monitored.

As described above at the Kids Need Dads site, transfer centers attempt to recruit monitors of both genders in order to provide a high degree of comfort to each parent. In the typical case, a mother will bring her child to the center at a designated time and then wait until the father picks up the child ten minutes later (Ellis and Levy 2003). Parents can be segregated into different waiting areas if either one requests such privacy or if an order of protection is in place. The process later repeats itself in reverse when the child needs to be returned back to the mother. Trained monitors keep a log of successful and unsuccessful child exchanges to submit to the courts if requested. Transfer centers typically do not charge for any of these services, as they are guided by the philosophy that parents should not have to pay to see their children.

Although only a handful of fathers' rights groups offer these types of services, they are emblematic of another key "personal" goal of fathers' rights groups: to improve the relationship between fathers and their children during and after the family dissolution process. As with their antistate approach to improving men's relationships with their ex-partners, fathers' rights groups view current services affiliated with the government in this sphere to be inadequate. More specifically, not all fathers are required to attend court-based divorce education programs, and not all of these programs address parent-child relationships. To the extent that these programs do cover child-oriented issues, they tend to treat children as autonomous units in the family by, for example, focusing on their individual reactions to the dissolution process rather than on what happens to the parent-child relationship over time. Fathers' rights groups, on the other hand, maintain that strong father-child links are essential to familial healing over the long run and strive to promote the protection of this bond at every opportunity by providing their own services rather than relying on state-run programs. What then does the academic research say about the factors that lead to better relations after a family dissolution, and how effectively do the practices of fathers' rights groups match these recommendations?

Parent-Child Relationships after the Family Dissolves: What Hurts? What Helps?

Without a doubt, the process of parental separation and divorce takes a substantial toll on children (Amato 2000; Kelly 2000; Kelly and Emery 2003). When compared to children growing up with married parents, children of divorce are more likely to have significant academic, psychological, and social problems. In the academic arena, children of divorce have lower scores on achievement tests and are more likely to drop out of school entirely, even after controlling for income and socioeconomic status (McLanahan 1999). Psychologically, children of divorce have more frequent clashes with authority figures and exhibit conduct problems with others that are not as prevalent in children from intact families (Hetherington and Kelly 2002). Compared to their peers who grew up with continuously married parents, children of divorce marry earlier as adults, report higher levels of dissatisfaction with their marriages, and divorce at a higher rate (Amato 1999; Amato 2000; McLanahan and Sandefur 1994).

What factors cause these types of hardships for children from dissolved families? Of course, the major forces driving these negative outcomes are complex, intertwining, and oftentimes difficult to disentangle. Initially, the stress of the separation process itself can be very overwhelming, especially if parents provide little-to-no information about the reasons behind their decision to part ways (Dunn et al. 2001). Children are frequently left to wonder where, exactly, they will live and who will take care of them. This uncertainty can be devastating, especially as young children rely on, become accustomed to, and value caretaker routines in structuring their daily lives. In addition, ongoing parental conflict can be especially damaging when adults use children as vehicles for expressing their anger toward one another by prohibiting discussion of the other parent or by demanding that the children "carry messages" to the other parent (Buchanan, Maccoby, and Dornbusch 1991; Johnston 1994). Families also experience economic decline in the immediate wake of a dissolution, which can have obvious adverse consequences for child well-being by intensifying stress levels for all members of the household (Duncan and Hoffman 1985; Kelly and Emery 2003). So what, if anything, can either parent, but especially fathers, do to insure that their children are as resilient as possible in the face of this undeniably negative event of a family breakdown? It turns out that they can make a difference by engaging in one central activity that, although commonsensical, is quite difficult to execute in practice: to stay involved in their children's lives.

Remaining engaged as parents is not an easy task for many fathers, as the data on postdissolution interactions suggest. In fact, some studies report that 18–25 percent of children have no contact with their fathers *at all* only three years following the divorce (Braver and O'Connell 1998; Hetherington and Kelly 2002; Maccoby and Mnookin 1992; Seltzer 1998). For families reporting at least some type of weekly contact, older children see their fathers less than infants, toddlers, and grade-school children (Stephens 1996). There is no one, simple explanation for either the total loss of contact or declining levels of contact over time; instead, a variety of factors seem to be at play. Some fathers clearly and willfully remove themselves from their children's lives (Arendell 1995). Their anger over their relationship ending with their partner spills over into their relationship with their children, and they want nothing more to do with any reminder—including their children—of that former life. Under another pessimistic interpretation, other fathers may simply choose to father "socially" rather than biologically. In other words, they elect to engage in serial parenting, whereby once they find a new partner, they stop being a father to their biological children. Rejecting their old responsibilities, they simply take up the task of parenting their new partners' children and whatever new biological children they produce as a result of this union (Dowd 2000).

However, researchers also note that for some fathers, the overwhelming sadness and corresponding confusion regarding their family's dissolution may make them disinclined to parent enthusiastically in the future. Before a separation or divorce, every family has clearly defined roles for each participating member. When the family breaks down, these roles are significantly altered and often subject to contestation (Fox and Blanton 1995). For example, a father who viewed himself as the head of the household in terms of economic provision may experience a crisis of meaning when he no longer resides with his partner and children and thus no longer directly sees his material contribution on a daily basis. Overall, then, fathers may no longer know how to comport themselves within the shifting definition of their family, a problem scholars have identified as "role ambiguity" (Madden-Derdich and Leonard 2000). Indeed, fathers may have less experience than mothers in the full array of caregiving skills that they need—such as adapting to the developmental requirements of their offspring at different stages of their lives—to raise their children on their own. As a result, fathers' confidence in their ability to guide their children effectively as well as their satisfaction as parents overall may substantially decline in the immediate postseparation years (Minton and Pasley 1996). Reducing or avoiding contact altogether with their children may be one way for fathers to cope with these overwhelming feelings of loss.

Others scholars note that explicit, conscious, and negative maternal behaviors further limit father-child contact over the long run. Simply put, fathers may be discouraged in pursuing contact with their children if they feel that they do not have the full support that they need from their ex-partners in order to be effective parents (Fox and Blanton 1995; Hoffman 1995). For example, mothers might impose on fathers carefully restrictive visitation rules and other types of constraints on contact (Kelly 1993b; Pleck 1997). This dynamic, also known as maternal gatekeeping, may function to depress paternal involvement because fathers may come to resent jumping through a series of hoops in order to see their own offspring (Allen and Hawkins 1999). Custodial parents, most frequently mothers, might also choose to or need to move away from the noncustodial parent for employment or other types of personal reasons, thereby further limiting contact (Braver, Ellman, and Fabricius 2003; Kelly and Lamb 2003; Leite and McHenry 2002). Finally, the issue of remarriage also can inhibit fathers. If the mother remarries, fathers may feel as if they have to take a "back seat" to the new step-father on issues of parenting (Furstenberg and Nord 1985). Under this scenario, dropping out of their former families' lives may become a more attractive alternative than competing with another man for their children's attention.

The amount of time fathers spend with their children, then, may clearly suffer after their adult relationships end. In addition, some evidence shows that as the *quantity* of parenting time declines in the post-dissolution period, the *quality* of this parenting might be declining as well (Wallerstein and Kelly 1980). Consumed by the end of their relationship, both parents often struggle with their own adjustment to new patterns of daily living. Their preoccupation with their depressed feelings can result in less-than-optimal monitoring of their children's behavior and in less emotional openness to truly hearing their children's needs. Gaps might also occur in the supervision of their children's behavior. A mother may assume that the father is handling one aspect of their children's lives, such as attending the children's sporting events or taking them to the doctor, while the father may at the same time erroneously assume that the mother is taking charge of the same duties. If this miscommunication persists, the children will have no one attending their activities or regularly taking them to the doctor, resulting in a potential blow to their self-esteem, confidence, and even health. Coordination regarding the instillation of important values may also falter. For instance, if each parent falsely believes that the other is reinforcing the importance of community service and voluntarism such that only one or even no parent ends up instilling this principle, children may be confused and uninterested in engaging in these activities as they grow older.

Fathers who counter these trends provide their children with an important buffer against many of the negative outcomes associated with family dissolution (Kelly and Emery 2003). Clearly, a relatively high level of frequency of contact with fathers matters in improving children's adjustment after a separation, although this is usually only the case when parental conflict is low (Hetherington and Kelly 2002). Intuitively, children will not do better emotionally or physically if they see both parents regularly, but their parents cannot stop arguing when they are together. With this exception in mind, fathers who do not see their children on a strictly scheduled basis simply cannot do a good job of parenting. Children require consistency in love, dedication, and discipline. Fathers who appear only on birthdays and major holidays will probably not be able to exert a positive influence on their children's lives nor contribute to the ultimate development of a positive relationship.

Yet insuring frequency of contact by itself is not enough for fathers who want to maintain positive relationships with their children (King 1994). Not surprisingly, a high *quantity* of parenting must be combined with a high *quality* of parenting in order to make a significant difference in fathers' relationships with their children (Amato and Gilbreth 1999; Simons et al. 1999). After a family dissolves, fathers can assume a variety of roles vis-à-vis their children (Acock and Demo 1994; Arendell 1995; Mott 1990; Rossi 1984). They can see their children as adult friends or distant relatives, thus relinquishing any type of corrective presence in their lives. They can also choose to only engage in "fun" activities with them, such as watching television, going to movies, visiting amusement parks, and eating out. They may favor these activities with an eye toward creating incentives for their children to express a desire to be with them in the future. Unfortunately, time with dad then becomes a constant vacation, and real life problems and stressors do not play the normal role in promoting the values of respect and responsibility that they would have if the family had stayed together.

In their critique of the "distant" or "fun" dad roles, researchers have stressed that achieving a high quality of parenting is attainable by all fathers and simply necessitates *structured involvement*. Fathers exhibiting high quality parenting behaviors do more on visitation days than take their children to the arcade or to the zoo (Lamb 1999). Instead, these fathers use effective, authoritative parenting skills to help their children with such tasks as completing homework and setting high expectations for their achievement overall (Amato and Gilbreth 1999). More specifically, the authoritative parenting approach outlined by developmental psychologists is one that emphasizes a nurturing attitude toward children but at the same time stresses the implementation of rules and limitations on personal behavior. In addition, under the guidelines of authoritative parenting, children are encouraged to voice an opinion on issues under discussion by the family, but parents have the final say over the choices that their offspring make. Authoritative parenting, by itself and especially when combined with strong financial support and a custodial parent who engages in similar parenting practices, results in children who do better in school, complete high school at higher rates, and are much less likely to engage in delinquent behaviors than children growing up in families without such involved fathers (Menning 2002; Simons 1996).

Fathers' Rights Groups Respond

Given these findings from the scholarly research on parenting in the postdissolution period, fathers' rights groups have taken it upon themselves to encourage men to stay involved with their children as much as possible, and, indeed, there is a certain urgency to their work. In the case of divorce, for example, scholars have characterized the family not as experiencing one critical, life-changing event in the form of family disintegration, but rather as undergoing a series of smaller transformations that each have the potential to impact father-child relationships over the long run (Wallerstein and Kelly 1980). In particular, the first year after a divorce or separation is especially critical, as many fathers make the determination by the end of this period as to whether or not they will retreat from their children's lives (Madden-Derdich and Leonard 2000; Seltzer 1991). Currently, beyond the court-affiliated divorce education programs, few resources exist for fathers to re-envision their role as valued parents in a dissolved family (Fox and Blanton 1995). Membership in fathers' rights groups, which can provide a safe network of support for recently separated and divorced fathers at this sensitive juncture in their lives, might therefore serve as a significant buffer against the potential decline in both the quantity and quality of contacts these men may experience with their children.

How then, specifically, do these groups provide the resources that fathers need to stay involved in their children's lives? Using a variety of techniques, including videos, brochures, speakers, posters, and informal conversation, fathers' rights groups have responded to these men in concrete ways. More specifically, they support and empower fathers regarding their irreplaceable roles in their children's lives; they give them child-centered skills and activity suggestions; and they offer them an important new philosophy or creed by which to re-envision their lives as parents.

Support and Empowerment

One of the most compelling ways that fathers' rights groups help fathers adapt to their new parenting roles is through the mutual support offered to all members as they go through this transformative process together. George, a father with sole custody of his young son, found himself in a desperate situation with respect to his ex-partner. She actually paid him child support, but because of her drug addiction had difficulty making her payments on time. George reported that within a short period, his ex-wife had gone from working as a highly skilled nurse to making ends meet as a strung-out car wash attendant. At the time of George's interview, she had just been incarcerated for her failure to financially support her child. George had many mixed feelings about the value of this punishment as a way to encourage her to fulfill her obligations; he particularly worried about how this penalty would affect his son. To help him deal with his feelings, George turned to the group as a supportive place where others reminded him that in the long run, his son would benefit from a relationship with both parents.

> I think [the group] helps a lot of guys because when you go into our meetings, we allow time to let everybody tell their stories and talk about them. I think it helps a lot of people—just having somebody [going through] a similar situation [who] kind of knows what you're talking about. You can sit down with a room full of people, be able to tell your story and be comfortable doing that. To me, it's a good surrounding and setting and it's people helping each other.   GEORGE

Like George, Samantha also found support and solace at her local fathers' rights group. Although she did not experience the family dissolution process herself, Samantha was motivated to join her local fathers' rights group by her brother-in-law's circumstances. He had significant difficulty seeing his son on a consistent basis and would often come to Samantha's house in tears. Things improved when he hired an attorney to secure regular access to his child, but he still experienced tremendous anxiety over future interactions with the child's mother. Like George, Samantha described the role of her group as important in providing fathers with an opportunity to share their feelings with one another as they seek to improve their relationships with their children.

> Well, first of all [our group tries to help] by letting [fathers] talk about [their problems] without making some kind of judgment on them because that's what happened to them; everywhere they go, they are judged. We say you can say anything you want to here, it stays here. Nobody is going to talk about it outside this place. [This is] kind of like an Alcoholics Anonymous [AA] meeting, sort of. We also try to hook them up [with other members]; we try to do a...mentoring kind of thing where...the guys will go out for coffee with each other and one will say, "You know, I had [a problem] just like yours and here is what I found was the best way to handle it." So that kind of mentoring was just so helpful.   SAMANTHA

For Samantha, the key distinguishing feature of these groups is their "AA-like" atmosphere. Parents feel free to express themselves without fear of being exposed in their distraught emotional state by other individuals involved in the group. Reed, a separated father who reported that he had a distant relationship with his two children, echoed Samantha's points on the importance of the group in providing support for fathers involved in similar circumstances. He also argued that the group played a fundamental role in giving fathers a network of individuals to tap both for knowledge and emotional comfort when attempting to reconnect with their children.

> It seems when somebody wants to cause these problems, [he or she] can make you look so defensive and bad that there is almost no way to overcome it. It is sort of like a hopeless type situation. Even if you are an optimist...it is like, how many times can you beat your head

on the wall and what is the point of this when these children aren't pawns, they are not cattle; these are human beings and they are being shown something that is about money and they are being told that somebody doesn't love them anymore. The group tries to overcome that through networking. Basically, it is very helpful when people can talk about this. There is access to people who [describe] their situations and we all have similar cases. REED

For some fathers, the main advantage of the group is that it makes them feel less alone as they try to build new lives for their families. Michael found that his relationship with his twelve-year-old daughter suffered a series of setbacks immediately after the family split apart. His former wife moved to another town in a concerted effort, Michael claims, to push him out of his daughter's life. Michael ultimately went to court in order to secure more consistent access, but the struggle to obtain more access definitely placed a severe psychological strain upon him. At an extremely dark point in his life, the group stepped in with the support that he needed to focus on his child's long-term needs for parental involvement.

> What [the group] did, at least initially, was encouraged me in the fact that I realized I wasn't alone. [The group showed me that] it wasn't me per se doing anything wrong; there are a lot of vindictive custodial parents out there. So at least [members of the group] consoled me and encouraged me a little bit to try to pursue visitation and continue seeing my daughter, because I was about ready to give up. MICHAEL

All of these individuals—George, Samantha, Reed, and Michael—experienced a common dilemma as they or someone whom they loved went through the family dissolution process: a feeling of being isolated in their quest to see their children more often. Fortunately, fathers' rights groups provided them with an essential comfort—a sense of common understanding—as they attempted to move forward in their lives.

Another fundamental component to this support process is the empowerment these groups can provide to anguished parents who fear losing contact with their children after the family dissolves. Strongly reflecting this view, Lawrence found his local fathers' rights group to be an excellent source of support regarding the changes in his life that he was experiencing as a parent of a nine-year-old daughter; more specifically, he felt that the group instilled in him an enormous sense of internal strength to continue in his parenting role. Lawrence described his relationship with his ex-partner as one that had evolved over time. It was decent for up to five years after the divorce. After that point in time, she became engaged and ultimately remarried. With a new man in the family, Lawrence's ex-wife dramatically reduced the time that he was allowed to spend with his daughter. Whereas before his ex-wife remarried she was quite flexible with the conditions under which he could see his daughter, after her remarriage she became quite rigid. She limited his visits strictly to the letter of the divorce decree and would not schedule any make-up time if Lawrence could not see his daughter during his formally prescribed parenting time. Initially discouraged by these new limitations, Lawrence argued that the group was an excellent place where he could feel emboldened once again to exert a strong, positive influence on his daughter's well-being.

> I felt a sense of empowerment because prior to my involvement with [the group], I had an overwhelming sense of helplessness and hopelessness. I felt like I was the only father in the world who wasn't allowed to see his child as much as he wanted or as much as what would be considered reasonable. That's [what I have taken away from the group] mostly in a nutshell; is the sense of empowerment that I have gotten. LAWRENCE

As he detailed, without the group Lawrence felt like he was the only man in his community missing his child. The group thus provided an important normalizing experience for Lawrence in that other fathers were with him in spirit throughout this difficult journey of familial transition.

The last way that the group provides support for fathers with respect to their children is by communicating to them that they are acting in their children's best interest by staying involved in their lives. For example, in Jackson's case, the group instilled in him the needed reassurance to feel that he was doing the right thing by never giving up in his

commitment to spend time with his daughter. Once he divorced his
ex-wife, he received the standard visitation arrangement of every other
weekend, summer time, and alternating holidays. Jackson reported that
even though this visitation plan was clearly spelled out in the divorce
decree, his ex-wife would fight with him over specific days or purposely
schedule parties for his daughter during his parenting time. Exacer-
bating this tension, over the years his daughter had gradually shown
a greater interest in being with her friends than with him, a development that could be expected given the normal cycle of social matura-
tion. Despite these challenges, Jackson made a point of attending her
soccer and basketball games whenever he could, even though she lived
135 miles away. He, in essence, became more flexible with his expectations of the conditions under which he could spend time with her and
less concerned with defending his rights to a rigid predetermined access
schedule.

> I think [the group] encourages you to continue on, to have that time,
> not to give up seeing your daughter, which I think is very good be-
> cause there are a lot of guys [who do give up]. [They think that their]
> time is gone and they go on to something else. [But the group is] very
> encouraging [in terms of] keeping in contact with your daughter and
> [telling you] not to get discouraged with access problems and stuff.
> I think it helps. JACKSON

Ross, father of a son and a daughter, had a different set of difficulties
than those faced by Jackson. He maintained that his ex-wife consistently promised to reward his children with love and affection when they
exhibited feelings of hatred toward him. Interestingly, his children had
two separate reactions to his ex-partner's efforts to poison them against
him. Ross reported that his son stood up to his mother when she criti-
cized his role as a father; however, his daughter attempted to play each
parent off the other. For example, when his daughter got into his car in
front of her mother, she screamed and yelled that she did not want to go
with him. However, when the car pulled out of the mother's driveway,
the ranting immediately stopped. Nonetheless, the fact that his daughter repeated this behavior every time they initially interacted with one
another was extremely disturbing. Luckily for Ross, throughout all of

these ordeals the group stood by him in his efforts to preserve his relationship with both of his children.

> I think one of the biggest things [the group does] is affirming that the guys [who reach out to their kids] are doing the right thing and lets them know that what [they are] doing is worth it. Maybe you don't have the answers or question that you [are] doing the right thing, [but] the kids know that you love them because they see that you're fighting to protect them. You're not running away.   Ross

Many fathers experiencing the family dissolution process are so disturbed by their own child support and child custody issues that they choose to disengage entirely from the process of parenting. As Ross pointed out, however, fathers' rights groups provide an extraordinary service to men throughout the country by convincing them that simply fleeing from these problems is not in their best interest nor in the best interests of their children.

Giving Members Child-Centered Skills and Sponsoring Child-Centered Activities

Mutual support and personal empowerment through the group are clearly important factors that help fathers improve their relationships with their children over time. But the nuts-and-bolts of every day parenting also must be considered, and fathers report strong needs in these areas as well. One of the most important ways the groups assist fathers in their daily parenting duties is by bringing in speakers to address their concerns and by training them in basic to advanced parenting skills. For example, fathers' rights members reported that psychologists and social workers dispensed excellent advice at meetings about how to interact with their children in the post-breakup context. Blayne, who maintained that he became a visitor in his own three-year-old daughter's life after his adult relationship broke down, appreciated that the group brought in these speakers to lecture on topics of interest to fathers who must adapt to new parenting roles. On many occasions, for instance, Blayne needed direction in setting appropriate developmental boundaries for his rambunctious daughter.

> A guy came in and [talked about] child development and behavior, the stages of development and stuff like that. [He explained] what type of discipline works for what age group. If they do X, you do Y for actions [for] this age group.   BLAYNE

Blayne had never been married and had never had a child before his girlfriend gave birth. Without any experience in the parenting arena, Blayne found the speakers that the group recruited for their monthly meetings to be extremely helpful.

As a much more extreme example, Casey had a difficult time seeing his seven-year-old daughter in the first few years of her life. He separated from his wife when his daughter was only two months old, and Casey reported that his ex-wife withheld her from him while she was a baby and then a toddler. Later, when she was only four or five years old, his ex-wife accused him of molesting his daughter. The police, family court, child protective services, and psychologists all became involved in investigating the case. The results of the investigation were "inconclusive"; as a result, the district attorney's office never brought charges against him. Yet simply because an investigation had taken place, Casey maintained that parts of his life were completely ruined. He could not participate in his daughter's after school activities, for example, because the school's background check would have revealed that a molestation investigation had taken place. Still reeling from these circumstances, Casey was desperate for any type of information that he could use to help restore his connection to his daughter in a healthy way.

> [The speakers that] I find the most interesting are the psychologists. They come from the point of view more than everyone else, I think, [of] what is best for the child.... I think all the speakers do to a certain extent.... The end result is obviously to be involved in your children's lives, but I think the psychologists still come from a unique perspective and they are the first ones to ask, "What do you think would help?" They ask tougher questions, let's just say. They are pretty no-nonsense. The [child support] people all try to be political; the [child protective services] people are political. The psychologists don't have to be political and they just level some tough questions [at you] like,

why don't you move closer to your daughter? Why don't you take off work on Friday afternoon? Why don't you take a job that pays less so [that] you can spend more time with her?   Casey

For fathers involved in the family dissolution process, social service professionals whom they encounter seem to be "political" in nature, meaning that they seem to have an agenda that might not comport with their children's best interest. For example, in their view, child support workers want to collect all possible money to the exclusion of protecting father-child relationships; child protective workers tend to believe all accusations of abuse at the expense of fathers. On the other hand, Casey perceived that the mental health professionals who speak at fathers' rights group meetings articulate concerns that are fundamental to the well-being of children, who have a strong need to maintain ties with both parents. They also challenge fathers to think about their children's interests in novel, innovative ways, for example by encouraging them to work less and spend more time at home.

Other speakers instruct fathers in being better parents, not only to get themselves through the divorce process, but to provide them with valuable parenting lessons that will last for a lifetime. Vince indicated that he had left his lucrative career in order to spend more time with his children after his family dissolved and appreciated that the group attracted speakers who could counsel members in disciplining and loving their children.

[At the last meeting] we had this lady Charlene, who is an attorney. She has her master's degree in counseling and she is a minors' counselor, too; I think they call them [guardians] ad litem out there. She is amazing. She talks about how as a counselor for children what she has to look for. [Educators like her] teach you what the courts look for in your behavior, in your reactions, and they tell you how you can improve your relationship with your children.   Vince

Like other fathers in his group, Vince prized a strong relationship with his children and was willing to make professional sacrifices in order to improve those bonds. Through his conversations with other members of the group, Vince found that he as well as other fathers lacked rudimentary parenting skills because they never had a positive paternal role model when they were growing up. Invited professional speakers like Charlene can help these fathers fill in the gap with respect to their basic parenting competencies.

These groups also recommend age-appropriate activities with which fathers can engage their children. Mel described his relationship with his fourteen-year-old son (recall from chapter 5 that his other three children were adults) as being better than it was when the family was intact. At the time of his interview, Mel was spending a great deal of time with his son through activities such as the Boy Scouts. Mel also realized, however, that not all fathers are in his enviable position, and therefore he worked with the group to sponsor more activities to promote father-child relationships. For example, most groups have some type of festive event on Father's Day, when fathers are likely to be with their children.

> [The group has] things like on Father's Day; we'll get together, have a barbecue in the park, and ask the news media to kind of see what we're doing. There's a children's festival the next town over and we put a booth together and paint the kids faces so [that fathers can] do some kind of crafty thing with the kids. We'll give out bumper stickers. There is a fair amount of that stuff going on. MEL

Mel emphasized the importance of these gatherings for fathers and their children, but also pointed out that they serve an additional purpose in attracting the local media to cover the cause of fathers' rights.

Leon, father of a son and a daughter, received a standard visitation order when he separated from his wife. His son, who had attention deficit disorder, was on multiple medications under the supervision of his mother. Leon disagreed with what he viewed as an overly aggressive medical approach to his son's health but found that there was little he could do to assert his paternal rights until the entire family-law system was overhauled. Like Mel, therefore, he echoed the idea that group-sponsored Father's Day events can serve multiple ends.

> Usually every year on Father's Day, we have a picnic. One year we had it down at the amusement park. Then we will get together once

during the summer and have a picnic and a pig roast at somebody's house. [The event] promotes some activities but the goal is political in order to improve the…parent-child relationship with the noncustodial parent.   LEON

In Leon's view, like that of Mel, the activities that the groups hold are good not only for encouraging parent-child interaction, but also for drawing public attention to the fact that fathers need to have more time with their children.

Another critical task for these groups is to stress that fathers need to do their best in order to make their houses feel like their children's homes when their sons and daughters do come over. A warm, welcoming environment might prompt otherwise sad, confused, or reluctant children to transition more easily between their parents' houses. Tito, for example, found that creating such a child-friendly living situation made a fundamental difference in the relationships that he had with his children. At the time of his interview, Tito had two teenage children—a son and a daughter—both of whom had their primary residence with their mother. He found that his son, even though he was at an age where friends tend to trump family as preferred associates, still spent significant time with him. Over the years, his daughter likewise expressed a strong desire to spend more time with him, even at one point asking to live with him. Although she eventually changed her mind, she still came to his house on a regular basis. He partially attributed his success in solidifying these bonds to the efforts that he expended in establishing a proper, child-friendly setting for them all to interact. Learning from his own personal experiences, Tito explained that it is critical for fathers to create a home environment that will be comfortable for their children, both physically and emotionally.

[It is really important for the children to have] personal stuff, even if dad lives in a studio apartment, at dad's house.…[Dads should] have a special drawer in [their] dresser, one for each child. That's for their stuff and that way it feels like it's their home. We encourage [fathers] to make their new living arrangements [feel like] home [for their children] and also use a lot of the language—this is dad's house, this is mom's house—[that make children comfortable].   TITO

Successfully adapting to a two-home situation is very important for children experiencing the family dissolution process. Fathers' rights groups, as Tito explained, do extremely significant work by raising the issue of comfort in both homes to the forefront of members' minds. For children to adjust properly over the long run, they must see that their parents value their presence to the point where they sense that their need for personal space and personal property are protected and respected, even when they are not physically there.

Providing Group Members with a New "Philosophy"

Perhaps the most important initiative undertaken by fathers' rights groups to promote the improvement of members' relationships with their children is the propagation of a specific, child-oriented philosophy among their members. This is not a formal creed that is posted in the group's meeting rooms, nor is it necessarily documented on each group's Web site. Rather, it is an ethos or "way of being" that is advanced by group leaders and members who have been part of the organization for a long time. Members describe the sanctity of this philosophy in a variety of ways, with some making parallels to traditional religious dogmas. Recall from chapter 7 that Alvin, for example, had a good relationship with his ex-wife and three children at the time of the interview, but that this had not always been the case. In addition to experiencing tensions with his ex-wife after the divorce, he sadly became estranged from his children in the first few years following the family's dissolution. His local fathers' rights group, however, gave him the "new religion" that he needed to get through what he described as incredibly dark days.

> I kind of feel like it's a fraternity and sorority of like-minded people who [have] accepted this creed of, put the children first and [establish] child-centered arrangements....Demilitarize what you're into and that's the reason I joined up, that's what I believe and that's what's been stoked. I compare it kind of to religion, you know, you accept the creed and you become family and friends with other members of your church and that's what happened in this. It was a philosophy that made sense; it was sensible for my kids and all kids and my court case

and all court cases. I bought into it first based on what I heard of that philosophy and the magnetism of [the group's leader] and then that's just been stoked. The more I learn, the more I experience [the more I agree; that energy's] just been stoked. ALVIN

Not all group members infused their organization's philosophy with the same religious overtones as Alvin, but the ones who articulated the importance of this belief system tended to do so in equally dramatic ways. Recall from chapter 6 that Ashton was the father of a nine-year-old girl. In reflecting on his own parenting experiences, he declared that his relationship with his daughter had actually improved over time because he actively worked at making her feel as comfortable as possible when they were together. But he also attributed this positive outcome to what he called his group's "white hat" philosophy.

When [members] start to get back involved with their children, that is when we start working on, okay, [their] attitude, [their] desires, [their] wants. How you perceive things to be is how you are going to perceive them. If you walk in there with your head down low and you are crying, [that is terrible]. The mommy is terrible for doing that to you. Guess what? It ain't going to be good for the children. They are going to hate their mommy; they are going to hate you. Why would you want to do that? You are going to walk in with your head held high. Be the guy with the white hat. That is one of our biggest things; be the guy with the white hat. ASHTON

For Ashton, the most important goal to communicate to all members is this "white hat" belief system. The central tenet behind this philosophy is to always act in accordance with what you perceive to be your child's best interests. This is difficult because, as Ashton pointed out, it requires significant restraint, especially if a father feels as if he has been wronged during the dissolution of his adult relationship. But for Ashton, the long term benefits of such a stance are worth the sacrifice because the children are then protected from the unnecessary harm that would come if they were exposed to interparental warfare. In addition to the "religious" and white-hat models, other group members articulated their organization's philosophy in much plainer terms as simply "group rules." These are child-centered, lifestyle-guiding principles which all members are encouraged to heed. For instance, Carlos, father of one daughter and two sons, maintained that his relationship with his three children remained quite strong, even after the divorce. He believed that he was able to actually enhance these relationships over time because he was well-educated and could present himself well in court. He also tried to live his life by the informal group rules that he helped develop and propagate.

> I say to parents that they have three jobs. They need to keep them separate in their own minds and they need to keep them in the right prioritized [order]....The first one is to be the best parent that they can be to their children within whatever constraints there are, and if that's supervised visitation, which sometimes is ordered completely unjustifiably because of false allegations or something, then, you know, don't go in there in any of your supervised visitations complaining to your child....If you're having problems with the enforcement of parenting time and stuff like that, don't bleed over onto your children about all of that. Just make sure that the time you spend with your children is the best time for them that it could be and so forth, and then we [can] talk about other things that you can do when you're not with your children. I mean, if the children are away, [use] mail and e-mail and the phone and all that stuff. The second task is to make your situation with your child, your legal situation with your child, as good as possible. That means working on your own case if you now don't have your kids very much, then working to get more time with your children and so forth. Then the third one is changing the system, so we try to talk a lot about that. So in going through these three tasks and trying to get people to separate these, I have certain exemplars of people who have violated these in mind. We've got a guy who's sort of been tangentially connected with the group. He's a member, but I wish he wouldn't be, [and] he has confused all of these. I mean, he is fighting his legal battle like a maniac, thrashing around at everything and anyone, threatening to sue anything and everyone and so forth. He's done it to the point where he'll be preparing his briefs when his daughter is actually with him, and he could be spending time with her, so, we talk about those sorts of things. CARLOS

One of Carlos's most significant fears, clearly articulated in the above quote, is that members sometimes become overly consumed with the legal fight for equal time with their children or with what in their minds would constitute a fair child support obligation. In doing so, they lose sight of what their most important goal should be: maximizing the quality of the relationship that they have with their children.

Although these fathers expressed their organizations' overarching philosophies in slightly different ways, they all had in common a unified belief in placing their relationship with their children at the forefront of their lives. How, then, are these critical philosophies actually carried out on a routine basis? One of the most significant day-to-day principles that these groups attempt to inculcate among their members is that any and all time they spend with their children is precious. As described in chapter 7, Gilbert was the father of two boys, ages three and six. At the time of his interview, Gilbert was struggling with the reality that after his divorce he saw his children much less frequently than he desired. This upset him greatly, because he missed experiencing their achievements and helping them recover from their disappointments, all of which constituted a normal part of supervising the growing up process. His own sense of loss, however, helped him warn other fathers who took the time that they had with their children for granted.

> Let's put it this way. When I see a father saying in conversations that he is always working or he is always going fishing with his buddies, I'll just pop in some questions like, did you bring your little boy with you or your little girl with you when you go fishing? No, [they say,] they are usually home with the new wife. I try to encourage them [by saying] well, what is wrong with (especially when the child is at a good age, five or six) that child of yours going fishing with you? That is quality time right there. That means more to that child than you can imagine. GILBERT

Like Gilbert, George, described above, expressed a similar concern over making sure that all fathers cherish the time they have with their children. When faced with the challenges related to his ex-partner's drug addiction, George found that the group helped him gather the psychological strength he required to be there for his child during this period of grave need.

> Well, [the group] helped me realize that any moment you get with your child is precious, [and] that you need to enjoy every bit of it, every second of it. The only thing about that is it makes you want more [time]. You hear other people's stories; you hear some guys talk about how they haven't seen their child in three and four years. You see grandparents and you watch them cry because they can't see their grandchildren. It makes you wonder.... But for those who are getting to see their kids and are still complaining about not getting to see them very much, they need to be thankful for what time they do have. There are some people out here that don't have any.   George

Vic also found that his group stressed the importance of simply spending time with his fourteen-year-old son. After his divorce, Vic remained highly active in his son's life by coaching both his soccer and football teams. He also established strong links with his child's school and always knew who his son's friends were. He maintained that part of the motivation behind his involvement was the organization's effort to show fathers that they should strive to be active parts of their children's lives, no matter what barriers they confront.

> [Our group stresses that all members should] always be involved in the lives of the children. One example comes to mind. [I had an employee of the] court come in and talk about [the fact that] during the summer months, you [can] take the child and have [him or her] go to one house one week [and the other house another week if the other parent agrees.]...I brought that in and I said, guys, you heard this, it's a good situation and it's a great start....If anything, being involved in my group has made me closer to my son.   Vic

For Vic, the most important task of groups like his is to make sure that fathers learn as many ways as possible to maximize the time they have with their children. As in this case, where Vic's group brought in a court employee to discuss opportunities for parents to spend time with their children during the summer months, fathers must be creative in expanding their availability to their sons and daughters after their families dissolve. They can no longer rely on mere convenience, which may have worked well in terms of making plans when all members of the family lived under one roof.

Maintaining this positive attitude about spending time with the children and actually implementing the religious, "white hat," or "group rules" philosophy is not always easy. For example, when Barry was living with his wife, one of the greatest joys he experienced was giving his young daughter a kiss goodnight. After he separated from his wife, he realized how much he missed this moment of interaction. He also came to see that raising his daughter in the most loving environment possible was his central mission in life and began an almost evangelical mission to make sure that other fathers viewed their parental role in the same way. In these efforts, Barry reported that initially, when fathers first come to the group for assistance, they are deeply embittered about the details of their own particular cases. Barry uses this opportunity to provide a counterweight to these intense feelings by stressing to all fathers that they must overcome the challenges that are to be expected when parenting in a dissolved family.

> We do try to encourage people to spend as much time as they can with their child. And usually [the father complains that the ex-partner is] not paying [him] for the time that [he has] them or, [he's] paying for it even if [his] children are with [him]....It throws me off, and I usually will counter with, "It doesn't matter. Spend as much time as you possibly can, because for one, you'll enjoy it, [and] for two, your children will need it." It should be the other way around. First they will need it and then you'll enjoy it, and in the end it will help you when it comes to the court.   BARRY

The lesson Barry took away from these experiences in the meetings is simple. Thoughts about money and proper remuneration for time spent with one's children should never become so strong as to interfere with a father's commitment to stay involved with his children.

Another challenge preventing fathers from implementing a child-oriented philosophy has to do with managing provocations from ex-partners. For example, like Barry, Samuel had a strong tie with his infant daughter; he cherished holding, feeding, and bathing her. In fact, as she grew into a toddler, he found that his bond with her only intensified. At the time of his interview, he had recently bought her a bicycle to ride in his neighborhood and was spending significant time with her outdoors, which she loved. Most important, he remarked that he is able to engage in all of these activities even though his relationship with his ex-wife can sometimes be tense. Even so, Samuel continued to emphasize at his monthly fathers' rights group meetings the importance of containing his reactions to his ex-partner's verbal sparring. As he explained,

> One question came out [at the meeting] last week. If your child comes to you and says, "Gee, mommy says daddy is no good," what is your response? The response was to tell your child [that] you love [him or her]. Don't answer a negative with a negative, and that was a very good emotional thing. So that [philosophy] comes out via the membership. You know, various levels of this [type of] experience [exist in the group]. Like, I am three years into it, another guy is six, another guy is ten [years into it]....Like a new guy coming in doesn't know anything, you know, [and] so he starts picking up things from more experienced people....So you do get things from guys who know more than you, and then you can sometimes pass something on to a guy who doesn't know maybe quite as much about this stuff as you do.   SAMUEL

Although refraining from negative interactions with one's ex-partner may be impossible all of the time, it is essential if members are to carry out the group's child-oriented philosophy practically and effectively on a regular basis. This means that the majority of time spent with children should be positive, educational, and love-filled.

This is not to say that every interaction should provide pure entertainment for the involved children. Many fathers in this study warned against the impulse of becoming "Disneyland Dads." This is a well-known phenomenon among single fathers, especially noncustodial fathers, whose time with their children is very limited. Because of their constraints, fathers feel overwhelming pressure to provide their children with a "good time," filled with constant fun when they do happen to interact. The hope is that this type of engagement will then entice children to want to spend more time with their fathers, perhaps even prompting them to request from the court a modification in visitation time. But fathers' rights activists warn that this strategy of winning children over through Disneyland techniques will backfire over the long run, and the scholarly research on the importance of fatherly involvement stresses authoritative parenting, not father-child "friendship," as the key to child well-being. Children need to know that when they go to their father's house, they will have responsibilities just like they do at their mother's house. Neither home should be a place where children can live without rules and restrictions, and both places should be residences where each parent wields respect.

As mentioned in chapters 5 and 6, Elliot was a father of four (a son and three daughters) and an active member of his local fathers' rights group. Elliot reported that he had learned the "Disneyland Dad" lesson the hard way. Initially, and much to his chagrin, Elliot quickly discovered that when his children came over to his house, they expected to be entertained. They did not want to be bothered with any of the chores that they normally would have had to assume when the family was intact. At first Elliot was tempted to give them exactly what they wanted; he desperately desired a positive relationship with them and did not want to cause any further acrimony after the divorce. However, he soon realized that by acquiescing to their demands, he was abdicating his role as a father.

[The group encourages us all to] enjoy your children when they [are with you], [but] don't be a Walt Disney dad or mom. Do have a good time with them, enjoy them when they are there. [The group lays] out a few things: here are some ways that you can bond with your kids, quick weekend activities, things that you can do that are inexpensive. [This is important] because a lot of times...when you are initially divorced, you don't have a lot of money because you end up paying for all the lawyers and stuff like that. You don't have a lot of funds available, so [you need to come up with alternative] things that you can do with restricted resources.... [But I know that being a Walt Disney dad can be very attractive.] So every time [they] come, it's like, let's go to Disney World! We are going to the movies! We are going to have fun! But dad is still dad and there is still a normal life there. So that means [that] when [the kids] come, there's going to be chores to do, there's going to be responsibilities, and expectations. [It is not going to be] you come and you just get to sit around.... [It is not going to be that] we are going to get up in the morning and we are going to go to the carnival, and then...we are going to eat out, and we are going to the movies. ELLIOT

Like other activists in fathers' rights groups, Elliot recognized that the time he had with his children was precious. He also acknowledged that it was easy to give in and grant their every wish when they came to his home for brief periods of time. However, he also was able to resist that temptation by drawing on the strength of his local fathers' rights group. Equally important to spending time with one's children, according to the child-centered philosophy of the groups, is that the time should involve the teaching of values and responsibility.

When the Group Does Not Help Parents Improve Their Relationships with Their Children

As we have seen, fathers' rights groups can be effective in helping parents improve their relationships with their children over time. For some fathers, however, as in the case of interparental relationships, the group does little or nothing to enhance parent-child bonds. Fathers in this category pointed to three primary reasons for the group's ineffectiveness in this area: a wider culture that devalues fatherhood, competing organizational priorities, and individual circumstances.

First, some fathers feel that the groups cannot help improve parent-child relationships because the culture in which these organizations operate is overwhelmingly "anti-father." In other words, the groups may try to help fathers enhance their relationships with their children, but they cannot do so for legal reasons and because fathers have a generally low status in society. Robert, father of two adult daughters, has been active in fathers' rights groups for many years, beginning when he was just a teenager when he decided to join out of sheer empathy with the cause. He separated from his wife when his daughters were two and six years old, and ironing out the details of his divorce took four years. After this dissolution period, one of his daughters was repeatedly molested and then raped by a male adolescent who was in the mother's house during the time when his daughter should have been with him according to the visitation schedule. Robert remarked that he felt powerless to protect his daughter and even more powerless as a father in contemporary culture.

> Well, the groups...can't change the laws or change the problems.... This is part of the perspective that impugns the legitimacy of fa- thers....Fathers are not permitted to [have] their own standards or show how to be a father [to their sons] or simply to be a father. This is why fatherhood has been so doomed.... Fathers are excluded, and then the young men don't know how to be a father because they were not permitted to have a father. And the young women don't know how to choose good men because their fathers were excluded, so they don't know what a good man is or what a good man does. And this contin- ues to the university level, where they have women's studies but they don't have men's studies or professors who teach men's studies get drummed out of the way. Robert

Robert's critique, then, was not merely of the groups themselves; it was of the more global context in which these groups operate that forces them to the margins of society. Indeed, Robert's comments demonstrate a common theme among fathers' rights advocates: society shortchanges men in a variety of arenas, whereas women reap the rewards of being more privileged members of the family.

Second, for other families, competing group priorities can prevent these organizations from assisting in improving adult-child relation- ships. In his own case, Pepe acknowledged his role and responsibility in weakening the bonds with his two daughters, ages nine and fourteen, when he separated from his wife. His relationship with his daughter in elementary school was still resilient, but his teenage daughter no lon- ger wanted to be with him, and perhaps for good reason. While she was away at camp, he moved in with his new girlfriend. His older daughter hated this new arrangement, prompting Pepe to look for ways to im- prove their dialogue on the issue, but to no avail. Nonetheless, despite these enormous difficulties, he still had a much better relationship with his daughters than most other fathers in his group.

> People tend to be in more desperate situations [in the group and do not focus on parent-child relationships]....It is more important that you figure out how to handle an order of protection at a given moment,

or an order for child support that you can't afford or that would put you in the poor house or make you homeless or something.   PEPE

Fathers facing these crisis situations come to depend on their groups to assist them in their time of need; the focus of these groups is therefore on helping fathers secure their rights to their children. In Pepe's view, improving relationships is a luxury topic that groups like his cannot currently afford to address.

A third reason why groups sometimes do not make a difference in improving parents' relationships with their children relates to individual circumstances. One of the most significant challenges in this regard pertains to the composition of the groups themselves. Many fathers who join these groups are in extremely difficult positions with respect to their children. They do not have regular access to them for a wide variety of reasons—including geographical distance, an allegation or the presence of domestic violence that enforces a separation, logistical difficulties in arranging regular contact, and so forth—so the idea that the group can expeditiously help improve their relationships with their children is simply irrelevant. As Jonathan, father of two young children with much less time and access to them than he desired stated, his group rarely involves itself in this volatile issue.

> [Improving relationships with children is] a touchy subject because most of the people [in the group] don't have that opportunity....It's a horrible loss that these children and these parents must feel when separated....Sometimes there are things going on but to me, it's a very superficial kind of a thing. Parenting is a profound relationship and can't really be done on the kind of time most people have with their kids....It's not a big emphasis in the group because most of the guys don't really have experience with having that much access; it's not an essential component of what the guys there are facing. They're facing trying to get access at all, not [wondering] what can I do with my kid.   JONATHAN

Mickey echoed Jonathan's concerns. For him, the group was not a place where deadbeat dads get together to discuss how to avoid paying child support, as the organizations are often portrayed in the media. Rather, it is a place where men congregate in order to find solace with similarly situated adults who cannot see their children. Indeed, Mickey considered himself to be one of the luckiest members in the group. He had a horrible relationship with his son and daughter after his divorce. He reported that his ex-wife had alienated his daughter from him, and his son, although engaged with him on a marginal level, constantly challenged him over chores he was expected to do while he was residing with him. Nevertheless, at least he was able to see his children. Although he might have liked the group to discuss issues related to improving these strained relationships, he also recognized that this was not a relevant concern to most members.

> Everyone that I know in the group right now is fighting with everything they have got to stay in their kids' lives. These aren't the... deadbeat dads coming to a fathers' group because they won't pay their child support. The guys in this group are just like me. They love their kids and their kids have been ripped out of their lives. These guys are hurting. It's not [about] having to coax a father back into their child's life. MICKEY

For Jonathan and Mickey, then, the law has created such a desperate situation for men that having any relationship at all with their children would be a positive step. Only then would these fathers be able to focus on actually improving their relationships in a group setting.

In a subset of these cases, groups cannot help improve parent-child relationships because the children themselves do not want to participate in such efforts. In one such family, Veronica, mother of three sons and one daughter, joined her local fathers' rights group because—in her assessment—her children were poisoned by her ex-husband to hate her. Because of this brainwashing, her group could not help her improve her relationships with her children at all.

> [First] I went to the group Tough Love—in the beginning when I was still in the house—because my kids were acting so badly. They had outings for parents and kids. Then I went to Parents Without Partners and they had outings for parents and kids. But [in our fathers' rights group we have] parents who haven't seen their kids; they have no right

to take them anywhere. I couldn't even take my kids on an outing....
I have to laugh....Some of my friends say, "Oh, you are coming over,
why don't you bring your son with you?" I laugh. They won't go anywhere with me; it is against their father's rules....They don't agree to
go anywhere. We go bowling maybe once a year; we go to the movies
maybe once a year. They understand clearly, whether it is spoken or
unspoken, that if they actually really go out and have fun with me
[that] they are crossing a line.   VERONICA

As Veronica's own words detail, there is little that her fathers' rights
group can do to assist her at the current time. Because of her own difficult personal situation, Veronica concentrates her efforts on advocacy
work in this area, where she believes she can make a more significant
difference in the lives of other families.

Re-envisioning Father-Child Ties

For the fathers discussed in this chapter, not all was lost with their
children after their families broke up. A significant number of fathers
reported that their relationships with their children quickly stabi-
lized after the family unit dissolved. And as the children grew older,
fathers adapted in their ways of relating and interacting with their offspring. In addition, a surprising number of fathers declared that their
relationships with their children were actually *better* after the family
broke-up. In these cases, fathers claimed that the stress surrounding
the divorce and breakup was so devastating that things could only get
better. Over time, these fathers adjusted to their new roles as parents
living on their own, and their children came to understand that simply
because their parents no longer resided in the same household did not
mean that their connections to each parent as individuals could not
continue to strengthen. Fathers in this category also reported that the
separation process and the possibility that they could lose access to
their children forever made them appreciate their children even more
than fathers in intact families.

In these more positive cases, fathers' rights groups clearly offered
much-appreciated and critical personal services in the area of improving

parent-child relationships. These services are different, and in the opinion of fathers' rights groups, more suited to the needs of their members, than the information presented in government-affiliated divorce education programs. Indeed, in contrast to their approach to child support and child custody policy, their antistate attitudes in the area of relationship-building have led them to develop viable, alternative services. More directly, these services reflect the academic research that stresses the importance of fathers remaining involved with their children after their family dissolves. By offering emotional support and empowerment, providing advice on child-rearing skills, planning age-appropriate activities, and encouraging a unique, child-centered philosophy by which to encourage men to live their lives, these organizations create an atmosphere whereby fathers can work to successfully rebuild their relationships with their children over time.

This is not to say that fathers' rights groups get it right all of the time with respect to service provision. For many of the fathers involved in this study, minimal or no contact with their children became the norm after their families broke down. Some blamed a culture that devalues fatherhood overall for this drop-off in contact. Others placed responsibility with the court system that prevented them from having ready access to their children through restrictive parenting time plans or orders of protection due to allegations of physical or sexual abuse. Finally, some cited alienation by their ex-partners as a reason for having no contact with their children; in these extreme circumstances, fathers reported being vilified by their ex-partners to the point where their children no longer expressed a desire to spend time with them. In all of these worst-case scenarios, their own fathers' rights groups seemed to offer them little in terms of assistance.

Elsewhere, Flood (2006) has suggested that fathers' rights groups themselves can do much more to help fathers mend their ties to their children. For fathers who believe that the culture devalues fatherhood, fathers' rights groups can encourage men to take a more active role in parenting while their families are intact; this will undoubtedly raise their currency in the postdissolution phase of their lives. For those fathers who become bogged down in the minutiae of their own legal fights for their "rights" to their children, fathers' rights groups should refocus their vision on the needs of their children. Life is complex; at times it may be extremely difficult to reconcile a father's desire to see his children on a rigid schedule and his children's need to grow up in a happy and stable home. In these circumstances, fathers' rights groups should encourage men to put their children's needs before their own immediate claims to ongoing access. Moreover, as this chapter has shown, fathers may need to give children the space that they need to recover emotionally from their family's breakdown. In these cases, fathers' rights groups would do well to emphasize the concept of care—broadly defined as placing their children's mental and physical well-being first—in moving families toward postdissolution healing.

Yet considered overall, and in contrast to their political goals, the personal goals of fathers' rights groups in the areas of improving interparental and parent-child relations have significant merit. Undoubtedly, the pain of a family unit breaking up is extraordinary, awakening deep and long-lasting feelings of loss. The key question is how parents choose to react to this devastation. Although significant sadness, depression, anger, and guilt may all be normal human responses, fathers' rights groups can promote the redirection of these volatile emotions toward recovery. This educational process may be very short or may take a significant period of time. In either case, with the coping techniques and skills that they learn through these organizations, fathers can take the first step toward making their new lives as single parents whole and fulfilling once again.

9

"Crooked Trees," Activism, and Healing in Dissolved Families

RESEARCHER: "Just so I have an understanding of your family situation...I always like to draw a family tree for all individuals participating in this study. Do you have custody of your son?"
DEVIN: "No, I do not....It's a crooked tree."

The fathers who are the subject of this book had complex stories to tell
about their family lives. Many were understandably angry that their adult
relationships had fallen apart. Many were also sad and depressed that
their wives or girlfriends had left them, or that they had felt, for whatever
reason, the need to be the one to leave. Of course, breakups when children are involved are rarely pleasant. As this book has illustrated, when
a family dissolves, accusations of physical and sexual abuse can occur.
Infidelity charges can rage. Drug and alcohol abuse can take its toll on
desperate parents. Mothers and fathers can call on friends and family
to take sides in their disputes, and police interventions over explosive
arguments can become grindingly habitual. Yet for many fathers, these
challenges only represent the beginning of the heartache and injustice to
come as they sort through their new familial roles.

Far worse than this initial emotional turmoil for these fathers was
what happened to them at the hands of the family law system. After

undergoing the gut-wrenching experience of an adult breakup, they now faced the prospect of paying child support until their children reached adulthood. These payments, they argued, were grossly unfair in the ways in which they were calculated and collected. In addition, fathers were often shocked to discover that they no longer had regular access to their children. Sole custody or joint physical custody were simply nonstarters in the courts as acceptable parenting arrangements. Instead, as they saw it, the court system forced them into the role of visitor to their own children. No longer were they able to kiss their children in the morning, send them off to school, eat dinner with them, and tuck them into bed at night. Instead, they had to squeeze their fatherly attention to their children into short periods of time, typically every other weekend between 6:00 p.m. on Fridays until their 7:00 p.m. Sunday drop-off at their ex-partner's house. Overall, what they viewed as oppressive child support and child custody policies forced them to conclude that they did not have a chance of recovering—financially or emotionally—unless the rules of the family-law game dramatically changed.

So what did they do when faced with these challenges? They organized, forming fathers' rights groups throughout the country. They gathered, usually in someone's home, a church, or some other informal setting, and planned comprehensive strategies to effect change. In observing these organizations and interviewing their members, what quickly became clear was that these groups served two fundamental functions: they were a focal point for political activism and a site for providing personal services for their members. The political activity of fathers' rights groups is much more well-known, as their demonstrations, lobbying efforts, and writings continue to garner widespread media attention. At the top of their agenda, of course, are child support and child custody reform. Although their particular policy recommendations vary by individual member and by group, the majority of fathers' rights groups would identify a utopian world as one in which no child support would be exchanged between parents and where both parents would share joint physical and legal custody of their children automatically in cases of familial dissolution. The personal service activities of fathers' rights groups, on the other hand, are less widely known. Through videos, lectures, speakers, and most predominantly informal advice, fathers' rights groups aim to guide fathers in improving their relationships with their ex-partners as well as their children as they embark on a new stage in their familial lives.

Despite this discrepancy in public awareness of the two faces of the fathers' rights agenda, what *was* uniform across both areas of activity was a strong antistate sentiment. In the political arena, these activists argued—quite correctly, if we consider simply the recent waves in family-oriented legislation—that the government was intruding into their lives as never before both in child support and child custody policy. Some members perceived government action in the area of family law as corrupt and abusive, and others maintained that it was completely unnecessary. Still others complained that government officials overly identified with women as a collective interest group. This antistate critique of public policy also permeated the construction of the personal services that fathers' rights groups offered. These activists have rejected the court-affiliated divorce education programs that have been sprouting up all across the United States in recent years as illegitimate vehicles for resolving their interpersonal issues with their ex-partners and children. As fathers and as men, they maintain that they have unique concerns when their families dissolve, and they have looked toward their own groups for self-help in fulfilling these particular needs.

Although this antistatism was noted throughout the book, a functional explanation for this pervasive belief system has not yet been offered. One way to understand the prevalence of this philosophy is to place it within the context of broader political trends contemporaneously occurring in the United States beginning in the 1980s. More specifically, this antistatist sentiment is consistent with the emergence of neoconservatism in recent American politics (O'Connor, Orloff, and Shaver 1999).[1] At its core, neoconservatism supports freedom as its highest value, a principle understood in its purest form as the right of individuals to interact with each other without interference from the state. Particularly in the post-Reagan era, proponents of the neoconservative view have focused their efforts on restraining the impact of government growth in all areas of everyday life. More specifically, neoconservatives aim to

1. Neoliberalism is the term commonly used to describe this type of politics throughout the world; however, in the United States, the term neoconservatism is more typical and is thus used here.

both (re)establish the role of the market in areas of life where previously the state had dominated and protect the capacity of individuals to carve out niches of privacy in their personal lives (Orloff and Monson 2002). In pursuing this vision, neoconservatives advocate a reduction in the role of the welfare state, promote deregulation and privatization wherever possible, and reassert the importance of individuals in solving their own family problems (Connell 2005b). In terms of partisan affiliations, most neoconservatives self-identify as conservative Republicans or Libertarians.

For women, this "turning away" from government has particular importance because the state has been the primary vehicle supporting their basic citizenship, social, and economic equality throughout the past century. From the passage of the Nineteenth Amendment, which gave women the right to vote, and especially beginning with the activism of the 1960s, feminists have consistently pressed all branches of government to guarantee them equality with men. In 1971, for example, the Supreme Court struck down the differential treatment of men and women for the first time in *Reed v. Reed*, which had challenged an Idaho law that required probate courts to appoint the father over the mother as executor of a deceased child's estate.[2] In this ruling, the court rejected the notion that the Idaho legislation had a rational relationship to an important government objective. In 1976 the Supreme Court took equality a step further beyond *Reed*. In *Craig v. Boren*, the court examined whether an Oklahoma law permitting vendors to sell low-alcohol beer to women between the ages of 18 and 21 but not to men was constitutional.[3] In its decision, the court determined that the states could categorize individuals by sex only under the condition that the classification held a substantial relationship to an important government objective. This was a less stringent test than used in cases of race-based classifications, but more stringent than the rational test laid out by *Reed*. This new, intermediate standard contained in *Craig* made labor laws that discriminated against women in the areas of pay and work hours certainly unconstitutional. Differences in the ways in which married women were treated—often as subordinates to their

2. *Reed v. Reed*, 404 U.S. 71 (1971).
3. *Craig v. Boren*, 429 U.S. 190 (1976).

husbands—as well as disparities in pension and Social Security benefits, also became presumably unconstitutional. So were differences in criminal sentencing. In the area of reproductive rights, in 1973 the Supreme Court handed down *Roe v. Wade*, which protected a woman's right to an abortion under a fairly liberal framework.[4] With successes in the judicial arena, women looked to their elected representatives as well to further the march of progress. Congress quickly came on board with increasingly strong legislative statements against discrimination, passing such laws as Title IX of the Education Amendments of 1972 (which prohibited discrimination in education programs receiving federal funding), the Women's Educational Equity Act of 1974 (which provided grants to programs offering educational opportunities to women), and the Pregnancy Discrimination Act of 1978 (which banned employment discrimination based on pregnancy status). Affirmative action policies for women, especially in government agencies or in contracting firms working for the government, also became commonplace. In sum, the Supreme Court, Congress, and federal agencies all began to challenge laws that were overtly discriminatory and to usher in a new era of autonomy for women in the process.

The neoconservative view of the minimal role for the state is, therefore, unsettling to many women who have viewed the government as an agent of progress. In the area of family policy, these fears are not misplaced. Although not necessarily a problem in terms of personal service provision to help improve intrafamilial relationships, neoconservatism with respect to child support and child custody policy, as we have seen, does pose a threat to women's and children's overall well-being. The question then becomes, How closely allied are neoconservatives with fathers' rights activists? The conventional wisdom is that they are one and the same, populated by the same personalities who have similar world views on a variety of issues affecting public and private life. In fact, progressive women's groups frequently label fathers' rights groups as part of the "reactionary right," a movement that wants nothing more than to return to a time in American history when women were treated as second class citizens. The reality, of course, is much more complex.

---

4. *Roe v. Wade*, 410 U.S. 113 (1973).

As chapter 3 of this book demonstrated, leaders and members of fathers' rights groups come from all political persuasions, including Republicans, Democrats, and Independents. They also take affirmative positions on a range of other contentious policy issues, including many that are regarded as extremely liberal, such as pro-animal rights initiatives, antiwar platforms, and environmental protection measures.

Much more likely, then, is that fathers' rights groups are using antistatism not as a statement of pure alliance with neoconservatism but rather as an opportunistic type of political strategy. More pointedly, fathers' rights activists describe their opposition to current child support and child custody laws in ways that imply that Americans have *always* resisted the influence of the state in their lives at the expense of individual freedom. In other words, they argue that antistatism is a persistent value in American culture that needs to be protected across time and space. In contrast, Quadagno and Street (2005) have insightfully described the ideology of antistatism as a relatively *inconsistent* theme in American politics. Indeed, as evidence they note that the supposedly timeless ethos of rugged individualism was not so strong as to prevent the implementation of a universal public education system by the end of the nineteenth century, Social Security for aging and disabled workers in 1935, or health insurance for senior citizens in the form of Medicare in 1965. Instead, Quadagno and Street assert that powerful interest groups use antistatist rhetoric at advantageous points in time—when the country is turning right ideologically or is otherwise more receptive to conservative partisan appeals—to promote their own political agendas. During the 1930s, for example, southern Democrats successfully used antistatist rhetoric to argue against the inclusion of mostly black agricultural and domestic workers in programs like unemployment insurance and allow local welfare agencies dominated by whites the authority to administer their own means-tested programs for the poor, primarily Aid to Dependent Children and Old Age Assistance. These racist policies—which ended up distributing very little public assistance—were intended to keep black Americans from experiencing upward economic mobility and the benefits of full citizenship. More recently, the Health Insurance Association of America, the American Hospital Association, and the National Federation of Independent Businesses all successfully used antistatist rhetoric to prevent President

Clinton from persuading Congress to pass the Health Security Act in 1993, a revolutionary reform that would have guaranteed health care coverage for all (Skocpol 2003). These groups maintained that their economic interests were going to be threatened by this comprehensive initiative, and they mounted a deliberately aggressive campaign to warn the public against the possibility of "Big Government" controlling their own personal health care decisions.

The use of antistate rhetoric by fathers' rights groups, therefore, does not signify that their members are closely allied with neoconservative activism—although clearly some of them are—nor are these types of claims indicative of an immutable political philosophy held by most Americans in a reflexive way. Instead, fathers' rights groups are taking advantage of an important moment in political time to strategically align their arguments with the belief systems of a significant share of American voters. In fact, if the political winds were to shift among the public at large, it is likely that the nature of fathers' rights appeals would change as well.

Fathers' Rights Groups: What Now?

This book has focused on the beliefs, practices, and attitudes of fathers' rights group leaders and members in the United States at a critical point in their organizational history: their emergence onto the policy scene. But what, if anything, have they actually *accomplished?* The simple truth is that although fathers' rights groups have succeeded in becoming important venues where the views of their membership can be shared, channeled, and packaged, they have yet to achieve major legislative gains in line with their preferred policy positions. In fact, and contrary to the efforts of fathers' rights groups, throughout the past thirty years Congress and the states have increasingly toughened the enforcement of the child support collection regime through stiffer penalties, such as the seizing of assets and threats of imprisonment. Moreover, although child custody laws in the states have advanced in the direction of promoting more shared parenting, it is difficult to pinpoint the exact role of fathers' rights groups in effecting this shift. In addition, and as noted earlier, most of these changes have had to do with the creation of joint legal custody provisions rather than joint physical custody laws, a movement that in many ways represents only a symbolic victory for these groups as they attempt to shift the public consciousness on parenting matters.

Simply because these groups have yet to make a strong policy difference in terms of results, however, does not mean that they are unimportant. In fact, it can be argued that a necessary precursor to shaping public attitudes and then the law is by first establishing oneself as a formidable policy entrepreneur. In this case, I extend the term "policy entrepreneur" beyond the scope of consideration in chapter 4 solely of leaders with a strong motivation for change to both leaders and members bonding together on behalf of a common cause. To understand and predict the future success of policy entrepreneurs considered in this broader fashion, I have argued in previous work that it is important to answer three critical questions (Crowley 2003): *Who* are these policy entrepreneurs? *Why* do they attempt to innovate in the field of public policy? And exactly *how* do they innovate?

In terms of the "who" question, political scientists have focused on three characteristics that determine whether someone ultimately will be victorious in influencing public policy: alertness, the capacity to engage in rhetorical ingenuity, and persistence. As described in chapter 4, these factors are of particular importance to group leaders. Kingdon (1984) highlighted the importance of alertness when he argued that policy problems and potential solutions are constantly floating around in the policy "ether." Policy entrepreneurs are those individuals who are alert enough to capitalize on a window of opportunity to match a problem with their preferred policy solution. Second, talented policy entrepreneurs must have considerable rhetorical skills to frame their issues in ways that maximize their appeal to the public at large. They must be able to effectively take the pulse of the citizenry and present their arguments in ways that tap into popularly held sentiments concerning the future direction of public policy. Finally, persistence also matters. Entrepreneurs who are committed to a cause cannot decide to quit working on behalf of their issue simply because they initially fail to promote change. Instead, they must be prepared to log long hours, days, years, and even decades in their fight to win over their opponents.

Answering the "why" concerning entrepreneurship is also important, and for this question, we can consider the motivations of both group leaders and members who wish to effect change. Entrepreneurs attempt to mold public policy in ways that directly benefit themselves or others for whom they claim to speak. In other words, they aim to redirect public resources away from past uses and toward their preferred policy outcomes. These resources may be material in nature, for instance when groups try to encourage the government to transfer wealth from one part of the citizenry to another or reduce their tax burden relative to other, less-powerful populations, and so on. Or these resources may be psychological in nature, for instance when entrepreneurs try to establish themselves as notable leaders, skilled spokespeople, or credible decision-makers when engaging in critical policy debates. In either case, what they are seeking is the same: a solid advantage in the marketplace of scarce goods.

Exactly "how" they go about instituting a policy revolution is a bit more complicated. More so than the "who" and even the "why" of entrepreneurship, this answer necessarily involves the activities of the entire membership of a group rather than primarily the leadership. Two factors related to planning are crucial in this process of promoting change: (1) devising strategies to overcome the competition and (2) properly managing risk. First, successful entrepreneurs must effectively "shakeout" their competition. This term, borrowed from the field of economics, involves the tactics entrepreneurs use in their attempt to dislodge the current groups holding power over the particular issue domain under contestation. To be effective, policy entrepreneurs must pursue strategies that are perceived as legitimate by the public, such as lobbying and media campaigns, rather than illegitimate strategies, such as force, coercion, illegal activities, and undemocratic tactics. Second, any group aiming to redefine public policy must face risk in doing so, with risk having two core components: the startup costs involved in organizing their political movement and the uncertainty that is necessarily present as they mobilize potential followers. To successfully reduce risk, smart entrepreneurs are those who come together to create wide-scale, durable, and flexible organizations—through techniques called cooperative strategies—to sustain pressure on policymakers over the long run rather than rely on one sole ringleader's engaging personality—also known as an individualized strategy—to push their ideas forward. After all, one individual can easily rise and fall in the eyes of the public with only one misstep. Policy entrepreneurs who use both legitimate and cooperative strategies will thus be in the best position to produce the politics of innovation in their favor.

So how well do fathers' rights groups meet these requirements for effective policy entrepreneurship? Throughout their history, their leaders appear to be alert, increasingly skilled at using rhetorical ingenuity to positively frame public debates about issues that are of grave concern to them, and persistent in their mission (the "who" of entrepreneurship). Their leaders and members have also articulated a particular set of policy goals that they wish to achieve to redirect public resources in their favor (the "why" of entrepreneurship). The problem for these groups, however, lies in the execution of their vision, or the "how" of entrepreneurship. Although they are quite adept at using legitimate means to shake out their competition, these groups still struggle to establish self-sustaining organizations composed of vigorously energized members who are committed to their movement's goals over the long run.

Two recent examples of potentially important political mobilization moments for fathers' rights groups demonstrate this struggle in graphic relief: the plight of the young Cuban boy, Elian Gonzalez, during the years 1999–2000, and the confirmation of Samuel Alito to the Supreme Court in 2005–2006. Elian Gonzalez, six-years-old at the time of his ordeal, was rescued off the coast of Florida on November 25, 1999, while fleeing Cuba with his mother and eleven others. He survived along with two of his fellow travelers, but sadly his mother perished during the journey. Almost instantaneously, his rescue set off a heated debate in the United States as to whether he should live in Miami with his distant relatives or be reunited with his father back in Cuba. Fathers' rights groups weighed in on this important issue, but did not do so with the overwhelming force that might have been expected from groups composed of thousands of members across the country. Instead, the response was much more individualized—with a few pundits raising their concerns in various government and media outlets—rather than cooperative in nature or engaging the mass membership of these organizations to lobby for comprehensive change. For example, activist Robert Hirschfeld of the National Congress of Fathers and Children filed an amicus brief with the Supreme Court in favor of returning the boy to Cuba and his father; Fatherhood Coalition spokesperson Mark Charalambous called the case an important time to raise public consciousness about fathers' rights; and leader Ned Holstein of Fathers and Families cynically asked how an ordinary father "whose wife or ex-wife kidnaps the kids to Arizona" would have any chance of success if Gonzalez could not be reunited with his father with the help of the Justice Department (Hirschfeld 1999; Weber 2000). Yet although these spokespeople provided their groups with a modicum of publicity, after the crisis ended with Gonzalez's return to Cuba, the momentum for further action quickly dissipated. The rank-and-file membership of fathers' rights groups across the United States was not galvanized nor energized enough to move its comprehensive public policy agenda forward.

The fragility of their organizational framework overall was once again on display with the confirmation proceedings for Samuel Alito to the Supreme Court in 2005–2006. The passionate debate involved Alito's involvement in the case *Planned Parenthood of Southeastern Pennsylvania v. Casey (1992)*. As part of its continued fight on behalf of reproductive rights in the United States, Planned Parenthood filed suit against the state of Pennsylvania for requiring women to inform their husbands of their intention to seek an abortion.[5] Alito sided with the state in this case while he was on the U.S. Court of Appeals for the Third Circuit, arguing that the legislature "could have rationally believed that some married women are initially inclined to obtain an abortion without their husbands' knowledge because of perceived problems—such as economic constraints, future plans or the husbands' previously expressed opposition—that may be obviated by discussion prior to the abortion." Although women's groups collectively decried this reasoning as a threat to female privacy rights, fathers' rights activists, in contrast, were much less unified and once again much more individualized rather than cooperative in vocalizing their support for Alito. These scattered voices of support for Alito included that of radio personality and fathers' rights sympathizer Glenn Sacks, who argued that men should have rights in these cases because they will be held responsible for child support for

5. *Planned Parenthood of Southeastern Pennsylvania v. Casey*, 505 U.S. 832 (1992).

the next eighteen years—whether they wanted the child or not—and Jeffery M. Leving, outspoken fathers' rights attorney, who noted that the outrage over Alito's opinion shows how few rights men have over their reproductive futures (Leving 2005; Sacks 2005). But what emerged were the voices only of leaders and notable sympathizers with the movement, not the energy of the rank-and-file membership. No cohesive, grassroots energy was available to push the goals of fathers' rights groups even marginally toward realization.

Fathers' Rights Groups: What's Next?

What, then, lies ahead for fathers' rights groups in the United States? Why is their rank-and-file so ineffective at political action? Are they forever to remain in the role of outside agitators rather than insider political activists? The answers to these questions are dependent on a variety of factors, but at the very least pivot on these groups' ability and willingness to engage in three critical activities: (1) self-examination regarding whom they claim to represent, (2) a lasting, committed decision regarding how they handle extremism within their membership, and (3) a proactive engagement with reforming their own goals.

One of the most important determinants of the future of fathers' rights groups in the United States is their capacity to embark on a critical journey of self-examination. Undoubtedly, the majority of respondents interviewed in this study were strongly dedicated to their children as well as very upset with the current state of family law, which in their minds unjustifiably restricts their access to their offspring while requiring that they make unfair child support payments. However, membership in fathers' rights groups is still very small, and leaders expressed frustration at their inability to recruit new members and to retain over the long run members who ultimately did decide to join. This problem of numbers raises the question of how well fathers' rights groups actually represent most fathers experiencing the family dissolution process in America today.

In *Redefining Fatherhood*, Dowd (2000) argues that although most men in the United States become biological fathers by their mid-thirties, there are strong differences among them in terms of their capacity to engage in *social fathering*. Social fathering involves all those tasks, emotions, and behaviors that men perform with and for their children to help them grow into responsible, loving adults. For Dowd, men fall into five categories with respect to social fathering. At one extreme, nurturing fathers are those who parent in extremely attentive ways. They are similar to mothers in the levels of physical and emotional care that they provide for their children. Second are nurturing fathers in step-families, blended families, or cohabiting with their partners. The key difference between these men and those in the first category is that a biological or adoptive tie to their children may not be present. However, these men behave in a similarly responsible way as nurturing fathers, offering an abundance of love and support for the children who are a fundamental part of their daily lives.

The final three categories of fathers, according to Dowd, embody much less positive parenting styles; the contemporary notion of the "good father," in other words, has not caught up with these men. More specifically, the third type are minimally engaged fathers, who may live with their adult partners but participate much less in the nurturing activities of parenting than their children's mothers. They see the goal of breadwinning as the most fundamental role that they can play in their families and defer to their partners in taking care of their children's other physical, emotional, and cognitive needs. In fact, if they separate from their partners and they no longer reside with their children, these fathers have a difficult time continuing any type of relationship with their offspring. This effect may be even more pronounced if they are struggling to provide them with financial support from geographically distant locations. Fourth are disengaged fathers, who play little to no role in nurturing their children and, by definition, live apart from, although still may financially support, their offspring. The marginal contact that they initially do have usually dissipates within two years after the family dissolves. The fifth and final category of fathers has no relationship with their children whatsoever. They may not know that their children exist, or they may have agreed to put them up for adoption. More commonly, these fathers simply reject any nurturing or economic role in their children's lives.

Part of the challenge for fathers' rights groups, and their problem of recruiting a growing, resilient, and easily mobilized membership over time, is determining where most men place themselves along Dowd's continuum. Are they more likely to be strong nurturers, or are they more likely to be disengaged, especially after their family dissolves? This book has documented the inner passion and drive of many committed leaders and members but also has portrayed many fatigued ones as well. It described numerous fathers who find their organizations to be very rewarding, but also many who, although they still call themselves members, derived very little benefit from their own groups at the time of this study. A central question for fathers' rights groups, therefore, is whether a critical mass of fathers overall care enough about the issues that fathers' rights groups are fighting for. If the answer is no, or even not enough, then fathers' rights groups might have to take a step back from any type of political activism to work on more fundamental, grassroots efforts to change the hearts and minds of those millions for whom they claim to be speaking. Undoubtedly this is a very difficult but fundamentally necessary task crucial to the success of these groups over the long run.

Beyond self-examination, fathers' rights groups also need to decide how they want to handle extremism in the forms of antifeminism and even overt negativity toward women that are currently infecting their organizations. Throughout this book, the interview and observational data demonstrated that a certain contingent of fathers' rights activists hold disturbing personal views both about the role of women in their lives and about women in society more generally. These views tend to be expressed in essentialist ways; that is, some father's rights activists argue that women have certain innate characteristics that make them behave in a detrimental fashion toward men. These members see women as single-minded gold diggers, or alternatively as overly emotional, crazy, slutty, frigid, lying, and manipulative creatures. Typical of this extremism is the Father's Manifesto, a web-based petition that activists circulated in the late 1990's and is still present on the Internet today. Signed by several prominent fathers' rights leaders, the Father's Manifesto argues for the repeal of the Nineteenth Amendment, which guarantees women's right to vote. In addition to this outrageous demand, the manifesto blames the women's movement for multiple social ills, including rising divorce levels, rampant crime, and widespread drug use, and calls for the restoration of patriarchal principles to govern contemporary society. Of course, these types of hostile proclamations about women—even those advocated by fringe components of these groups—should instantaneously ring serious alarms among those interested in pursuing a fully egalitarian society.

Disturbingly, however, these pernicious attitudes are often also accompanied by dangerous actions against women as a group. For instance, although not the central mission of fathers' rights groups, a variety of them spend a significant amount of energy and resources attempting to refute the claim that women are disproportionately affected by the problem of domestic violence. This position is just flat-out wrong. According to the U.S. Department of Justice, from 1998 to 2002, approximately 1.7 million violent crimes were committed between spouses and 2 million violent crimes were committed between boyfriends and girlfriends; of those committed between spouses, 84.3 percent of the victims were women, and of those committed between boyfriends and girlfriends, 85.9 percent of the victims were women (U.S. Department of Justice [DOJ] 2005). Even more tragically, in 2002 there were 787 spousal murders and 668 boyfriend/girlfriend related murders; 81 percent of the spousal victims were women and 71 percent of the boyfriend/girlfriend victims were women (DOJ 2005).

Despite these statistics, fathers' rights groups vehemently oppose the Violence Against Women Act (VAWA), originally passed in 1994, which, as described in chapter 6, provides women with specifically designed services to help them heal from domestic and dating violence, sexual assault, rape, incest, and stalking. When VAWA was up for reauthorization in 2000 and again in 2005, an active debate took place among fathers' rights group members as to how hard they should fight to ensure that men received equal funding with women as victims of domestic violence. This "battle" for equal protection is hard to understand except as a way to remove the protections that women have gained—and so desperately needed—against violence and threats of violence by their ex-partners. In addition, as described in chapter 3, fathers' rights groups also reported that they participate in "court watcher" programs, whereby one or more of the group's members will attend a judicial proceeding and sit in the public area of the courtroom to ensure that the presiding judge conducts business in a way that is fair to fathers. Members claim that these initiatives are designed to offer fathers emotional support when they need to go to court to present their case before a judge. However, this type of group activity can be extremely intimidating to women, especially those who have been victims of domestic violence. It is difficult enough for a woman to sit through a hearing with an abuser close by. It is even more psychologically damaging when she has to do so under the watchful eyes of other men who purport to be allied with her abuser. A final concern related to domestic violence is that some fathers' rights groups have secured federal funding to operate the child access centers described in chapter 8. If these groups continue to marginalize the domestic violence problem, women might be both afraid and unwilling to use these centers to transfer their children to their former partners, and all parties will end up losing.

These types of beliefs, attitudes, and activities, although not espoused by all members, are nonetheless loudly championed by a certain contingent of those involved with fathers' rights organizations. Indeed, because of their extremism, these zealots can seize an extraordinary amount of press coverage at the expense of their more moderate counterparts as they pursue their version of a just society. Making matters worse, the largest and most mainstream fathers' rights groups do not seem to denounce these strategies, a quiescence that can seem disturbingly like acquiescence. The organizational recommendation in this book, therefore, is clear. For fathers' rights groups to move forward into the realm of potent political visibility, they must overtly condemn extremists and ostracize those who perpetuate sexist and damaging practices. If they do not, then they will have bound themselves to a future of well-earned political marginalization.

Third, as fathers' rights groups refocus their vision on their future, they must engage in active reform of their goals. In the area of politics, as this book has demonstrated, fathers' rights groups are demanding equality with women in terms of economic support for their children and parenting time. Taken to the extreme, fathers' rights groups want children to live with each parent for approximately half the year, an arrangement that would ultimately lead to (and justify, in their minds) the complete abolition of all child support payments. These positions reflect a belief that the women's movement beginning in the 1960s has been 100 percent successful in achieving equality for the sexes in the economic and family spheres. In fact, as their words have documented, many fathers' rights group members contend that the women's movement has gone too far, with women now holding an advantage in both of these realms.

Of course, nothing could be farther from the truth. Women continue to earn less than men, are occupationally segregated into low-paying jobs, do most of the caretaking of children that are produced in their relationships, and suffer dramatic financial and emotional losses when they are forced by a dissolution into the role of heading their own families. So where does this misperception of current "equality" come from? Two reasons are most paramount, one pertaining to the decline of women's political mobilization on these issues and the other pertaining to the power of the concept of equality of opportunity over equality of outcomes in American society.

During the 1980s, as chapter 5 clearly documented, women's groups such as the National Organization for Women (NOW) and grassroots organizations such as For Our Children and Us, Incorporated, the Association for Children for Enforcement of Support (ACES), the Organization for the Enforcement of Child Support (OECS), and For Our Children's Unpaid Support (FOCUS), were on the forefront of advocacy when it came to economic equality issues, especially for single mothers. When Congress ultimately strengthened child support enforcement laws in 1984 and again in 1988, most of these grassroots groups disappeared (except ACES), and NOW moved on to other issues. This left a political vacuum that fathers' rights groups quickly occupied, notably without stirring a round of countermobilization by women.

In addition to the folding and redirection of advocacy groups that put single mothers' interests at the core of their concerns, significant public tension arose around whether America should be a country that promotes equality of opportunity or equality of outcomes. Simply put, those who espouse equality of opportunity principles are those who believe that men and women should be treated equally in every permissible area of their lives. This means that in family law courts should be gender-blind in making child support and custody decisions; 50–50 should be the guiding rule. Those who espouse equality of outcomes, on the other hand, argue that men and women—for a variety of reasons—are differentially situated in terms of their economic and social standing and that women need to be compensated for their relative disadvantage.

Fineman (1991) has argued that historically—and to their ultimate disservice—women's organizations as well as feminists more broadly have tended to promulgate the equality of opportunity rule over the equality of outcomes ideal for a variety of reasons. First, if women demanded preferential treatment as embodied by the equality of outcomes principle upon divorce or dissolution, this stance would presumably work against their claim for complete egalitarianism within the family while it was intact. Second, such differential treatment upon familial dissolution might spread to other areas of women's lives—especially the labor market. If women are believed to need special treatment within the family, this line of reasoning suggests, they might need special protection from riskier, higher paying, male-dominated jobs. Third, the principle of equality of outcomes could reinforce the notion that "biology is destiny" and that all women want custody of their children more so than men, which could unwittingly serve to further hamper women from making progress in the public world. Fourth and finally, if they were to affirm equality of outcomes, women's groups and feminists alike could propagate the false impression that because equality does not exist right now (thus necessitating the implementation of corrective policies), it might never be possible. Supporting the equality of opportunity principle, on the other hand, carries none of these intrinsic risks of misperception.

Fathers' rights groups, then, in many ways, have simply echoed the traditional mantra of mainstream women's organizations when they request "equality"; they are asking for equality of opportunity just as women's groups have done. In other words, fathers' rights organizations have framed their demands as simply extending this concept of equality of opportunity into the realm of family law, especially in cases of relationship dissolution. Indeed, the belief in equality of opportunity is so deeply ingrained in American culture today that it is becoming increasingly difficult for any political leader to argue with the claim that fathers should be treated "the same as" mothers. But the truth is that mothers remain at a severe disadvantage in their economic and child-rearing lives, and these inequalities will only be exacerbated if child support and child custody laws are modified in the manner in which fathers' rights advocates insist. Indeed, if fathers' rights groups get their way in these policy realms, mothers would experience greater financial insecurity, poverty, and potentially violence from their ex-partners, as well as much weaker relationships with their children over time.

Ironically, therefore, fathers' rights groups must first work for certain preconditions that promote equality of outcomes for women in order to advance their own political agenda. Two areas need their fundamental attention: the economic sphere and the child care sphere. Economically, they should join forces with national women's groups to improve the economic fortunes of women so that equal pay for equal work is the norm. They should also ally themselves with women's groups that focus on occupational desegregation so that women have the same opportunities to achieve high salaries in lucrative fields as their male colleagues. As a start, they need to support programs in public schools that aim to attract young girls into science and mathematics. Mentoring programs should also be created to encourage young women who demonstrate an interest and talent to pursue these areas in colleges and universities. But this is not all: Boys need to be encouraged to take up traditionally female careers so that parity can be achieved across all occupations, not just currently male-dominated ones.

In the child care sphere, fathers' rights groups must encourage men to become fully equal caretakers of their children, both when their relationships with their partners are solid and when they are less stable. How can they effect this type of change? They can lobby employers to provide more flexible schedules, which would allow men to share jobs, work from home, and more generally be available to their children, as needed. They can also pressure employers to provide more than three months of unpaid family leave, which is current public policy. Critically, though, they also need to take this leave once it is offered. Researchers have noted that fathers on average take less than one week off when they have a new child (Nepomnyaschy and Waldfogel 2007). Clearly, fathers should do much more child care sharing with mothers in the early stages of their babies' lives, which would then serve as the foundation for equal caregiving down the road. Overall, then, only when these preconditions are met can the claims of fathers' rights groups for reform in the areas of child support and child custody be seriously considered for possible action.

Of course, these are only several of the many long-term solutions *fathers* can take to close the current equality gap between men and women in family life. But what about the interim? How can *policymakers* most expeditiously make family life more fair for all involved participants, such that if a family breaks down, neither mother, nor father, nor child unnecessarily suffers? In other words, how can the equality of outcomes principle best be achieved in the near future? Given a proper commitment to equality, policymakers could make two immediate changes that would create an environment where men and women would be held harmless for the economic and child care decisions they make while their family unit is intact.

First, achieving equality of outcomes would focus on the financial risks and rewards each partner takes as a parent. If one parent, typically the mother, takes on more of the domestic responsibilities in the home rather than in the marketplace, she should be compensated for that decision if her marital partnership ends (Carbone 1994; Okin 1989). More precisely, the way society thinks about the income earned by a family unit needs to be reconsidered. Currently, each individual earns his or her own income while a member of the family, and by law these earnings are considered separate and distinct. An improved system—a post-divorce income-sharing system—would treat all earnings made while a couple is married as common income. If the partners then decide to separate, their earnings would continue to be pooled and divided to preserve everyone's standard of living equally for a designated period of time. This arrangement would protect the quality of life of both halves of the couple, and thus make explicit both their employment and child care contributions before they were separated.

Second, achieving the equality of outcomes principle would mean taking concrete steps to reward caregiving involving children. This would mean that states would enact primary caregiver rules to supersede the best interest of the child standard for custody, which would serve to place the child with the parent who engaged in the most critical child care activities while the family was intact. This rule is gender-neutral in that it does not specify whether the child should live with the mother or father. However, it does create an incredibly powerful incentive structure for each parent to pull his or her own weight in child care activities. If each parent is to be judged in a custody trial in terms of the level of child care provided in the unfortunate event that a family dissolves, fathers may start doing more of their share.

In contrast to their political goals, which require fundamental transformation, in the personal service realm fathers' rights groups are already providing valuable benefits to their members. Through videos, speakers, reading materials, and plain-old informal advice, these organizations encourage their members to work through their differences with their ex-partners in order to minimize conflict. More specifically, they offer members legal information so that they can understand their rights as their court proceedings unfold, and they also instruct their members in the art of communication so as to avoid contentious hot spots regarding potential disputes. In addition, these groups give assistance to fathers wishing to reconnect and strengthen the ties with their children, bonds that may have been sadly frayed during the family dissolution process. As a result of these services, which in contrast to their public policy goals *are* reflective of best practices as suggested by the academic literature on family dynamics, fathers report a much greater capacity to piece their interpersonal lives together once again so as to best experience fulfilling, interpersonal relationships in the future.

However, as fathers' rights group members in this book noted themselves, the provision of these personal services is not perfect. For these services to have maximum positive impact, certain preconditions must be attained across the board. In terms of helping men deal with their ex-partners more effectively, fathers' rights groups need to promote a pro-parental partnership rather than a victimhood agenda. In addition, these groups also need to do everything in their power to decrease the levels of hostility that some men continue to harbor toward the women who used to play a fundamental role in their daily lives. With respect to improving their relationships with their children, fathers' rights groups need to stake out a clear position that men need to be involved in the caretaking of their children while their families are together, not simply when they dissolve. Groups should also promote flexibility in access to children rather than focus only on rights-based claims to them, and allow children the time and space that they need to recover from the initial shock of the family breakup. In some cases, this will mean putting their children's interests and needs before their own immediate claims for ongoing access.

Once these preconditions are met, personal service provision could be further improved in two areas: consistency and professionalization.

Although all fathers' rights groups analyzed in this study offered personal services, a few only did so sporadically. Members attributed this unevenness to many factors, including the existence of other group priorities, personality conflicts or animosities that were too overwhelming to fix, and pervasive feelings of hopelessness due to the low status of fathers in contemporary American society. Given the importance of these services to those men who did receive them, however, fathers' rights groups should make them priority action items at every meeting. After all, for those men unable to afford the services of an attorney, the group setting might be the only opportunity that they have to acquire information about the judicial process. And for those men who do not have the luxury of visiting a counselor or who resist seeking out more formal sources of emotional help in relating to their ex-partners and children, fathers' rights groups might be their only resource for obtaining the practical tools necessary for their eventual emotional wellness and recovery.

The fact that fathers' rights groups might represent the only channel for many men to obtain interpersonal assistance leads to the second recommendation for these organizations in this area: the need for enhanced professionalization of services offered. Even in the groups that had a strong emphasis on the provision of both legal and interpersonal information, these resources tended to be dispensed quite informally. For example, other members, rather than attorneys, provided newcomers with tips for pursuing legal strategies. The same was true for the guidance offered in the areas of communicating with their ex-partners and children; other members, rather than professional social workers, psychologists, and mental health counselors, typically supplied the majority of instruction related to navigating the emotional minefields of family relations in the postdissolution context. This is not to say that these types of professionals were never present at meetings, nor is it to denigrate the valuable experiences that laypeople can offer one another during difficult times. The introduction of consistent, professionally run sessions, however, would help to fill in the blanks on new issues faced by the group in an ever-changing legal and social environment. It would also help to correct misinformation that could be circulating on the issue of relationship dynamics, as well as introduce cutting-edge communication techniques for fathers to use in moving forward interpersonally at a critical juncture in their lives.

Without question, these are ambitious goals for fathers across the board. Why should men alter their political agenda to help secure equality for women? Why should they invest resources in the personal service arena to be both more consistent across meetings and more professionalized in content? The long-term gains, of course, are clear; arguments in favor of "true 50–50 treatment" in the child support and child custody arenas are more likely to have resonance in a world where men and women experience a semblance of equality in their own economic and home spheres prior to a family dissolution. And fathers who receive enhanced training in interpersonal relationship skills are likely to be better parents and raise more well-adjusted children. But in interest group politics, it is often difficult to encourage individual players to think "long-term." In the short term, fathers' rights groups will undoubtedly need to make significant modifications in both their philosophies and strategies that many members will quite consciously view as against their own immediate well-being.

But hopefully with sufficient introspection, these modifications need not be perceived as sacrifices for long. After all, fathers are not autonomous individuals, operating in isolation from the world around them (Connell 2000, 2005a; Pease 2000). Instead, they are deeply enmeshed with the fate of women everywhere. They have sisters and mothers, nieces and aunts, grandmothers and great-grandmothers. Most important, they have daughters. If they see their work as benefiting their own girls as they grow up to parent successfully in a more egalitarian society, perhaps they, too, can find the capacity to mobilize around a new set of family-empowering policy goals and relationship practices in the not-too-distant future.

Appendix A

Research Methodology

Three main research methodologies were used in the production of this book: in-depth interviews, observational analysis, and an intensive document review. First, I was interested in securing individual accounts of participation in fathers' rights groups through interviews. As a female scholar, I clearly was not a natural member of these groups, yet I had to achieve access in order to conduct the one-hour-long telephone interviews with members and leaders that form the backbone of this project. Because no centralized list of fathers' rights groups exists, I first searched the Internet and nonprofit directories for possible groups to investigate.

Complicating matters, and as noted in the text, organizations that are involved in this movement describe themselves in many ways. Some prefer the term "fathers' rights" group. Others identify themselves as "children's rights" groups and adamantly deny that they are interested in "fathers' rights." Still others designate themselves as "family rights" groups. Further confounding this task is the fact that many of these groups are ephemeral in nature. Intragroup infighting is common, leading to the rapid birth and demise of these organizations over short periods of time. I therefore had to create a sampling strategy that would

enable me to research a set of similarly situated groups that would remain stable over the study period.

In deciding which groups to include in this analysis, therefore, I first
looked at an individual group's array of activities, mission statement,
and goals. If child support and child custody reforms were primary, that
particular organization was included in the pool of groups that could be
studied. Groups also had to meet two other criteria. First, all selected
groups had to be truly active at the time the research was conducted;
that is, they could not simply be post office boxes without members.
More specifically, all groups had to engage in a certain threshold of regularly scheduled activities, including in-person meetings. I therefore
excluded Internet chat rooms, online groups (where some fathers' rights
organizations provide "virtual" advice and support only and do not meet
in person), private companies attempting to profit from collecting child
support, publishing houses and magazines devoted to these issues, and
individually sponsored Web sites. Using these standards, I estimate that
there were approximately one to two groups per state that were viable
for study purposes.[1] Second, I chose groups that would provide the research project with maximum geographic and thus membership diversity. In the end I had a potential sampling pool of fifty groups.

Next I attempted to make contact with each group's leader to deliver
a general statement of research intent. I expressed to each potential participant (leaders, and then members if access was granted) my interest
in obtaining information about his or her involvement in the fathers'
rights movement and parental rights in general. I also stated that another
aim of this project was to understand how each potential participant's
organization helps parents achieve the goals that they desire in their
family lives.[2] In the end, four leaders declined participation on behalf
of their groups. In addition, two leaders declined because their groups
were no longer active at the time of my interview requests. Finally,

1. I used 50 of these approximately 100 groups as my sampling pool to provide the
study with geographic diversity. This 100-group estimate is different than I reported
in 2003, primarily because of intervening organizational turnover and a new counting methodology in this study that separated lower-level organizational units from
higher-level units. For more information on organizational structure, see chapter 2 of
this volume and Crowley 2003, 174–79.

2. For more information on the opportunities and challenges presented in studying these groups, see Crowley 2007.

fourteen group leaders did not respond to my query for information, and the contact information for four group leaders was no longer valid. This left me with a final sample of twenty-six groups, including seven from the Northeast, eight from the Midwest, nine from the South, and two from the West.[3]

Once the group's leader agreed to be interviewed, I then requested permission to pass around a signup sheet on the research project to all members if I planned to attend a group meeting, to post a message on the group's Web site, or send an e-mail message concerning the study to the group's Listserv if I did not plan to physically meet with the group. This is a typical snowball sampling technique, a procedure that is necessary when group members are difficult to reach.

Although most leaders were helpful and forthcoming during the interview process, a small minority assumed more protective or antagonistic roles in the process of information exchange. These diverse reactions translated into highly differing levels of success in recruiting potential members to my study. The maximum number of interviews I obtained from any one group was twenty, and the minimum was only one. In the end, I secured a total of 158 interviews. I asked all of my respondents questions related to six topics, which are detailed in appendix B: (1) demographics, (2) group patterns of recruitment and goals, (3) relationships with ex-partners, (4) relationships with their children, (5) political behavior, and (6) challenges related to leadership (asked of leaders only). These interviews were deliberately unstructured in nature in order to put the respondents at ease and in order to maximize the contextual depth of the information provided.

After these taped interviews were transcribed, I analyzed the interview data utilizing grounded theory methods with the assistance of the qualitative software analysis program Atlas.ti. Coding the data by theme, I was able to draw on the words of each of my respondents to create categories of meaning across the interviews (Strauss and Corbin 1990). I constantly compared, developed, and refined these categorical

---

3. These twenty-six groups constitute each respondent's primary affiliation. Some were members of multiple groups at one point in time—belonging to other groups in my study or, in most cases, groups that I did not have permission to study (counting these second and third affiliations would bring the total number of groups studied to thirty-four).

structures in order to produce the theoretical understandings of these groups and their members that are presented in the book. It is also important to note that throughout the book I have illustrated my most compelling arguments with quotes taken from my research participants. All quotes that are incorporated into the book are verbatim. Sometimes I inserted words for grammatical clarity or to protect the identity or personal characteristics of a person or organization; these word insertions are always noted by brackets. I added punctuation marks to clarify the meaning of the quote and utilized ellipses to indicate breaks in the text of the interviews. In addition, all names of groups, names of respondents, names of their family members and friends, and the geographic locations for these groups have been changed to protect their identities.

The second methodology used in this book involved conducting observational research on a limited sample of the groups whose members and leaders were interviewed over the phone. Observation of eight groups located across the country provided a more complete picture of group demographics and issues facing these members, and thus offered an important check on the interview data. In general, I began each attempt to observe a group "in action" by contacting the group leader. Only after I received written permission to attend a group session did I present myself at a meeting. All but one of the meetings that I attended were general informational meetings. The single exception was a training session for individuals interested in becoming monitors at a child access transfer center, which provides a neutral, safe location for parents—especially those engaged in high-conflict disputes—to exchange children under the supervision of volunteers. In addition, one group gave me permission to attend its meetings for five months. I took advantage of this opportunity to learn something about the breadth, depth, and dynamic nature of a single fathers' rights organization over time. The groups I observed ranged in size from five to twenty-four persons, including the group leader.

Before every meeting began, I introduced myself to the group leader. Then, under his or her direction, I introduced myself and the project to the members in attendance. I asked for each individual's permission to be there and to take confidential notes on the proceedings. I explained that I would not be recording any individual's name or any other identifying characteristic in my notes, only the general flow of the dialogue. I also gave everyone in the room the opportunity to "opt out" of being observed; this meant that I would not record what that individual said or did during the meeting. No one ever opted out.[4] However, an important qualification must be made in terms of reporting these results. Each chapter begins with observations from selected group meetings that I attended all throughout the country. These discussions were not tape-recorded; however, the text represents my best attempt to reconstruct from my extensive notes the meeting conversations that took place.

The third methodological strategy involved collecting as much primary material from the groups included in this study as possible. These materials include new membership packets, commonly distributed information sheets, and group bylaws or governing documents, where available. I supplemented these primary materials with secondary resources as well. All of the above research was conducted from 2003 to 2004.

---

4. I tried to minimize the disruption in the meetings due to my presence; nevertheless, it is impossible to know for sure how much members and leaders modified their behavior in the presence of a researcher. However, in the one group that I attended over a five month period, the content and presentation styles of the participants remained largely constant.

Appendix B

Unstructured Interview Guide

Demographics

1. What is your age?
2. What is your occupation?
3. What is your highest level of education?
4. How would you identify yourself racially or ethnically?
5. Are you religious? Which group do you belong to?
6. Are you currently separated or divorced? If so, for how long?
7. How many children do you have, and what are their ages? Do you have custody of these children? If not, do you have visitation? Explain.
8. Do you have an order to pay child support? If so, can you give me the approximate amount you pay per month?

Patterns of Recruitment and Goals

9. What fathers' rights group do you belong to?
10. How long have you been a member of this organization? How did you hear about it?
11. Why did you join this organization?
12. Have you recruited others to join this or other groups like this? If so, how did you recruit them?

13. What would you say are the most important goals of this organization?
14. Describe a typical meeting.
15. Some people have said that child support laws are unfair. Do you think that this is true?
16. Some people have said that custody and visitation laws are unfair. Do you think that this is true?
17. Are there any interest groups or sets of people that you think are mobilized against you?

Relationships with Past Partners (Mothers of Your Children)

18. How would you describe your relationship with the mother of your children right now?
19. How do you think this relationship affects your children?
20. What impact does the fathers' rights group have on this relationship? (Better or worse and why?)

Relationships with Children

21. What was your relationship with your children like before the family split up?
22. What has your relationship with your children been like since the family split up?
23. What role does your fathers' rights group play in impacting your relationship with your children?

Politics and Political Involvement

24. Did you vote in the last presidential election? Are you a regular voter?
25. Do you consider yourself a Republican, a Democrat, or neither?
26. Do you consider yourself a politically active person? Do you consider this fathers' rights organization to be a "political group?" Why or why not?
27. Is this the first time you have been involved in a "political activity"?
28. Do you consider your group to be part of a social movement?

For Leaders Only
1. How did you become the leader of this organization?
2. How are leaders normally selected (i.e., elected, volunteers)?
3. How do decisions get made in your organization (i.e., by consensus, by the leadership, by voting)? Are there official rules that govern this organization?
4. Are members ever expelled from this group for any reason? If so, why?

Appendix C

No-Fault Divorce Legislation Dates, by State

No-Fault Divorce Legislation Dates, by State

State	Decision Date	State	Decision Date
Alabama	1971	Montana	1973
Alaska	1963	Nebraska	1972
Arizona	1973	Nevada	1967
Arkansas	1991	New Hampshire	1971
California	1970	New Jersey	1971
Colorado	1972	New Mexico	1973
Connecticut	1973	New York	1967
Delaware	1968	North Carolina	1965
Florida	1971	North Dakota	1971
Georgia	1973	Ohio	1982
Hawaii	1972	Oklahoma	1953
Idaho	1971	Oregon	1971
Illinois	1984	Pennsylvania	1980
Indiana	1973	Rhode Island	1975
Iowa	1970	South Carolina	1979
Kansas	1969	South Dakota	1985
Kentucky	1972	Tennessee	1977
Louisiana	1979	Texas	1970
Maine	1973	Utah	1987
Maryland	1983	Vermont	1972
Massachusetts	1976	Virginia	1975
Michigan	1972	Washington	1973
Minnesota	1864	West Virginia	1977
Mississippi	1976	Wisconsin	1978
Missouri	1974	Wyoming	1977

Source: Vlosky, Denese Ashbaugh and Pamela A. Monroe. 2002. "The Effective Dates of No-Fault Divorce Laws in the 50 States." *Family Relations* 51(4): 317–24.

Appendix D

Number, Rate, and Percent of Births to Unmarried Women and Birthrate for Married Women

Unites States, 1950–2003

Number, Rate, and Percent of Births to Unmarried Women and Birthrate for Married
Women: United States, 1950–2003

Year	Number of Births to Unmarried Women	Percent of All Births to Unmarried Women	Birth Rate per 1,000 Unmarried Women 15–44	Birth Rate per 1,000 Married Women 15–44
1950	141,600	4.0	14.1	141.0
1951	146,500	3.9	15.1	N/A
1952	150,300	3.9	15.8	N/A
1953	160,800	4.1	16.9	N/A
1954	176,600	4.4	18.7	N/A
1955	183,300	4.5	19.3	153.7
1956	193,500	4.7	20.4	N/A
1957	201,700	4.7	21.0	N/A
1958	208,700	5.0	21.2	N/A
1959	220,600	5.2	21.9	N/A
1960	224,300	5.3	21.6	156.6
1961	240,200	5.6	22.7	155.8
1962	245,100	5.9	21.9	150.8
1963	259,400	6.3	22.5	145.9
1964	275,700	6.9	23.0	141.8
1965	291,200	7.7	23.4	130.2
1966	302,400	8.4	23.3	123.6
1967	318,100	9.0	23.7	118.7
1968	339,200	9.7	24.3	116.6
1969	360,800	10.0	24.8	118.8
1970	398,700	10.7	26.4	121.1

Year	Number of Births to Unmarried Women	Percent of All Births to Unmarried Women	Birth Rate per 1,000 Unmarried Women 15–44	Birth Rate per 1,000 Married Women 15–44
1971	401,400	11.3	25.5	113.2
1972	403,200	12.4	24.8	100.8
1973	407,300	13.0	24.3	94.7
1974	418,100	13.2	23.9	94.2
1975	447,900	14.3	24.5	92.1
1976	468,100	14.8	24.3	91.6
1977	515,700	15.5	25.6	94.9
1978	543,900	16.3	25.7	93.6
1979	597,800	17.1	27.2	96.4
1980	665,747	18.4	29.4	97.0
1981	686,605	18.9	29.5	96.0
1982	715,227	19.4	30.0	96.2
1983	737,893	20.3	30.3	93.6
1984	770,355	21.0	31.0	93.1
1985	828,174	22.0	32.8	93.3
1986	878,477	23.4	34.2	90.7
1987	933,013	24.5	36.0	90.0
1988	1,005,299	25.7	38.5	90.8
1989	1,094,169	27.1	41.6	91.9
1990	1,165,384	28.0	43.8	93.2
1991	1,213,769	29.5	45.2	89.9
1992	1,224,876	30.1	45.2	89.0
1993	1,240,172	31.0	45.3	86.8
1994	1,289,592	32.6	46.9	83.8
1995	1,253,976	32.2	45.1	83.7
1996	1,260,306	32.4	44.8	83.7
1997	1,257,444	32.4	44.0	84.3
1998	1,293,567	32.8	44.3	85.7
1999	1,304,594	33.0	43.9	87.3
2000	1,347,043	33.2	44.0	87.4
2001	1,349,249	33.5	43.8	86.7
2002	1,365,966	34.0	43.7	86.3
2003	1,415,995	34.6	44.9	88.1
2004	1,470,189	35.8	46.1	87.6

Source: Centers for Disease Control and Prevention. National Center for Health Statistics. 2000. "Nonmarital Childbearing in the United States, 1940–1999." *National Vital Health Statistics Reports* 48(16). All other years, see Centers for Disease Control and Prevention. National Center for Health Statistics. 2005. "Births: Final Data for 2003." *National Vital Health Statistics Reports* 54(2).

References

Acock, Alan C., and David H. Demo. 1994. *Family Diversity and Well-Being.* Thousand Oaks, CA: Sage.

Adamsons, Kari, and Kay Pasley. 2006. "Coparenting Following Divorce and Relationship Dissolution." In *Handbook of Divorce and Relationship Dissolution*, edited by M. A. Fine and J. H. Harvey, 241–61. Mahwah, NJ: Lawrence Erlbaum Associates.

Afifi, Tamara D., and Kellie Hamrick. 2006. "Communication Processes That Promote Risk and Resiliency in Postdivorce Families." In *Handbook of Divorce and Relationship Dissolution*, edited by M. A. Fine and J. H. Harvey, 435–56. Mahwah, NJ: Lawrence Erlbaum Associates.

Ahmeduzzaman, Mohammad, and Jaipaul L. Roopnarine. 1992. "Sociodemographic Factors, Functioning Style, Social Support, and Fathers' Involvement with Preschoolers in African-American Families." *Journal of Marriage and the Family* 54 (3): 699–707.

Ahrons, Constance R. 1994. *The Good Divorce.* New York: Harper Collins.

Ahrons, Constance R., and Roy H. Rodgers. 1987. *Divorced Families: A Multidisciplinary Developmental View.* Markham, ON: Penguin.

Aldous, Joan, Gail M. Mulligan, and Thoroddur Bjarnason. 1998. "Fathering over Time: What Makes the Difference?" *Journal of Marriage and the Family* 60 (4): 809–20.

Allen, Sarah M., and Alan J. Hawkins. 1999. "Maternal Gatekeeping: Mothers' Beliefs and Behaviors That Inhibit Greater Father Involvement in Family Work." *Journal of Marriage and the Family* 61 (1): 199–212.

Amato, Paul R. 1999. "Children of Divorced Parents as Young Adults." In *Coping with Divorce, Single Parenting, and Remarriage*, edited by E. M. Hetherington, 147–64. Mahwah, NJ: Lawrence Erlbaum.

———. 2000. "The Consequences of Divorce for Adults and Children." *Journal of Marriage and the Family* 62 (4): 1269–87.

Amato, Paul R., and Joan G. Gilbreth. 1999. "Nonresident Fathers and Children's Well Being: A Meta-Analysis." *Journal of Marriage and the Family* 61 (3): 557–73.

Anderson, Elaine A., Julie K. Kohler, and Bethany L. Letiecq. 2002. "Low-Income Fathers and 'Responsible Fatherhood' Programs: A Qualitative Investigation of Participants' Experiences." *Family Relations* 51 (2): 148–55.

Arbuthnot, Jack, and Donald A. Gordon. 1996. "Does Mandatory Divorce Education Work?: A Six-Month Outcome Evaluation." *Family and Conciliation Courts Review* 34 (1): 60–81.

Arbuthnot, Jack, Kevin M. Kramer, and Donald A. Gordon. 1997. "Patterns of Relitigation Following Divorce Education." *Family and Conciliation Courts Review* 35 (3): 269–79.

Arditti, Joyce A., and Michalena Kelly. 1994. "Fathers' Perspectives of Their Co-Parental Relationships Postdivorce: Implications for Family Practice and Legal Reform." *Family Relations* 43 (1): 61–67.

Arditti, Joyce A., and Debra Madden-Derdich. 1997. "Joint and Sole Custody Mothers: Implications for Research and Practice." *Families in Society* 78 (1): 36–45.

Arendell, Terry. 1995. *Fathers and Divorce*. Thousand Oaks, CA: Sage.

Barnes, Stephanie. 1999. "Strengthening the Father-Child Relationship through a Joint Custody Presumption." *Willamette Law Review* 35: 601–28.

Bartfeld, Judi. 2000. "Child Support and the Postdivorce Economic Well-Being of Mothers, Fathers, and Children." *Demography* 37 (2): 203–13.

Baruch, Grace K., and Rosalind C. Barnett. 1981. "Fathers' Participation in the Care of Their Preschool Children." *Sex Roles* 7 (10): 1043–55.

Baum, Nehami. 2004. "Typology of Post Divorce Parental Relationships and Behaviors." *Journal of Divorce and Remarriage* 41 (3/4): 53–79.

Baumgartner, Frank R., and Bryan D. Jones. 1993. *Agendas and Instability in American Politics*. Chicago: University of Chicago Press.

Bauserman, Robert. 2002. "Child Adjustment in Joint-Custody Versus Sole-Custody Arrangements: A Meta-Analytic Review." *Journal of Family Psychology* 16 (1): 91–102.

Beck, Connie J. A., and Bruce D. Sales. 2000. "A Critical Reappraisal of Divorce Mediation Research and Policy." *Psychology, Public Policy, and Law* 6 (4): 989–1056.

Bender, William N. 1994. "Joint Custody: The Option of Choice." *Journal of Divorce and Remarriage* 21 (3/4): 115–32.

Bertoia, Carl, and Janice Drakich. 1993. "The Fathers' Rights Movement: Contradictions in Rhetoric and Practice." *Journal of Family Issues* 14 (4): 592–615.

Bianchi, Suzanne M., John P. Robinson, and Melissa A. Milkie. 2006. *Changing Rhythms of American Family Life.* New York: Russell Sage Foundation.

Bianchi, Suzanne M., Lekha Subaiya, and Joan R. Kahn. 1999. "The Gender Gap in the Economic Well-Being of Nonresident Fathers and Custodial Mothers." *Demography* 36 (2): 195–203.

Blaisure, Karen R., and Margie J. Geasler. 2006. "Educational Interventions for Separating and Divorcing Parents." In *Handbook of Divorce and Relationship Dissolution,* edited by M. A. Fine and J. H. Harvey, 575–602. Mahwah, NJ: Lawrence Erlbaum Associates.

Blankenhorn, David. 1995. *Fatherless America: Confronting Our Most Urgent Social Problem.* New York: Basic Books.

Blau, Francine D., Marianne A. Ferber, and Anne E. Winkler. 2001. *The Economics of Women, Men, and Work.* Upper Saddle River, NJ: Prentice-Hall.

Bly, Robert. 1990. *Iron John: A Book About Men.* Reading, MA: Addison-Wesley.

Bowman, Madonna E., and Constance R. Ahrons. 1985. "Impact of Legal Custody Status on Fathers' Parenting Postdivorce." *Journal of Marriage and the Family* 47 (2): 481–88.

Boyd, Susan B. 2003. *Child Custody, Law, and Women's Work.* Don Mills, ON: Oxford University Press.

——. 2006. "Robbed of Their Families? Fathers' Rights Discourses in Canadian Parenting Law Reform Processes." In *Fathers' Rights Activism and Law Reform in Comparative Perspective,* edited by R. Collier and S. Sheldon, 27–51. Oxford: Hart.

Braver, Sanford L., Ira M. Ellman, and William V. Fabricius. 2003. "Relocation of Children after Divorce and Children's Best Interests: New Evidence and Legal Considerations." *Journal of Family Psychology* 17 (2): 206–19.

Braver, Sanford L., and Dianne O'Connell. 1998. *Divorced Dads: Shattering the Myths.* New York: Tarcher, Putnam.

Braver, Sanford L., Peter Salem, Jessica Pearson, and Stephanie R. DeLuse. 1996. "The Content of Divorce Education Programs: Results of a Survey." *Family and Conciliation Courts Review* 34 (1): 41–59.

Braver, Sanford L., Sharlene A. Wolchik, Irwin N. Sandler, and Virgil L. Sheets. 1993. "A Social Exchange Model of Nonresidential Parent Involvement."

In *Nonresidential Parenting: New Vistas in Family Living*, edited by C. E. Depner and J. A. Bray, 87–108. Thousand Oaks, CA: Sage.

Brinig, Margaret F., and Douglas W. Allen. 2000. "'These Boots Are Made for Walking': Why Most Divorce Filers Are Women." *American Law and Economics Review* 2 (1): 126–69.

Brown, Susan. 1984. "Changes in Laws Governing Divorce: An Evaluation of Joint Custody Presumptions." *Journal of Family Issues* 5 (2): 200–23.

Buchanan, Christy M., Eleanor E. Maccoby, and Sanford M. Dornbusch. 1991. "Caught between Parents: Adolescents' Experience in Divorced Homes." *Child Development* 62 (5): 1008–29.

Budig, Michelle J., and Paula England. 2001. "The Wage Penalty for Motherhood." *American Sociological Review* 66 (2): 204–25.

Buehler, Cheryl. 1995. "Divorce Law in the United States." *Marriage and Family Review* 21 (3/4): 99–120.

Buehler, Cheryl, and Catherine Ryan. 1995. "Former-Spouse Relations and Noncustodial Father Involvement during Marital and Family Transitions: A Closer Look at Remarriage following Divorce." In *Stepparenting: Issues in Theory, Research, and Practice*, edited by K. Pasley and M. Ihinger-Tallman, 127–50. Westport, CT: Greenwood.

Burgess, Adrienne. 1997. *Fatherhood Reclaimed: The Making of a Modern Father.* London: Vermilion.

Burnes, Ailsa, and Cath Scott. 1994. *Mother-Headed Families and Why They Have Increased.* Hillsdale, NJ: Erlbaum.

Camara, Kathleen A., and Gary Resnick. 1989. "Styles of Conflict Resolution and Cooperation between Divorced Parents: Effects on Child Behavior and Adjustment." *American Journal of Orthopsychiatry* 59 (4): 560–75.

Carbone, June. 1994. "A Feminist Perspective on Divorce." *The Future of Children* 4 (1): 183–209.

———. 2000. *From Partners to Parents: The Second Revolution in Family Law.* New York: Columbia University Press.

Centers for Disease Control and Prevention. National Center for Health Statistics. 2000. "Nonmarital Childbearing in the United States, 1940–1999." *National Vital Health Statistics Reports* 48 (16).

———. 2005. "Births: Final Data for 2003." *National Vital Health Statistics Reports* 54 (2).

Coates, Christine A., Robin Deautsch, Hugh Starnes, Matthew J. Sullivan, and BeaLisa Sydlik. 2004. "Parenting Coordination for High-Conflict Families." *Family Court Review* 42: 246–60.

Cohen, Philip N., and Suzanne M. Bianchi. 1999. "Marriage, Children, and Women's Employment: What Do We Know?" *Monthly Labor Review* 122 (12): 22–31.

Coleman, Marilyn, Lawrence Ganong, and Mark Fine. 2000. "Reinvesting Remarriage: Another Decade of Progress." *Journal of Marriage and the Family* 62 (4): 1288–1307.

Collier, Richard. 1995. *Masculinity, Law and the Family.* London: Routledge.

——. 2006. "The Outlaw Fathers Fight Back: Fathers' Rights Groups, Fathers 4 Justice and the Politics of Family Law Reform——Reflections on the UK Experience." In *Fathers' Rights Activism and Law Reform in Comparative Perspective,* edited by R. Collier and S. Sheldon, 53–77. Oxford: Hart Publishing.

Collier, Richard, and Sally Sheldon. 2006. "Fathers' Rights, Fatherhood and Law Reform: International Perspectives." In *Fathers' Rights Activism and Law Reform in Comparative Perspective,* edited by R. Collier and S. Sheldon, 1–26. Oxford: Hart Publishing.

Coltrane, Scott. 1989. "Household Labor and the Routine Production of Gender." *Social Problems* 36 (5): 473–90.

——. 2001. "Marketing the Marriage 'Solution': Misplaced Simplicity in the Politics of Fatherhood." *Sociological Perspectives* 44 (4): 387–418.

Coltrane, Scott, and Neal Hickman. 1992. "The Rhetoric of Rights and Needs: Moral Discourse in the Reform of Child Custody and Child Support Laws." *Social Problems* 39 (4): 400–20.

Comanor, William, ed. 2004. *The Law and Economics of Child Support Payments.* Northampton, MA: Edward Elgar.

Connell, R. W. 2000. *The Men and the Boys.* Cambridge: Polity Press.

——. 2005a. "Change among the Gatekeepers: Men, Masculinities, and Gender Equality in the Global Arena." *Signs: Journal of Women in Culture and Society* 30 (3): 1801–25.

——. 2005b. *Masculinities.* Berkeley: University of California Press.

Cooney, Teresa, Frank A. Pedersen, Samuel Indelicato, and Rob Palkovitz. 1993. "Timing of Fatherhood: Is 'On-Time' Optimal?" *Journal of Marriage and the Family* 55 (1): 205–15.

Coverman, Shelley, and Joseph F. Sheley. 1986. "Change in Men's Housework and Child-Care Time, 1965–1975." *Journal of Marriage and the Family* 48 (2): 413–22.

Crittenden, Ann. 2001. *The Price of Motherhood.* New York: Henry Holt and Company.

Crowley, Jocelyn Elise. 2000. "Supervised Devolution: The Case of Child Support Enforcement." *Publius: The Journal of Federalism* 30 (1/2): 99–117.

——. 2001. "Who Institutionalizes Institutions? The Case of Paternity Establishment in the United States." *Social Science Quarterly* 82 (2): 312–28.

——. 2002. "The Rise and Fall of Court Prerogatives in Paternity Establishment." *Justice System Journal* 23 (3): 363–76.

——. 2003. *The Politics of Child Support in America.* New York: Cambridge University Press.

——. 2006a. "Adopting 'Equality Tools' from the Toolboxes of Their Predecessors: The Fathers' Rights Movement in the United States." In *Fathers for Justice? Fathers' Rights Activism and Legal Reform in Comparative Perspective,* edited by R. Collier and S. Sheldon, 79–100. Oxford: Hart Publications.

——. 2006b. "Conflicted Membership: Women in Fathers' Rights Groups." *Working Paper.*

——. 2006c. "Organizational Responses to the Fatherhood Crisis: The Case of Fathers' Rights Groups in the United States." *Marriage and Family Review* 39 (1/2): 99–120.

——. 2007. "Friend or Foe? Self-Expansion, Stigmatized Groups, and the Researcher-Participant Relationship." *Journal of Contemporary Ethnography* 36 (6): 603–30.

Dewar, John. 1998. "The Normal Chaos of Family Life." *The Modern Law Review* 61 (4): 467–486.

Donnelly, Denise, and David Finkelhor. 1992. "Does Equality in Custody Arrangements Improve the Parent-Child Relationship?" *Journal of Marriage and the Family* 54 (4): 837–45.

Doolittle, Fred, Virginia Knox, Cynthia Miller, and Sharon Rowser. 1998. *Building Opportunities, Enforcing Obligations: Implementation and Interim Impacts of Parents' Fair Share.* New York: Manpower Demonstration Research Corporation.

Doolittle, Fred, and Suzanne Lynn. 1998. *Working with Low-Income Cases: Lessons for the Child Support Enforcement System from Parents' Fair Share.* New York: Manpower Demonstration Research Corporation.

Dowd, Nancy E. 2000. *Redefining Fatherhood.* New York: New York University Press.

Doyle, Richard. 1976. *The Rape of the Male.* St. Paul, MN: Poor Richard's Press.

Duncan, Greg J., and Saul D. Hoffman. 1985. "Economic Consequences of Marital Instability." In *Horizontal Equity, Uncertainty, and Economic Well-Being,* edited by M. David and T. Smeeding, 427–70. Chicago: University of Chicago Press.

Dunn, Judy, Lisa C. Davies, Thomas G. O'Connor, and Wendy Sturgess. 2001. "Family Lives and Friendships: The Perspectives of Children in Step-, Single-Parent, and Nonstep Families." *Journal of Family Psychology* 15 (2): 272–87.

Ellis, Alfred, and David L. Levy. 2003. *Establishing Safe Haven Child Access Centers Handbook.* Children's Rights Council.

Ellis, Elizabeth M. 2000. *Divorce Wars: Interventions with Families in Conflict.* Washington, DC: American Psychological Association.

Elrod, Linda D. 2001. "A Minnesota Comparative Family Law Symposium: Reforming the System to Protect Children in High Conflict Custody Cases." *William Mitchell Law Review* 28: 495–551.

Elrod, Linda D., and Robert G. Spector. 2002. "A Review of the Year in Family Law: State Courts React to Troxel." *Family Law Quarterly* 35 (4): 577–615.

Emery, Robert E., Lisa Laumann-Billings, Mary C. Waldron, David A. Sbarra, and Peter Dillon. 2001. "Child Custody Mediation and Litigation: Custody, Contact, and Coparenting 12 Years after Initial Dispute Resolution." *Journal of Consulting and Clinical Psychology* 69 (2): 323–32.

England, Paula, Carmen Garcia-Beaulieu, and Mary Ross. 2004. "Women's Employment among Blacks, Whites, and Three Groups of Latinas: Do More Privileged Women Have Higher Employment?" *Gender and Society* 18 (4): 494–509.

Eriksson, Maria, and Keith Pringle. 2006. "Gender Equality, Child Welfare and Fathers' Rights in Sweden." In *Fathers' Rights Activism and Law Reform in Comparative Perspective,* edited by R. Collier and S. Sheldon, 101–23. Oxford: Hart.

Fabricius, William V., and Jeffrey Hull. 2000. "Young Adults' Perspectives on Divorce Living Arrangements." *Family and Conciliation Courts Review* 38 (4): 446–61.

Ferreiro, Beverly Webster. 1990. "Presumption of Joint Custody: A Family Policy Dilemma." *Family Relations* 39 (4): 420–26.

Fineman, Martha. 1991. *The Illusion of Equality: The Rhetoric and Reality of Divorce Reform.* Chicago: University of Chicago Press.

Flood, Michael. 1998. "Men's Movements." *Community Quarterly* 46 (June): 62–71.

———. 2004. "Backlash: Angry Men's Movements." In *The Battle and Backlash Rage On: Why Feminism Cannot Be Obsolete,* edited by S. E. Rossi, 261–342. Philadelphia: Xlibris.

———. 2006. Separated Fathers and the Fathers' Rights Movement. Paper read at Feminism, Law, and the Family Workshop, at Law School, University of Melbourne.

Fox, Greer Litton, and Priscilla White Blanton. 1995. "Noncustodial Fathers following Divorce." *Marriage and Family Review* 20 (1–2): 257–82.

Friedman, Debra. 1995. *Towards a Structure of Indifference: The Social Origins of Maternal Custody.* New York: Aldine De Gruyter.

Fullerton, Howard N. 1999. "Labor Force Participation: 75 Years of Change, 1950–98 and 1998–2025." *Monthly Labor Review* (December).

Furstenberg, Frank F., and Andrew J. Cherlin. 1991. *Divided Families: What Happens to Children When Parents Part.* Cambridge, MA: Harvard University Press.

Furstenberg, Frank F., and Christine Winquist Nord. 1985. "Parenting Apart: Patterns of Childrearing after Marital Disruption." *Journal of Marriage and the Family* 47 (4): 893–904.

Garfinkel, Irwin. 2001. "Child Support in the New World of Welfare." In *The New World of Welfare*, edited by R. M. Blank and R. Haskins, 442–60. Washington, DC: Brookings Institution Press.

Gavanas, Anna. 2004. *Fatherhood Politics in the United States: Masculinity, Sexuality, Race, and Marriage.* Champaign, IL: University of Illinois Press.

Geasler, Margie J., and Karen R. Blaisure. 1998. "A Review of Divorce Education Program Materials." *Family Relations* 47 (2): 167–75.

——. 1999. "Nationwide Survey of Court-Connected Divorce Education Programs." *Family and Conciliation Courts Review* 37 (1): 36–63.

Goldberg, Herb. 1976. *The Hazards of Being Male: Surviving the Myth of Masculine Privilege.* New York: Nash.

Goldberg, Stephanie B. 1997. "Make Room for Daddy." *American Bar Association Journal* 82 (2): 48–51.

Gornick, Janet C., and Marcia K. Meyers. 2003. *Families That Work: Policies for Reconciling Parenthood and Employment.* New York: Russell Sage Foundation.

Gould, Jonathan W. 1998. *Conducting Scientifically Crafted Child Custody Evaluations.* Thousand Oaks, CA: Sage.

Grall, Timothy. 2003. "Custodial Mothers and Fathers and Their Child Support: 2001."*Current Population Reports*, U.S. Census Bureau. P60–225.

Griswold, Robert L. 1998. "The History and Politics of Fatherlessness." In *Lost Fathers: The Politics of Fatherlessness in America*, edited by C. Daniels, 11–32. New York: St. Martin's Press.

Guyot, Robert B. III. 2005. "Using a Parenting Coordinator in a High-Conflict Case." *American Journal of Family Law* 19 (3): 178–82.

Hetherington, E. Mavis. 2003. "Intimate Pathways: Changing Patterns in Close Personal Relationships across Time." *Family Relations* 52 (4): 318–31.

Hetherington, E. Mavis, and Joan B. Kelly. 2002. *For Better or for Worse.* New York: Norton.

Hirschfeld, Robert A. 1999. In the Matter of Elian Gonzalez, Petition for Writ of Habeas Corpus before the U.S. Supreme Court.

Hofferth, Sandra L., and Jack Sandberg. 2001. "Changes in American Children's Time, 1981–1997." In *Children at the Millennium: Where Have We Come from, Where Are We Going?* edited by T. Owens and S. Hofferth, New York: Elsevier Science.

Hoffman, Charles D. 1995. "Pre- and Post Divorce Father-Child Relationships and Child Adjustment: Noncustodial Fathers' Perspectives." *Journal of Divorce and Remarriage* 23 (1/2): 3–21.

Hoffman, Saul D. 1977. "Marital Instability and the Economic Status of Women." *Demography* 14 (1): 67–76.

Holden, Karen C., and Pamela J. Smock. 1991. "The Economic Costs of Marital Dissolution: Why Do Women Bear a Disproportionate Cost?" *Annual Review of Sociology* 17: 51–78.

Huang, Chien-Chung, James Kunz, and Irwin Garfinkel. 2002. "The Effect of Child Support on Welfare Exits and Re-Entries." *Journal of Policy Analysis and Management* 21 (4): 557–76.

Huang, Chien-Chung, Ronald Mincy, and Irwin Garfinkel. 2005. "Child Support Obligations and Low-Income Fathers." *Journal of Marriage and Family* 67 (5): 1213–25.

Ishii-Kuntz, Masako, and Scott Coltrane. 1992. "Predicting the Sharing of Household Labor: Are Parenting and Housework Distinct?" *Sociological Perspectives* 35 (4): 629–47.

Jacob, Herbert. 1988. *Silent Revolution: The Transformation of Divorce Law in the United States.* Chicago: University of Chicago Press.

Johnston, Janet R. 1994. "High-Conflict Divorce." *Future of Children* 4 (1): 165–82.

——. 1995. "Children's Adjustment in Sole Custody Compared to Joint Custody Families and Principles for Custody Decision Making." *Family and Conciliation Courts Review* 33 (4): 415–25.

Johnston, Janet R., Marsha Kline, and Jeanne M. Tschann. 1989. "Ongoing Postdivorce Conflict: Effects on Children of Joint Custody and Frequent Access." *American Journal of Orthopsychiatry* 59 (4): 577–92.

Kelly, Joan B. 1993a. "Current Research on Children's Postdivorce Adjustment: No Simple Answers." *Family and Conciliation Courts Review* 31 (1): 29–49.

——. 1993b. "Developing and Implementing Post-Divorce Parenting Plans: Does the Forum Make a Difference?" In *Nonresidential Parenting: New Vistas in Family Living,* edited by J. H. Bray and C. E. Depner, 135–55. Newbury Park, CA: Sage.

——. 2000. "Children's Adjustment in Conflicted Marriage and Divorce: A Decade Review of Research." *Journal of Child and Adolescent Psychiatry* 39 (8): 963–73.

Kelly, Joan B., and Robert E. Emery. 2003. "Children's Adjustment following Divorce: Risk and Resilience Perspectives." *Family Relations* 52 (4): 352–62.

Kelly, Joan B., and Michael E. Lamb. 2003. "Developmental Issues in the Resolution of Relocation Cases Involving Young Children: When, Whether, and How?" *Journal of Family Psychology* 17 (2): 193–205.

Kenedy, Robert A. 2004. *Fathers for Justice: The Rise of a New Social Movement in Canada as a Case Study of Collective Identity Formation.* Ann Arbor: Caravan.

Kimmel, Michael S., and Michael Kaufman. 1993. "The New Men's Movement: Retreat and Regression with America's Weekend Warriors." *Feminist Issues* 13 (2): 3–21.

King, Valerie. 1994. "Nonresident Father Involvement and Child Well-Being: Can Dads Make a Difference?" *Journal of Family Issues* 15 (1): 78–96.

King, Valerie, and Holly E. Heard. 1999. "Nonresident Father Visitation, Parental Conflict, and Mother's Satisfaction: What's Best for Child Well-Being?" *Journal of Marriage and the Family* 61 (2): 385–96.

Kingdon, John. 1984. *Agendas, Alternatives, and Public Policies.* Boston: Little, Brown.

Kline, Marsha, Janet R. Johnston, and Jeanne M. Tschann. 1991. "The Long Shadow of Marital Conflict: A Model of Children's Postdivorce Adjustment." *Journal of Marriage and the Family* 53 (2): 297–309.

Kline, Marsha, Jeanne M. Tschann, Janet R. Johnston, and Judith S. Wallerstein. 1989. "Children's Adjustment in Joint and Sole Physical Custody Families." *Developmental Psychology* 25 (3): 430–39.

Kramer, Laurie, and Amanda Kowel. 1998. "Long-Term Follow-up of a Court-Based Intervention for Divorcing Parents." *Family and Conciliation Courts Review* 36 (4): 452–65.

La Rossa, Ralph. 1997. *The Modernization of Fatherhood: A Social and Political History.* Chicago: University of Chicago Press.

Lamb, Michael E. 1999. "Noncustodial Fathers and Their Impact on the Children of Divorce." In *The Postdivorce Family: Children, Parenting, and Society,* edited by R. A. Thompson and P. R. Amato, 105–25. Thousand Oaks, CA: Sage.

Lee, Mo-Yee. 2002. "A Model of Children's Postdivorce Behavioral Adjustment in Maternal and Dual Resident Arrangements." *Journal of Family Issues* 23 (5): 672–97.

Leite, Randall W., and Patrick C. McHenry. 2002. "Aspects of Father Status and Postdivorce Father Involvement with Children." *Journal of Family Issues* 23 (5): 601–23.

Leving, Jeffery M. 2005. "Alito's Stance Supports Men's Right to Choose." *Chicago Sun-Times,* November 6.

Luepnitz, Deborah Anna. 1982. *Child Custody.* Lexington, MA: DC Heath and Company.

Maccoby, Eleanor E., Christy M. Buchanan, Robert H. Mnookin, and Sanford M. Dornbusch. 1993. "Postdivorce Roles of Mothers and Fathers in the Lives of Their Children." *Journal of Family Psychology* 7 (1) 24–38.

Maccoby, Eleanor E., Charlene E. Depner, and Robert H. Mnookin. 1990. "Coparenting in the Second Year after Divorce." *Journal of Marriage and the Family* 52 (1): 141–55.

Maccoby, Eleanor E., and Robert H. Mnookin. 1992. *Dividing the Child: Social and Legal Dilemmas of Custody.* Cambridge, MA: Harvard University Press.

Madden-Derdich, Debra A., and Joyce A. Arditti. 1999. "The Ties That Bind: Attachment between Former Spouses." *Family Relations* 48 (3): 243–49.

Madden-Derdich, Debra A., and Stacie A. Leonard. 2000. "Parental Role Identity and Fathers' Involvement in Coparental Interaction after Divorce: Fathers' Perspectives." *Family Relations* 49 (3): 311–18.

Masheter, Carol. 1997. "Former Spouses Who Are Friends: Three Case Studies." *Journal of Social and Personal Relationships* 14 (2): 207–22.

Mason, Mary Ann. 1994. *From Father's Property to Children's Rights: The History of Child Custody in the United States.* New York: Columbia University Press.

——. 1999. *The Custody Wars: Why Children Are Losing the Legal Battle, and What We Can Do About It.* New York: Basic Books.

May, Susannah. 2001. "Child Custody and Visitation." *Georgetown Journal of Gender and the Law* 2 (2): 382–401.

McClure, Thomas E. 2002. "Postjudgment Conflict and Cooperation Following Court-Connected Parent Education." *Journal of Divorce and Remarriage* 38 (1/2): 1–16.

McHale, James P., Regina Kuersten-Hogan, Allison Lauretti, and Jeffrey L. Rasmussen. 2000. "Parental Reports of Coparenting and Observed Coparenting Behavior during the Toddler Period." *Journal of Family Psychology* 14 (2): 220–36.

McHale, Susan M., and Ted L. Huston. 1984. "Men and Women as Parents: Sex Role Orientations, Employment, and Parental Roles with Infants." *Child Development* 55 (4): 1349–61.

McLanahan, Sara. 1999. "Father Absence and Children's Welfare." In *Coping with Divorce, Single Parenting, and Remarriage: A Risk and Resiliency Perspective,* edited by E. M. Hetherington, 117–46. Mahwah, NJ: Lawrence Erlbaum.

McLanahan, Sara, and Gary Sandefur. 1994. *Growing up with a Single Parent.* Cambridge, MA: Harvard University Press.

Mead, Lawrence M. 1999. "The Decline of Welfare in Wisconsin." *Journal of Public Administration Research and Theory* 9 (4): 597–622.

Menning, Chadwick L. 2002. "Absent Parents Are More Than Money: The Joint Effects of Activities and Financial Support on Youths' Educational Attainment." *Journal of Family Issues* 23 (5): 648–71.

Messner, Michael A. 1997. *Politics of Masculinities: Men in Movements.* Thousand Oaks, CA: Sage.

Metz, Charles V. 1968. *Divorce and Custody for Men.* New York: Doubleday.

Mincy, Ronald, and Hillard Pouncy. 1997. "Paternalism, Child Support Enforcement, and Fragile Families." In *The New Paternalism: Supervisory Approaches to Poverty,* edited by L. Mead, 130–60. Washington, DC: Brookings Institution Press.

——. 1999. "There Must Be 50 Ways to Start a Family." In *The Fatherhood Movement: A Call to Action,* edited by W. Horn, D. Blankenhorn, and M. B. Pearlstein, 83–104. New York: Lexington Books.

Minton, Carmell, and Kay Pasley. 1996. "Fathers' Parenting Role Identity and Father Involvement." *Journal of Family Issues* 17 (1): 26–45.

Mintrom, Michael. 1997. "Policy Entrepreneurs and the Diffusion of Innovation." *American Journal of Political Science* 41 (3): 738–70.

Moore, Robert, and Douglas Gillette. 1991. *King, Warrior, Magician, Lover.* San Francisco: Harper Collins.

Morgan, Leslie A. 1989. "Economic Well-Being following Marital Termination: A Comparison of Widowed and Divorced Women." *Journal of Family Issues* 10 (1): 86–101.

Mott, Frank L. 1990. "When Is a Father Really Gone? Parental-Child Contact in Father Absent Homes." *Demography* 27 (4): 499–517.

Nepomnyaschy, Lenna, and Jane Waldfogel. 2007. "Paternity Leave and Fathers' Involvement with Young Children." *Community, Work and Family* 10 (4): 427–53.

Nestel, Gilbert, Jacqueline Mercier, and Lois B. Shaw. 1983. "Economic Consequences of Midlife Changes in Marital Status." In *Unplanned Careers: The Working Lives of Middle-Aged Women,* edited by L. B. Shaw, 109–26. Lexington, MA: Lexington Books.

Nock, Steven L. 1998. *Marriage in Men's Lives.* New York: Oxford University Press.

Nock, Steven L., and Paul William Kingston. 1988. "Time with Children: The Impact of Couples' Work-Time Commitments." *Social Forces* 67 (1): 59–85.

O'Connor, Julia S., Ann Shola Orloff, and Sheila Shaver. 1999. *States, Markets, Families: Gender, Liberalism, and Social Policy in Australia, Canada, Great Britain, and the United States.* Cambridge: Cambridge University Press.

Office of Child Support Enforcement (OCSE). 2006. "Office of Child Support Enforcement, Fiscal Year 2005 Preliminary Report."

Okin, Susan Moller. 1989. *Justice, Gender, and the Family.* New York: Basic Books.

Orloff, Ann Shola, and Renee Monson. 2002. "Citizens, Workers or Fathers? Men in the History of U.S. Social Policy?" In *Making Men into Fathers: Men, Masculinities, and the Social Politics of Fatherhood,* edited by B. Hobson, 61–91. Cambridge: Cambridge University Press.

Pease, Bob. 2000. *Recreating Men: Postmodern Masculinity Politics.* London: Sage.

Peterson, Richard R. 1996. "A Re-Evaluation of the Economic Consequences of Divorce." *American Sociological Review* 61 (3): 528–36.

Phillips, Elizabeth, and Irwin Garfinkel. 1993. "Income Growth among Nonresident Fathers: Evidence from Wisconsin." *Demography* 30 (2): 227–41.

Pleck, Joseph H. 1997. "Paternal Involvement: Levels, Sources, and Consequences." In *The Role of the Father in Child Development,* edited by M. E. Lamb, 66–103. New York: John Wiley and Sons.

Polsby, Nelson W. 1994. *Political Innovation in America: The Politics of Policy Initiation.* New Haven, CT: Yale University Press.

Pool, Hannah. 2007. "A Parent Has 'Fewer Rights Than a Terrorist,' Says Fathers 4 Justice Founder Matt O'Connor. So Is Dressing up as Spiderman the Answer?" *The Guardian,* August 30, 2007.

Popenoe, David. 1996. *Life without Father: Compelling New Evidence That Fatherhood and Marriage Are Indispensable for the Good of Children and Society.* New York: Free Press.

Putnam, Robert. 2000. *Bowling Alone: The Collapse and Revival of American Community.* New York: Simon and Schuster.

Quadagno, Jill, and Debra Street. 2005. "Ideology and Public Policy: Antistatism in American Welfare State Transformation." *Journal of Policy History* 17 (1): 52–71.

Quicke, Andre, and Karen Robinson. 2000. "Keeping the Promise of the Moral Majority? A Historical Critical Comparison of the Promise Keepers and the Christian Coalition, 1989–98." In *The Promise Keepers: Essays on Masculinity and Christianity,* edited by D. S. Claussen, 7–19. Jefferson, NJ: McFarland and Company.

Radin, Norma. 1981. "Childrearing Fathers in Intact Families." *Merrill-Palmer Quarterly* 27 (4): 489–514.

Reece, Helen. 2003. *Divorcing Responsibly.* Oxford: Hart.

Rhoades, Helen. 2006. "Yearning for Law: Fathers' Groups and Family Law." In *Fathers' Rights Activism and Law Reform in Comparative Perspective,* edited by R. Collier and S. Sheldon, 125–46. Oxford: Hart.

Rickets, Martin. 1987. *The New Industrial Economics.* New York: St. Martin's Press.

Riker, William. 1986. *The Art of Political Manipulation.* New Haven, CT: Yale University Press.

Rimmerman, Craig A. 2002. *From Identity to Politics: The Lesbian and Gay Movements in the United States.* Philadelphia: Temple University Press.

Rossi, Alice S. 1984. "Gender and Parenthood." *American Sociological Review* 49 (1): 1–19.

Sacks, Glenn. 2005. "Alito and the Rights of Men." *Los Angeles Times,* November 1.

Salem, Peter, Andrew Schepard, and Stephen W. Schlissel. 1996. "Parent Education as a Distinct Field of Practice: The Agenda for the Future." *Family and Conciliation Courts Review* 34 (1): 9–22.

Sayer, Liana C., Suzanne M. Bianchi, and John P. Robinson. 2004. "Are Parents Investing Less Time in Children?" *American Journal of Sociology* 110 (1): 1–43.

Schepard, Andrew I. 2004. *Children, Courts, and Custody: Interdisciplinary Models for Divorcing Families.* New York: Cambridge University Press.

Schneider, Mark, and Paul Teske. 1995. *Public Entrepreneurs: Agents for Change in American Government.* Princeton, NJ: Princeton University Press.

Schwalbe, Michael. 1996. *Unlocking the Iron Cage: The Men's Movement, Gender Politics, and American Culture.* New York: Oxford University Press.

Seltzer, Judith A. 1991. "Relationships between Fathers and Children Who Live Apart." *Journal of Marriage and the Family* 53 (1): 79–102.

——. 1998. "Father by Law: Effects of Joint Legal Custody on Nonresident Fathers' Involvement with Children." *Demography* 35 (2): 135–46.

Shapiro, Adam, and James David Lambert. 1999. "Longitudinal Effects of Divorce on the Quality of the Father-Child Relationship and on Fathers' Psychological Well-Being." *Journal of Marriage and the Family* 61 (2): 397–408.

Shehan, Constance L., Felix M. Berardo, Erica Owens, and Donna H. Berardo. 2002. "Alimony: An Anomaly in Family Social Science." *Family Relations* 51 (4): 308–16.

Sheldon, Sally. 2003. "Unwilling Fathers and Abortion: Terminating Men's Child Support Obligations?" *Modern Law Review* 66 (2): 175–94.

Shifflett, Kelly, and E. Mark Cummings. 1999. "A Program for Educating Parents About the Effects of Divorce and Conflict on Children: An Initial Evaluation." *Family Relations* 48 (1): 79–89.

Shrier, Diane K., Sue K. Simring, Edith T. Shapiro, Judith B. Greif, and Jacob J. Lindenthal. 1991. "Level of Satisfaction of Fathers and Mothers with Joint or Sole Custody Arrangements: Results of a Questionnaire." *Journal of Divorce and Remarriage* 16 (3/4): 163–69.

Sigle-Rushton, Wendy, and Jane Waldfogel. 2007. "Motherhood and Women's Earnings in Anglo-American, Continental European, and Nordic Countries." *Feminist Economics* 13(2): 55–91.

Simons, Ronald L. 1996. *Understanding Differences between Divorced and Intact Families: Stress, Interaction, and Child Outcomes.* Thousand Oaks, CA: Sage.

Simons, Ronald L., Kuei-Hsiu Lin, Leslie C. Gordon, Rand D. Conger, and Frederick O. Lorenz. 1999. "Explaining the Higher Incidence of Adjustment Problems among Children of Divorce Compared with Those in Two-Parent Families." *Journal of Marriage and the Family* 61 (4): 1020–33.

Skocpol, Theda. 2003. *Diminished Democracy: From Membership to Management in American Civic Life.* Norman, OK: University of Oklahoma Press.

Smart, Carol. 2004a. "Changing Landscapes of Family Life: Rethinking Divorce." *Social Policy and Society* 3 (4): 401–408.

———. 2004b. "Equal Shares: Rights for Fathers or Recognition for Children?" *Critical Social Policy* 24 (4): 484–503.

Smart, Carol, and Bren Neale. 1997. "Good Enough Morality? Divorce and Postmodernity." *Critical Social Policy* 17 (53): 3–27.

———. 1999. *Family Fragments.* Cambridge: Polity.

Smart, Carol, Bren Neale, and Amanda Wade. 2001. *The Changing Experience of Childhood: Families and Divorce.* Malden, MA: Blackwell.

Smock, Pamela J. 1993. "The Economic Costs of Marital Disruption for Young Women over the Past Two Decades." *Demography* 30 (3): 353–57.

———. 1994. "Gender and the Short-Run Economic Consequences of Marital Disruption." *Social Forces* 73 (1): 243–62.

Sorenson, Elaine, and Chava Zibman. 2001. "Getting to Know Poor Fathers Who Do Not Pay Child Support." *Social Service Review* 75 (3): 420–34.

Stacey, Judith. 1998. "Dada-Ism in the 1990s: Getting Past Baby Talk About Fatherlessness." In *Lost Fathers: The Politics of Fatherlessness in America,* edited by C. R. Daniels, 51–84. New York: St. Martin's Press.

Stahl, Philip M. 1994. *Conducting Child Custody Evaluations: A Comprehensive Guide.* Thousand Oaks, CA: Sage.

Stephens, Linda S. 1996. "Will Johnny See Daddy This Week?" *Journal of Family Issues* 17 (4): 466–94.

Stirling, Kate J. 1989. "Women Who Remain Divorced: The Long-Term Economic Consequences." *Social Science Quarterly* 70 (3): 549–61.

Stone, Glenn, Kathleen Clark, and Patrick McHenry. 2000. "Qualitative Evaluation of a Parent Education Program for Divorcing Parents." *Journal of Divorce and Remarriage* 34 (1/2): 25–40.

Stone, Glenn, Patrick McHenry, and Kathleen Clark. 1999. "Fathers' Participation in a Divorce Education Program: A Qualitative Evaluation." *Journal of Divorce and Remarriage* 30 (1/2): 99–113.

Strauss, Anselm, and Juliet Corbin. 1990. *Basics of Grounded Theory: Grounded Theory Procedures and Techniques.* Newbury Park, CA: Sage.

U.S. Bureau of Labor Statistics (BLS). 2004. *Women in the Labor Force: A Databook.* Bureau of Labor Statistics, United States Department of Labor.

U.S. Census Bureau. 2002. "Profile of Selected Economic Characteristics." *Census 2000 Supplementary Survey Profile.* Table 3.

——. 2006. "Household Relationship and Living Arrangements of Children Under 18 Years, by Age, Sex, Race, Hispanic Origin: 2006." *America's Families and Living Arrangements, Current Population Surveys.* Table C2. http://www.census.gov/population/socdemo/hh-fam/cps2006/tabC2-all.xls.

——. 2007. *The 2007 Statistical Abstract.*

U.S. Department of Justice. 2005. *Family Violence Statistics.* Bureau of Justice Statistics.

U.S. Department of Labor. 2006. *Highlights of Women's Earnings in 2005,* Table 14. U.S. Bureau of Labor Statistics.

U.S. House of Representatives. House Committee on Ways and Means. 2004. *The 2004 Green Book.* Washington, DC: U.S. Government Printing Office.

van Krieken, Robert. 2005. "The 'Best Interests of the Child' and Parental Separation: On the 'Civilizing of Parents.'" *Modern Law Review* 68 (1): 25–48.

Ventura, Stephanie J., and Christine A. Bachrach. 2000. "Nonmarital Childbearing in the United States, 1940–99." *National Vital Statistics Reports* 48 (16).

Verba, Sidney, Kay Schlozman, and Henry E. Brady. 1995. *Voice and Equality: Civic Volunteerism in American Politics.* Cambridge, MA: Harvard University Press.

Vlosky, Denese Ashbaugh, and Pamela A. Monroe. 2002. "The Effective Dates of No-Fault Divorce Laws in the 50 States." *Family Relations* 51 (4): 317–24.

Waldfogel, Jane. 1997. "The Effect of Children on Women's Wages." *American Sociological Review* 62 (2): 209–17.

Waller, Maureen R., and Robert Plotnick. 2001. "Effective Child Support Policy for Low-Income Families: Evidence from Street Level Research." *Journal of Policy Analysis and Management* 20 (1): 89–110.

Wallerstein, Judith S., and Joan B. Kelly. 1980. *Surviving the Break-Up: How Children and Parents Cope with Divorce.* New York: Basic Books.

Wardle, Lynn D. 1991. "No Fault Divorce and the Divorce Conundrum." *Brigham Young University Law Review* 1991 (1): 79–142.

Weber, David. 2000. "Fathers' Groups Say Case Spotlights Custody Bias." *Boston Herald*, April 24.

Weiss, Robert S. 1984. "The Impact of Marital Dissolution on Income and Consumption in Single-Parent Households." *Journal of Marriage and the Family* 46 (1): 115–27.

Weissert, Carol. 1991. "Policy Entrepreneurs, Policy Opportunists, and Legislative Effectiveness." *American Politics Quarterly* 19 (2): 262–74.

Weitzman, Lenore J. 1985. *The Divorce Revolution.* New York: The Free Press.

Williams, Gweneth I., and Rhys H. Williams. 1995. "All We Want Is Equality: Rhetorical Framing in the Fathers' Rights Movement." In *Images of Issues: Typifying Contemporary Social Problems,* edited by J. Best, 191–212. New York: Aldine De Gruyter.

Williams, Joan. 2000. *Unbending Gender: Why Family and Work Conflict and What to Do About It.* New York: Oxford University Press.

Wilson, William Julius. 1996. *When Work Disappears: The World of the New Urban Poor.* New York: Knopf.

Zick, Cathleen D., and W. K. Bryant. 1996. "A New Look at Parents' Time Spent in Child Care: Primary and Secondary Time Use." *Social Science Research* 25 (3): 260–80.

Zimmerman, Diane K., Joe H. Brown, and Pedro R. Portes. 2004. "Assessing Custodial Mother Adjustment to Divorce: The Role of Divorce Education and Family Functioning." *Journal of Divorce and Remarriage* 41 (1/2): 1–24.

Index

Page numbers with a *t* indicates tables.